UNIVERSITY OF CAMBRIDGE DEPARTMENT OF APPLIED ECONOMICS

OCCASIONAL PAPER 38

THE DISTRIBUTION OF CONSUMER GOODS:
STRUCTURE AND PERFORMANCE

The distribution of consumer goods: structure and performance

T.S. WARD

CAMBRIDGE UNIVERSITY PRESS

Published by the Syndics of the Cambridge University Press
Bentley House, 200 Euston Road, London NW1 2DB
American Branch: 32 East 57th Street, New York, N.Y. 10022

ISBNs:
0 521 20145 4 hard covers
0 521 09791 6 paperback

First published 1973

Set in cold type by E.W.C. Wilkins Ltd,
and printed in Great Britain by Alden & Mowbray Ltd,
at the Alden Press, Oxford

Contents

List of Tables and Figures

FIGURES

Preface

This book is the final product in chronological terms of a research programme on the distributive trades, carried out in the Department of Applied Economics and financed by the Social Science Research Council. It represents the third study in this area to appear in the Occasional Paper series and consists, firstly, of an analysis of labour productivity in retailing and, secondly, of an examination of recent changes in the distribution of consumer goods.

The first part is based primarily on statistics for retailing in a sample of towns, and I am indebted to the people in the Business Statistics Office of the Department of Trade and Industry who painstakingly compiled the 1966 figures from the Census of Distribution for that year and who took much trouble over the inevitable problems that arose.

The major source of information for the second part consists of details collected from a number of manufacturing companies. Interviews with the representatives of these took place around the beginning of 1971 and the study is largely concerned with the developments that had occurred up to that time. Although they prefer to remain anonymous, I can at least record my gratitude to all those who supplied information and gave up their time to answer my questions, and without whose co-operation this part of the study would not have been possible.

My main indebtedness in the actual writing of the Paper is to Mr. K.D. George who was responsible for the two previous Occasional Papers on the distributive trades and who supervised the work contained here. He gave invaluable advice at each stage of the research and made countless suggestions for improvement to earlier drafts. I also owe a great deal to Professor W.B. Reddaway who acted as 'principal investigator' during the course of the project and as supervisor while Mr. George was on sabbatical leave.

In addition, I am grateful to the Director of the Department of Applied Economics, Mr. W.A.H. Godley, for his constructive criticism of the penultimate draft which led to a marked improvement in exposition, particularly with regard to the first three chapters, to Mr. G.E.J. Llewellyn and Mr. R.J. Tarling, whose comments on an earlier paper initiated changes in the structure of the first part of the study, and to the businessmen who read extracts from the second part.

Finally, I should like to express my thanks to the Department's assistant staff, most of whom have contributed in some way to the project. Mrs. Marion Hughes and her colleagues patiently carried out interminable computations, only a minute proportion of which are reproduced in the following pages; Mrs. Bobby Coe and

Co. cheerfully punched the data and controls for the computer; and Mrs. Lilian Silk and her typists suffered by obscure hand-writing over numerous drafts with hardly a complaint.

T.S. Ward
April, 1973

General Introduction

The aim of this study is two-fold: Part One sets out to analyse labour productivity in the retail trades, Part Two to examine the changes in the distribution of consumer goods that have occurred in recent years. The concern of the former is essentially to identify and to measure the quantitative importance of the main factors affecting the number of people employed in retailing a given volume of goods. The analysis is based on annual figures for the sector as a whole covering the period 1954 to 1970, on Census of Distribution statistics for individual categories of retailer for the years 1957, 1961 and 1966, but largely on data for retailing in a sample of large towns in the two years 1961 and 1966 — the details for the latter year being especially compiled for the study by the Department of Trade and Industry. The issues examined include the possible reasons for the sharp decline in the retail labour force in the period 1965 to 1970, the impact on employment of changes in the structure of the sector and the adoption of self-service methods of selling, and the effect on productivity of labour market conditions, the expansion of trade, the sales-size of shops and income per head. In addition, various hypotheses which have been advanced to explain productivity growth in the distributive trades are assessed in the light of the evidence accumulated.

Part Two of the study broadens the scope of enquiry to cover the whole process of the distribution of goods from manufacturer to final consumer. The principal concern is with the effects of the progressive abolition of resale price maintenance on channels of distribution, retail prices and distributive margins, which have been much more the subject of theoretical reasoning than of empirical investigation. This involves additionally examining the influence on these factors of structural changes in retailing and manufacturing and the imposition of the Selective Employment Tax. The discussion is conducted primarily in terms of six categories of commodity: tobacco, confectionery, domestic electrical appliances, hardware, carpets and pharmaceutical preparations, which have sufficiently different features to be representative of a wide range of consumer expenditure. The period covered is mainly that from 1965 to 1970, the former year being the one in which the Resale Prices Act of 1964 began to be applied. The primary source of information consists of details collected from a number of manufacturing concerns engaged in the production of the six groups. This, with the aid of various published statistics and information obtained from distributive organisations, is used to illustrate the nature of the relationship between the distributive process prevailing for each commodity group and the structural and other characteristics of the products, and to give an indication of the most important developments that have occurred in this area over the period in question.

1

PART I. PRODUCTIVITY GROWTH AND STRUCTURAL
CHANGE IN RETAILING

I
Introduction and Methodology

1. The Historical Perspective

A well-documented feature of the growth of industrialised economies is the tendency
for an increasing proportion of the labour force to be engaged in service activities.[1]
In the United States, for example, this proportion increased from about a quarter in
1870 to 40 per cent in 1929 and to 55 per cent in 1965.[2] Over the same period,
there was also a relative expansion of numbers engaged in the distributive trades,
which account for a significant part of employment in services. Between 1929 and
1965, however, the increase was much smaller than in the sector as a whole, with
the result that the distributive trades' share of the work-force employed in services
declined from 41 per cent to 34 per cent. In this country, a similar shift of labour
into services is also apparent, but up to 1965, the growth of employment in distribution was virtually the same as for the other service trades. Thus total persons
engaged in both services and distribution rose at an annual rate of about 2·5 per
cent between 1924 and 1937,[3] and by 1·5 per cent between 1950 and 1965.[4] In
both periods, these rates of growth were almost twice as high as the annual increase
in the total working population, and by 1965 over 40 per cent of the labour force
was employed in the service sector — which, it should be noted, was the stage
reached by the U.S. in the 1930's.

Such tendencies, of course, are difficult to interpret when divorced from information on changes in output. The problem here, however, is that output series for
services are in many cases very much less satisfactory than those for other sectors of
the economy, the major reason being that changes in inputs often represent the
only available indicator of movements in output, which necessarily denies the
possibility of any productivity growth taking place. Nevertheless the consensus of
opinion seems to be that the relative expansion of employment in services is not so

1   See, for example, Colin Clark, *The Conditions of Economic Progress*, Third Edition,
    Macmillan, 1957, Chapter IX; Simon Kuznets, *Modern Economic Growth*, Yale University
    Press, 1966; Maurice Lengellé, supplement to OECD, *Manpower Problems in the Service
    Sector*, 1967; and Victor R. Fuchs, *The Service Economy*, National Bureau of Economic
    Research, Columbia University Press, 1968, especially Table 7, p. 30.

2   Fuchs, *op. cit.*, Table 4, p. 24 and Table 2, p. 19.

3   C.H. Feinstein, 'Production and Productivity 1920–62', *London and Cambridge
    Economic Bulletin*, December 1963.

4   'Distribution of Total Working Population', *D.E.P. Gazette*. The figures are not adjusted
    for part-time working and taking account of this factor would reduce the rate of increase,
    but would not change the relative picture all that much.

3

much the reflection of a larger increase in output than in other sectors – or, in other words, of a higher income elasticity of demand – as of a slower rate of growth of labour productivity. According to Fuchs, for example, 'the major explanation for the shift of employment is that output per man has risen more rapidly in agriculture and industry than in services . . . . . It seems likely to me that we would find a differential in output per man even if we had perfect measures of output.'[1]

However the output series conventionally used in respect of distribution – the volume of retail sales – is perhaps more reliable than for other parts of the sector, in the sense that it does not necessarily incorporate a downward bias. Indeed, as we note later, a number of commentators have argued that the series may well overestimate the actual growth in the activities performed by the distributive trades. This measure of change does in fact tend to support Fuch's view, insofar as for both the U.S. and U.K. the growth of labour productivity in distribution calculated on this basis has generally been less than for the primary and secondary sectors. At the same time, it would appear that the differential has narrowed significantly in the post-war period. Thus in the U.S., output per man in the distributive trades increased at half the rate of that in manufacturing, for example, between 1929 and 1947, while in the U.K. the rise in output between 1924 and 1937 was actually lower than the increase in employment. Over the period 1947 to 1965 in the U.S., however, the productivity growth rate of distribution was 2·7 per cent as compared with 3·1 per cent in manufacturing, and the difference seems to have been of a similar order of magnitude in the U.K. between 1950 and 1965, if allowance is made for the rise in part-time working in the former sector.[2] Since 1965, moreover, the British pattern has shown an even more radical change, employment in distribution declining by about ten per cent between that year and 1970 – considerably greater than in manufacturing – and labour productivity rising by more than for the economy as a whole. By contrast employment in other services increased slightly in this period.

This brief summary of the historical evidence therefore seems to indicate a tendency for the relative productivity performance of the distributive trades to improve as economic growth proceeds and for their expansion in terms of employment to become less similar to that of the service sector generally. It is also possible that cyclical factors are of some underlying importance, in the sense that labour may gravitate into distribution during periods when there are few opportunities for work elsewhere. Comparatively little, however, is known about the determinants of productivity growth in this sector and the way in which such factors as labour market conditions or the expansion of trade affect employment. The limited

1 Victor R. Fuchs (editor), *Production and Productivity in the Service Industries*, National Bureau of Economic Research, Colombia University Press, 1969, p. 10. See also the same author's, *The Service Economy*, op. cit. and *The Growing Importance of the Service Industries*, National Bureau of Economic Research, Occasional Paper No. 96, 1965. For a critical appraisal of conventional measures of service output see A.D. Smith, *The Measurement and Interpretation of Service Output Changes*, N.E.D.O., 1972.

2 This is based, for the U.S., on Fuchs, *The Service Economy*, op. cit., Table 15, p. 51; for the U.K., on Feinstein, *op. cit.*, A.D. Smith, *op. cit.;* Table 2.6, p. 34; W.B. Reddaway, *Effects of the Selective Employment Tax, First Report*, H.M.S.O. 1970, Appendix F; and *D.E.P. Gazette.*

research that has been undertaken in this country suggests that these factors are of importance, although this has largely been based on comparing *levels* of retail sales per person engaged in different areas with differing characteristics.[1] An important recent exception to this method of approach was the enquiry into the effects of the Selective Employment Tax carried out in Cambridge, part of the concern of which was to explain year-to-year movements in the employment of the distributive trades.[2] The purpose of this study is to throw further light on the process of productivity growth in this sector. Specifically, it deals with retailing, in which about three-quarters of all distribution workers are engaged.

The prime concern is to identify the main factors influencing the number of people employed in the retail trades to distribute a given volume of sales. This essentially involves examining the relationship between movements in sales per person engaged — although differences in levels between towns are also examined — and changes in other variables, such as in the volume of sales, labour market conditions and the number of shops. It also entails saying something about how such factors affect the use of labour in retailing, or, in other words, about the process underlying the realisation of gains in labour productivity. In so doing, we shall attempt to consider the validity of various hypotheses that have been proposed as explanations of productivity change in this sector — or more accurately we shall consider whether the main hypotheses are consistent with the evidence available.

2. The Hypotheses

There are many views as to the major source of growth in the volume of sales per person engaged in retailing. They can, nevertheless, be classified into three groups, which are not however mutually exclusive, in the sense, for example, that any one commentator might advocate a different explanation at different points in time. The first consists of those which emphasize technical advance and improvements in efficiency made at the shop level; the second, of those which stress the gains accruing from the concentration of sales on fewer shops; and the third, of those which attribute a central role to a reduction in the activities performed by the sector, or to a decline in the amount of service provided with the goods sold. At the risk of distorting the balance of this section, we intend to devote most of our attention to describing the second hypothesis because a detailed exposition has never really been set out, while details of the other two views are readily available in other publications.

However, to briefly summarize the first group of hypotheses, technical advance is in some cases seen as occurring independently of changes in other factor inputs apart from labour, through the internal reorganisation of existing shops or businesses, but perhaps primarily it is regarded as a corollary of capital expenditure. This is likely to take the form of the construction of more up-to-date shopping facilities, or, in recent years, the conversion of existing stores to self-service or self-selection methods of selling, although such conversion does not necessarily involve a great deal of expenditure and may equally be regarded as an organisational change. The

1 See M. Hall, J. Knapp and C. Winsten, *Distribution in Great Britain and North America*, Oxford University Press, 1961 and K.D. George, *Productivity in Distribution*, Cambridge University Press, 1966.

2 See W.B. Reddaway, *op. cit.*, especially Chapter XI.

importance of technical progress is in some cases held to be supported by studies of output growth based on a production-function type of approach, which have commonly found a significant residual element after taking account of changes in physical inputs of labour and capital.[1] The rate of technical advance, and therefore of the increase in sales per person engaged, is either regarded as being largely autonomous or is seen as being greatly influenced by certain factors — most importantly, by conditions in the labour market and the market for goods. This is closely related to the model of productivity change formulated by Salter,[2] which ascribes a central role to the spread of new techniques through production units and postulates that the rate at which this occurs is determined primarily by the rate of output growth and the change in the real wages paid to labour. Both affect the level of gross capital investment, the former directly through the induced expansion of capacity, the latter indirectly through its effect on the substitution of capital for labour. Although Salter focused his attention on the manufacturing sector, his thesis may also be valid for retailing.

The second view is that held by Kaldor and underlies the imposition of the Selective Employment Tax on distribution.[3] Major emphasis is placed on the market characteristics of the retail trades, which are seen as being most appropriately described by the model of monopolistic competition. This carries the implication that excess capacity — or too many shops relative to the perfect competition ideal — is likely to prevail, the reduction in which would produce a gain in the productivity of the sector through concentrating sales on fewer stores. The essential mechanism inducing such a reduction is held to be an increase in real wages in retailing, which acts to reduce profits, because labour costs do not enter into the retail pricing decision, and therefore forces the least profitable shops out of business.

In more detail, the retail sector is regarded as being characterised by a large number of units, each enjoying some element of monopoly power — if only by virtue of its location relative to other outlets, in a market with easy entry conditions. Figure I.1 depicts the hypothetical situation with regard to two representative retailers, selling the same type of product, which they buy at a similar price, and facing the same demand conditions, but with different levels of operating efficiency, in the sense that one has higher unit fixed costs than the other — because of older premises, for example. The less efficient retailer is assumed to be just covering the costs of remaining in business and is denoted by the suffix m (for marginal) in the diagram; the other is denoted by the suffix I (for intra-marginal). The AFC curves show for each retailer the variation in average fixed cost per unit of sales as the volume of turnover changes; each curve includes some rate of return equivalent to

1 See, for example, Harold Barger, *Distribution's Place in the American Economy since 1869*, National Bureau of Economic Research, Princeton University Press, 1955; J.W. Kendrick, *Productivity Trends in the United States*, National Bureau of Economic Research, Princeton University Press, 1961; and for this country, K.D. George and P.V. Hills, *Productivity and Capital Expenditure in Retailing*, Cambridge University Press, 1968.

2 W.E.G. Salter, *Productivity and Technical Change*, Second Edition, Cambridge University Press, 1966.

3 It should be made clear that what follows represents the author's interpretation of Professor Kaldor's view of the main mechanism underlying productivity growth in this sector.

Figure I.1

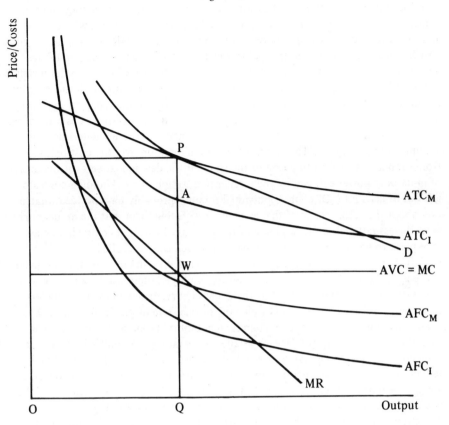

the opportunity costs of remaining in business for the trader concerned. The other fixed cost elements are such items as rent, rates and, most importantly in many cases, labour costs. Although the latter may vary with output – through the employment of part-time workers to cope with fluctuations in sales over the shopping week and year – Kaldor emphasizes that retailers tend to treat labour *as if* it were an overhead or fixed cost. At each level of output, therefore, the diagram indicates that the fixed costs of the marginal retailers are greater than those of the intra-marginal outlet. Average variable costs for both are shown by the horizontal line AVC. These largely consist of the cost of goods bought for resale which is assumed to be invariant with the volume sold;[1] they also include the cost of holding stock, which for any stocks–sales ratio is assumed to be proportional to the purchasing price. As average variable costs are constant, so is the marginal cost to each retailer of an additional unit of sales, and AVC equals marginal cost (MC). The ATC curves represent average total costs – the sum of AFC and AVC. Finally D and MR describe respectively the demand (or average revenue) and marginal revenue functions

1   Although this assumption is unrealistic in the majority of cases because of bulk-purchase discounts, a downward sloping AVC curve does not alter the argument greatly but merely serves to complicate the exposition.

facing each trader.

Under these circumstances, the output at which both retailers, acting independently, maximise their individual profits is, of course, given by OQ, where the additional revenue obtained from selling the marginal unit (MR) equals the marginal cost (MC). The retail price at this point is given by QP, which is made up of the wholesale price, QW, and the retail mark-up, WP. In this situation, the sales revenue obtained by the marginal trader just covers the costs of remaining in business, while the intra-marginal retailer earns a profit — over the opportunity costs of remaining in business — equal to AP per unit. It should be noted that overhead costs are of no relevance as far as the retail selling price is concerned, but merely determine the amount of profit earned. The extent of the retail mark-up over the cost of goods from suppliers is solely a function of the slope of the demand curve — or the degree of monopoly power enjoyed by the retailer in question, if stockholding costs are left out of account.[1] Of course, individual retailers probably have no idea whatsoever about the actual shape of the demand curve facing them, but the model might nevertheless rationalise the outcome of the process of trial and error which may take place to determine the optimal mark-up which can be applied.

A further point to note is that if the profit earned by the intra-marginal retailer exceeds the 'normal' rate of return on assets employed there will be a tendency for new entry to occur, which will shift the demand curve facing individual retailers to the left until tangential to ATC_I plus the normal rate of profit. Assuming that the situation described by the diagram is an equilibrium one however, it is clear that at the level of output OQ, each retailer is operating at a point where average total costs are decreasing. An expansion of turnover would therefore result in a reduction of average cost per unit of output — although of course it would lead to a bigger decline in average revenue. In this sense excess capacity is a feature of the equilibrium position and is a consequence of the downward sloping demand curve. The extent of excess capacity is given by the difference between the minimum point on the ATC curve and OQ, the former reflecting the turnover size of outlets in a perfectly competitive market. In other words, under perfect competition there would be fewer, larger shops.[2]

To demonstrate how productivity growth is seen to occur over time under these conditions, it is necessary to postulate that there is a tendency for overhead costs in retailing to increase relative to the ex-factory or wholesale price. Thus, for instance, there may be a general rise in wages which is offset to a greater extent by increased productivity in manufacturing than in retailing. Figure I.2 reproduces the picture shown in Figure I.1, which we take to represent the situation at time

1 The percentage mark-up is given by the inverse of $e/e - 1$, where e is the elasticity of demand.

2 It has been argued that if the model is extended to include selling costs — advertising expenditure, for example — excess capacity is no longer a necessary feature, on the grounds that these would be included in the ATC curve and are likely to vary with turnover, with the result that equilibrium might prevail at a point where average 'production' costs are at a minimum. See, for example, H. Demsetz, 'The Nature of Equilibrium in Monopolistic Competition', *Journal of Political Economy*, February, 1959, pp. 21–30. It is difficult, however, to ascribe much importance to this faint possibility, insofar as the validity, or even the feasibility of separating production costs from selling costs in this particular case is open to doubt.

Figure I.2

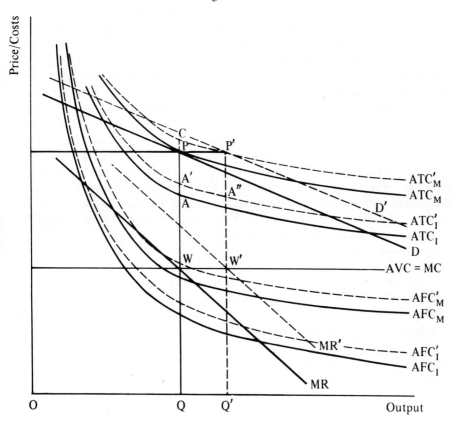

period 0. If to simplify the exposition we assume no change in the cost of goods to retailers, the cost functions after the rise in labour costs has occurred – that is, those prevailing at time period 1 – are shown in Figure I.2 by the dotted cost curves, denoted by the superscript 1. Assuming the increased labour costs have no effect on demand, the price and output at which profits are maximised are the same in the new situation as in the old. Nothing has happened to change MC and MR. Because of the increase in wages, however, the marginal retailer is no longer able to cover total costs and will be forced out of business. The intra-marginal retailer experiences an initial reduction in profit per unit to A'P, but at the same time will enjoy an expansion of trade in the form of the sales diverted from those shops no longer in business. In consequence the demand curve facing the intra-marginal outlet will tend to shift to the right, to a position such as depicted by the dotted line D' in the diagram. The new equilibrium situation therefore obtains at an output OQ' and a retail price Q'P', which is equal to QP, the price at time period 0, as long as the slope of the demand curve remains unchanged. Assuming the latter to be so, the retail mark-up, W'P' is also unaltered – the wholesale price not having changed – as is the level of profit per unit of sales, A"P'. All that has happened is that the level of output of the surviving retailers has increased, and hence the same volume of

trade is concentrated on fewer shops. In short, shops are of a nearer-to-optimal sales-size and fewer resources are employed in the retail sector.

Under this hypothesis, therefore, an increase in overhead costs in retailing leads to a reduction in the number of shops and this is associated with gains in both total factor productivity and labour productivity. As the basic operating unit is seen as the retail establishment, such a cost increase does not only affect unit retailers but may equally entail the closure of marginal branches of multiple organisations.

This process may be regarded as a decline in excess capacity, in the sense of being a movement towards the perfectly competitive market equilibrium point in terms of the scale of individual units and the resources employed in retailing. However this does not necessarily imply that such a movement would be desirable, as, if only by virtue of locational factors, the total number of retail outlets in existence is part of the service provided by the sector. The losses on the output side arising from a reduction in shops must therefore be considered along with the associated gains on the input side. In other words, the perfect competition model cannot tell us how many shops should exist, simply because it does not take account of the relative location of such shops, or indeed of consumer preference for a wide variety of shops.

A feature of the hypothesis which is apparent from the above exposition, however, is that the total number of outlets in existence at any one point in time is related to the level of overhead costs. Given demand and wholesale supply factors, the scale of individual units which can remain in operation is determined by average fixed costs in Figure I.1 above. As labour is often the most important overhead cost item, it follows that the extent of excess capacity on the above definition is a function of the level of real wages — the lower the latter, the greater, *ceteris paribus*, will be the number of shops in existence.

Turning to the third group of hypotheses, these consist of those commentators who attribute a central role to a decline in the amount of service offered with the sale of goods. The main reason why labour productivity, in the sense of the volume of sales per person engaged, has shown a tendency to increase is because of a concomitant reduction in the activities performed by the retail sector.

Adherents of this view have pitched their arguments at very different levels. At the one extreme, observers have merely pointed to the decline in the personal attention received from shop assistants and to the increase in self-service or self-selection methods of selling, without taking into account the fact that personal attention is only one aspect of retail service. At the other extreme, a few attempts have been made to justify this view by trying to assess the change in the actual work-load of retail employees. The most rigorous attempt to date is that by David Schwartzman in a study of the growth in labour productivity of the retail trade in the United States over the period 1929 to 1963.[1] Having found the usual substantial residual element remaining after allowing for estimated changes in the quantity and quality of labour, the quantity of capital and in the prevalence of excess capacity and economies of scale, he develops an explanation in terms of changes in average transaction size and service per transaction. Stated briefly, his hypothesis, 'emphasizes the rise in productivity in the economy as a whole and

1 David Schwartzman, *The Decline of Service in Retail Trade*. Bureau of Economic and Business Research, Washington State University, 1971.

suggests that it may have raised retail sales per manhour in two ways. First, the resulting increase in national income per family led consumers to buy more when they shopped, and the consequent increase in average transaction size was not associated with a proportional increase in service per transaction. Second, the growth of productivity in Retail Trade may have lagged behind that in the economy as a whole. The resulting increase in the price of retail service may have reduced the demand for service per transaction.'[1] In other words, the work required of employees in retailing has shown a tendency to progressively decline over time, as a result of increasing income per head and a reduction in the demand for retail service.

A further aspect of this tendency is seen by others to be a decrease in the functions that need to be performed at the retail level, in consequence of such factors as the increasing standardisation of products, the growing extent of brand advertising and improvements in packaging. In some degree, therefore, the growth of sales per person engaged in retailing is related to developments in the manufacturing and wholesale sectors. Similarly the gains in productivity arising from the adoption of self-service methods of selling can be regarded as being attributable to the willingness of retail customers to undertake work previously performed by shop assistants. In other words, this view emphasizes the inter-relationship between different parts of the economy, which implies that the sectoral responsibility for improvements in efficiency and their sectoral location are not necessarily identical.[2]

The adoption of this view therefore means that we may need to look outside the retail sector for the source of the growth in sales per person engaged, while the Schwartzman hypothesis implies that such growth is likely to be closely related to the expansion of sales and the rate of increase of retail operating costs (relative to the costs of production).

One final point to mention in this connection is that most commentators, whatever their views as to the most likely source of productivity growth over a period of time, would probably accept that fluctuations in the rate of growth of sales per person engaged might well occur as a result of short-term changes in the level of or quality of service provided. Such changes tend to be associated with time-lags and with the characteristic to some extent peculiar to retailing, that, in the short-run, sales are not closely related to retail capacity but rather to the demand for goods. Thus, for example, an expansion of trade is likely to mean an increase in sales per person engaged during the time it takes for retailers to adjust employment and capacity to the new equilibrium level. Over the adjustment period, shoppers will almost certainly have to wait longer before being served and service generally will tend to be less than previously. In the same way, changes in labour market conditions might lead to a similar outcome, insofar as retailers find it more or less difficult to replace staff that have left.

To sum up, all three views predict that we are likely to observe, for example, some relationship between changes in labour productivity in retailing and changes in the cost of employing labour. Similarly we could expect to find movements in

1 *ibid*, p. 10.

2 See, for example, A.D. Smith, *op. cit.*, pp. 94–105. Of course, it is equally true that developments in retailing have contributed to productivity gains in manufacturing or wholesaling, through the increasing size of individual orders, for example.

sales volume to be positively associated with productivity movements on the basis of each group of hypotheses. This is clearly the case in respect of the first and third groups identified, but it is also true of the second, according to Kaldor, 'as a reflection of the changing incidence of excess capacity generated by imperfect competition.'[1] As we are unable to observe the underlying mechanism at work this clearly makes it difficult to conclude that one view is in some sense more valid than another. However changes in other variables might give some indication of the process involved. For instance, if increases in real wages were accompanied by a decline in the number of shops per unit of sales, this would enable us to conclude that the evidence was at least consistent with the 'excess capacity' hypothesis, while if productivity gains occurred independently of a rise in sales per shop, this would suggest that another mechanism was at work.

Nevertheless it should be recognised at the outset that the nature of the problem and the data available are likely to enable any *firm* conclusion to be reached as to the prime source of productivity growth in this sector, if indeed such a source exists. To anticipate the results to some extent, the study in fact tends to emphasize the multiplicity of factors underlying the performance of the retail trades.

3. Outline of Analysis

The study is divided into two main sections. The first is concerned with the national picture, and looks firstly at the recent historical record with regard to productivity growth in retailing and compares this with the performance of the manufacturing sector. The association between the number of persons engaged in the retail trades and such factors as labour market conditions and the level of output is examined for the period 1954 to 1965 and the sharp reduction in employment per unit of sales after 1965 is discussed in the light of the events of that period. Secondly, we adopt a more disaggregated view and consider the experience of the different categories of retailer over the period 1957 to 1966, using the Census of Distribution information. This enables us to investigate the longer-term relationship between the movement in sales and productivity change and the influence of changes in the number and size of shops. In addition, we look at the structural changes and the development of self-service stores that occurred in the sector over this period, and attempt to indicate their effect on overall labour requirements.

The second section consists of an inter-town analysis of variations in productivity performance. This is based on the statistics published in the 1961 Census of Distribution and on 1966 data for the fifty largest towns in Great Britain outside the London area, which were especially compiled for the study by the Department of Trade and Industry. These enable us to pursue more fully the association between productivity growth and the above-mentioned factors, and to include other potentially important influences on sales per person engaged, particularly labour market conditions and income per head. Two aspects are examined: differences in the level of sales per person engaged between the towns in 1961 and 1966 (for 1961 our sample consists of 160 towns), and differences in the change in

---

1 N. Kaldor, *Causes of the Slow Rate of Economic Growth of the United Kingdom*, Cambridge University Press, 1966, pp. 17–18.

labour productivity over this five-year period. The two can be regarded to a certain extent as complementary insofar as differences at one point in time arise from variations in the rate of change over preceding years.

4. Methodology

One important issue needs to be cleared up at the outset. Throughout the study we adopt the convention of using the term 'productivity', whether qualified by 'labour' or not, to mean the volume of sales per person engaged (on a full-time equivalent basis). We take the view that changes in this concept are important to analyse for a number of reasons — in respect of manpower planning considerations, for example — but it should be emphasized that welfare implications can be drawn from the findings only with some trepidation. Thus the output of the retail trades is not the actual goods but rather the goods plus the service included with their sale.[1] From this it follows that a situation may arise in which an increase in the throughput of goods is more than offset by a reduction in service, with the result that output declines. In this case our measure of productivity change would tend to show an increase although a fall in productivity, in the welfare sense, might have taken place.[2] As we intimated above, it is a matter of continuing debate how far such an occurrence is the rule rather than the exception. We can say now that there seems to be no objective way of deciding what is essentially a subjective issue, about which different people are quite legitimately entitled to hold different opinions. All we can do is warn of the danger of attaching welfare connotations to the findings and re-emphasize that our concern is with variations in the number of people employed to retail a given volume of goods.

However, although there is no satisfactory measure of changes in retail service, one point is worth making in this context. Thus it is claimed by some that the development of self-service methods of selling, which has been an important source of reduction in the number of persons required to retail a given sales volume, is indicative of a decline in service. This it should be said, is by no means certain. Indeed a good case can be made out in support of the view that the introduction of self-service actually increased the service provided by the sector. Thus in respect of the grocery trade especially, there are many reasons for regarding the service offered by supermarkets as superior to that normally associated with traditional outlets. For example, it can be argued that supermarkets tend to stock a wider range of products, facilitate consumer choice between brands, encourage experimentation, are generally cleaner and more hygenic, reduce the time spent shopping, and increasingly tend to provide car parking facilities. To quote 'even when prices are known to be the same

---

1   It has been argued that the output of retailing is the service element alone, as this is what the sector adds to the value of the goods purchased from suppliers. However in our view, retailers are really selling a joint-product, goods and service, and it is not possible to separate one element from the other. Customers, in other words, are obliged to accept or reject the total package offered and are rarely in a position to purchase the goods they desire with the level and type of service they would prefer. On this see N. Kaldor, 'The Economic Aspects of Advertising', *Review of Economic Studies*, Vol. XVIII, pp. 1–27.

2   It is not possible to conclude that a fall had definitely taken place as restrictive agreements which have been especially rife in distribution may have led to an over-expansion of services in the initial situation.

in the self-service store, many customers deliberately choose this way of making their purchases. So long as counter-service remains available for those who want it, it seems perfectly legitimate to measure the output of retailing by reference to the volume of goods sold, even though an increasing proportion of them has been bought on a self-service basis: indeed, one might even argue that where self-service was not previously available for some types of goods, the introduction of this additional element of choice improves the position for the customer'.[1]

As far as the denominator of our measure is concerned, we calculate employment in terms of the number of persons engaged rather than in terms of the number of man-hours actually worked. Some allowance is made for part-time working by, in the main, counting two part-time workers as equivalent to one full-timer, but this adjustment gives only an approximate guide to hours of work.[2] Consequently variations in hours worked between towns or between kinds of business clearly might have some bearing on our findings. Similarly differences in the quality of labour might also be an important determinant of variations in sales per person engaged but again we have no way of including an allowance for these in the analysis.[3]

A further consideration is that we have no way of incorporating changes in factor inputs other than labour in our measure and this may also prejudice the findings. It is certainly true that the capital intensity of the retail operation has tended to increase over recent years, principally as a result of the development and spread of self-service methods of selling. For this reason alone, we would expect the amount of labour employed to retail a given volume of goods to decline over time. While we cannot measure the influence of capital intensity directly, to some

1 W.B. Reddaway, *Effects of the Selective Employment Tax, First Report*, H.M.S.O. 1970, p. 75. Interestingly, Schwartzman (*op. cit.*), estimates that food stores were the only sector to show any significant increase in service per transaction in the U.S. over the period 1929—63.
   An important point here is to differentiate between self-service and pre-packaging. The development of the latter has almost certainly led to a reduction in consumer choice in many instances, through forcing purchases to be made in certain quantities. Although the two phenomena have taken place at the same time, there is little evidence of any causal relationship.

2 The time-series analysis to which we refer in the next chapter in fact gives a smaller weight to part-timers, assuming a ratio of closer to three to one rather than two to one. Our choice of the latter was determined partly by the data available in the Census of Distribution for estimating changes in labour productivity over the period 1957—66, and partly out of a concern not to understate the relative contribution made to sales by the employment of part-timers, who tend to work during peak periods. It should be stressed that the absence of any reliable information means that there is no correct ratio even in terms of average hours worked.

3 It might be thought in some quarters that the use of wage-bill figures would have been preferable to persons engaged, insofar as they reflected the number of hours worked and the proficiency of the staff employed. Notwithstanding their non-availability — except for 1966 — they would not, however, have taken account of the self-employed and unpaid helpers who represented about 20 per cent of the total labour force in 1966. Moreover it would be heroic to assume that the relative earnings of, for instance, male and female shop assistants are an acceptable indicator of the relative quality of the labour input involved. In addition, wage-bill figures include an element of pay for over-time working and it is doubtful whether the excess over the normal rate can be regarded as recompense for additional work-effort.

extent it is likely to be closely related in its importance to other variables, such as the growth in the share of multiple retail organisations or the degree of tightness in the labour market, which enter into the explanation of variations in labour productivity. Insofar as this type of relationship exists, changes in capital expenditure can be regarded as a means through which such factors affect labour productivity, rather than an independent variable in its own right.

A further salutory consideration is that a number of studies have tended to show that movements in output per person engaged give a fairly good indication of variations in overall factor productivity, in the sense that results based on the use of labour as the sole input are not greatly changed by the inclusion of capital.[1]

---

1 See, for example, W.B. Reddaway and A.D. Smith, 'Progress in British Manufacturing Industries in the Period 1948–54', *Economic Journal*, March 1960, p. 29.

II
The National Picture – Productivity Growth in Retailing, 1954 to 1970

1. Changes in Output, Employment and Productivity, 1954 to 1970
Between 1954 and 1970, the volume of goods sold by the retail trades increased at an annual rate of 2·5 per cent while the number of persons engaged – on a full-time equivalent basis – declined by 0·3 per cent a year.[1] Labour productivity in retailing therefore rose at an average annual rate of 2·8 per cent over this period, which is the same as the growth rate in output per head in manufacturing. This is indicated in Table II.1, which shows the annual rates of change in output, employment and productivity for these two sectors from 1954 to 1970 and over the three sub-periods, 1954 to 1960, 1960 to 1965 and 1965 to 1970.

However although the productivity increase was the same in both sectors over the period as a whole, the pattern of change differed noticeably, as is shown by the figures for the three sub-periods. While these indicate an acceleration in the rate of productivity growth in both cases, this acceleration is much more marked in retailing. Thus whereas the gain in labour productivity in this sector was less than in manufacturing, over the first two sub-periods, between 1965 and 1970, the rate of gain in retailing averaged 3·5 per cent a year as against 2·9 per cent a year in manufacturing. For both sectors, the difference in performance between sub-periods is largely explicable in terms of differential rates of change in employment, the rate of output growth progressively declining over the period as a whole. Again, however, this feature is much more apparent with respect to retailing. In this sector, the increase in the volume of sales declined from an average rate of 3·4 per cent a year between 1954 and 1960 to only 1·2 per cent a year between 1965 and 1970, but this reduction was more than offset by the fall in persons engaged, which averaged well over two per cent a year in the five years after 1965.

Superficially, the performance of the retail trades in the period 1965 to 1970 might seem consistent with previous years, in as much as the movements in employment and labour productivity appear to embody the continuation of a decreasing trend and of an increasing trend, respectively. This applies *a fortiori* if consideration is given to the experience of the sector in the inter-war period. As described at the beginning of the study, employment in distribution increased at an annual average rate of about 2·5 per cent between 1924 and 1937,[2] which was greater than the

---

1   As described in the previous chapter, persons engaged are adjusted to a full-time equivalent basis throughout the subsequent analysis, unless it is explicitly stated otherwise.

2   We should emphasize that this rate of increase is based on estimates of total persons at work in this sector and is by no means as reliable as the changes calculated for the period 1954 to 1970. The same applies in some degree to the figure for output growth.

Table II.1 *Average Annual Changes in Output, Employment and Productivity in Retailing and Manufacturing, 1954 to 1970*

	Average rates of change per year:			
	1954 to 1970	1954 to 1960	1960 to 1965	1965 to 1970
Retailing				
Output	2·47	3·37	2·64	1·23
Employment	−0·29	1·16	−0·04	−2·28
Productivity	2·76	2·21	2·68	3·51
Manufacturing				
Output	3·06	3·39	3·26	2·47
Employment	0·30	0·89	0·38	−0·47
Productivity	2·76	2·50	2·88	2·94

Source: For retailing, W.B. Reddaway, *Effects of the Selective Employment Tax, First Report*, op. cit., Appendix F and *Final Report*, Cambridge University Press, 1973, Table VIII.1, p. 51. For manufacturing, *Monthly Digest of Statistics* for the years up to 1960 and *Department of Employment Gazette* for subsequent years.
Notes: For retailing, changes in employment are derived from figures for full-time equivalent persons engaged, an approximate adjustment being made for part-time workers. For manufacturing, employment changes are in terms of the total number of persons employed.

growth in output with the result that labour productivity is estimated to have declined on average by over 0·5 per cent a year. However closer inspection of the year-to-year changes over the period 1954 to 1970 reveals that the sharp decline in numbers engaged after 1965 represents a marked departure from the pattern of change which was evident before that year. This point is illustrated in the following two sections. The first describes the relationship between employment in retailing in each of the years 1954 to 1965 and other variables; the second compares the productivity performance of the sector which would have been expected to obtain over the period 1965 to 1970 on the basis of this relationship with the actual performance.

2. An Explanation of Employment in Retailing, 1954 to 1965
During the course of the enquiry into the effects of S.E.T. on the distributive trades, a number of different formulations were fitted to the experience of the period 1954 to 1965 in an attempt to predict the likely course of productivity movement in retailing after 1965, had things remained the same.[1] The equations which gave the best fit generally included a trend factor, the volume of sales and labour market conditions as the independent variables explaining either changes in employment or productivity. We have adopted a slightly different approach and have related the number of persons engaged in retailing in each of the years 1954 to 1965 relative to the number in 1954 − that is an index of employment based on 1954 − to the same explanatory variables identified by Reddaway. The result is summarized in the equation:

---

1 W.B. Reddaway, *Effects of the Selective Employment Tax, First Report*, Chapter XI and Appendix F, and *Final Report*, Chapter VIII and Appendix C.

$$\text{Log}_e \, E \;=\; 0\!\cdot\!8389 + 0\!\cdot\!8252 \, \text{Log}_e \, 0 - 0\!\cdot\!0179 \, (V - \overline{V}) - 0\!\cdot\!0192t$$
$$(0\!\cdot\!2144) \qquad\qquad (0\!\cdot\!0069) \qquad\qquad (0\!\cdot\!0067)$$

$$\overline{R}^2 = 0\!\cdot\!92 \quad \text{S.E.} = 0\!\cdot\!0070 \quad \text{D.W.} = 1\!\cdot\!67$$

where the dependent variable is the logarithm of the index of employment and 0 is the index of sales volume, both with $1954 = 100$, $V - \overline{V}$ is the difference between the tightness of the labour market — measured in terms of percentage unfilled vacancies — in any year and the average degree of tightness over the period 1954 to 1965, and t represents time, assuming an initial value of one for 1954. The figures in brackets are the standard errors of the regression coefficients and $\overline{R}^2$, S.E. and D.W are, respectively, the coefficient of determination adjusted for degrees of freedom, the standard error of the residuals and the Durbin—Watson statistic.[1]

The equation indicates, firstly, that the level of employment in the years 1954 to 1965 was a function of the volume of retail sales. While the regression coefficient in respect of the latter variable is less than unity, which would imply a tendency for the number of persons engaged to increase less than in proportion to sales growth, the standard error shows that it is not significantly so. We cannot therefore conclude that a higher level of output as between two years would necessarily be associated, *ceteris paribus*, with a higher level of output per person engaged, or labour productivity.

However a tendency does emerge for labour productivity to be positively related to the degree of tightness in the labour market, other things being equal, inasmuch as employment in retailing tended to be lower than it otherwise would have been in those years when percentage vacancies were abnormally high.[2] Thus the equation indicates that, for given values of the other two explanatory variables, a difference of one percentage point in the value of $V - \overline{V}$ would have been associated with a difference of almost two per cent in numbers engaged.

The possible rationale underlying this feature of the equation is that, as we mentioned in the previous chapter, when there are abundant job opportunities in other sectors, retailers as a whole find greater difficulty both in retaining employees

1   The equation used in Reddaway, *First Report* was

$$\Delta E = 0\!\cdot\!786 + 0\!\cdot\!793 \, (\Delta 0 - \overline{\Delta 0}) - 2\!\cdot\!010 \, (V - \overline{V}) + 1\!\cdot\!246 \, D$$
$$(0\!\cdot\!173) \qquad\qquad (0\!\cdot\!999) \qquad\quad (0\!\cdot\!443)$$

$$\overline{R}^2 = 0\!\cdot\!62 \quad \text{S.E.} = 0\!\cdot\!67 \quad \text{D.W.} = 1\!\cdot\!30$$

where Δ refers to the percentage change between adjacent years and D to the initial deficiency or excess of employment, defined as employment required on the basis of trend productivity and actual output, minus actual employment as a percentage of 'required' employment. The other symbols are the same as in the text. The different formulation adopted here was inspired by some misgivings concerning the D term and by a desire not to include both changes and levels in the same equation.

2   This is the measure of labour market tightness adopted by Reddaway, *op. cit.* A measure incorporating unemployment as well as vacancies would be more satisfactory for this particular period, but the change is the relationship between the statistics for these two variables which occurred after 1967 means that for purposes of predicting the pattern of events over the period 1965 to 1970, the use of either one is preferable to the use of both. The stability of the relationship between vacancies and unemployment over the period 1954 to 1965 implies that the results would not be greatly altered by including the latter in the measure.

and in recruiting suitable staff, to replace those who have left to fill vacancies elsewhere or to meet any rise in the volume of trade. This is especially so as wages in other sectors tend to be higher than in retailing in most parts of the country. Retailers may therefore be forced to operate with less staff than they ideally require, which would mean that the assistants who remain are likely to have to cope with an increased work-load. The consequent rise in sales per person engaged in such periods would thus tend to entail a reduction in the amount or quality of retail service included with the goods sold, shoppers being obliged, for example, to wait longer before being served. The reverse side of the coin, however, is that relatively slack labour market conditions were associated, over the period 1954 to 1965, with employment in retailing being higher than it otherwise would have been. Thus as percentage vacancies followed a cyclical pattern over this period — a complete cycle covering about four years — the higher level of sales per person engaged and lower level of service in tight periods can be regarded as a relatively short-term phenomenon, employment in retailing tending to increase as the overall demand for labour declined.

This particular explanation of the relationship in question seems more plausible in this connection than either of the first two hypotheses described in the introductory chapter, there perhaps being insufficient time for labour scarcity and the possibly associated rise in real wages to affect methods of working or the number of outlets in the years when they were most pronounced. Such effects are likely to be spread over a number of years and therefore may well be concealed in the trend factor, which is the last term in the above equation. This indicates a tendency for the numbers engaged in retailing to have declined by about two per cent a year between 1954 and 1965, given the values for the other two variables, and hence reflects the upward trend in productivity.

3. Changes in Productivity, 1965 to 1970
It is clear that the above equation fits the annual data for the period 1954 to 1965 very closely. If however we apply it to the period after 1965, a significant part of the variation in employment, and hence labour productivity, remains unexplained. This is demonstrated in Table II.2, in which the actual index of productivity for the years 1965 to 1970 is compared with the index predicted on the basis of the above equation — the latter being derived by dividing the actual index of sales volume by the predicted index of employment. Thus over this period — with the exception of an apparent break in 1969 — there was an increasing deviation of retail productivity from that which we would have expected to observe had past relationships continued to hold good. The result was that by 1970, employment in retailing was about eight per cent lower and the index of productivity almost nine per cent higher than predicted on the basis of the experience of the preceding 11 years.[1] In other words, the increase in labour productivity over the period 1965 to 1970 was 19·2 per cent as against an expected rise of 10·2 per cent.

The divergence of the actual growth in productivity in this period from that expected to occur can essentially be rationalised in two ways. Firstly, it is possible to argue that some new factor (or factors) emerged after 1965 to influence the course

1 This is similar to the difference derived by Reddaway on the basis of the equation he used.

Table II.2   *Actual and Expected Index of Retail Productivity, 1965 to 1970*

Year	Actual index of productivity, 1954 = 100	Expected index of productivity[a]	Difference between actual and expected indices
1965	130·6	129·8	0·8
1966	133·8	132·6	1·2
1967	138·4	134·3	4·1
1968	145·2	137·6	7·6
1969	147·1	140·2	6·9
1970	155·7	143·1	12·6

a Expected on the basis of the regression equation:

$$\text{Log}_e \, E = 0.8389 + 0.8252 \, \text{Log}_e \, 0 - 0.0179 \, (V - \overline{V}) - 0.0192t$$

where the variables are as described in the text.

of events. By definition these are not taken into account by the equation derived for earlier years. On this reckoning, the difference between actual and expected productivity can be regarded as reflecting the effect of the new factor(s). Secondly, it is possible to dispute the stability of the equation itself, in the sense that the coefficients computed for the explanatory variables from the data for the period 1954 to 1965 may not reflect their influence on employment over the period after 1965. In other words, instead of looking to the emergence of new factors, the apparent divergence might be explained in terms of a change in the relationship between 'old' factors and the numbers engaged in retailing.

There is no sure method of deciding which of these two views is the correct one. It is really only possible to apply a 'plausibility' test. The adoption of the first hypothesis would clearly seem to require the new factor(s) to be identified and a plausible reason advanced as to why it (or they) should have caused a 'jump' in retail productivity of the magnitude described. The requirement of the second approach is that a plausible explanation be given as to why the relationship between the numbers engaged in retailing and other variables should have changed or why the trend rate of productivity increase should have accelerated.[1]

When one actually comes to look at the explanations advanced by commentators, the immediately striking feature is the profusion of special factors obtaining during the period, which could conceivably have caused the productivity gain that occurred. Indeed the difficulty is not one of identifying potential candidates but one of choosing among them.

4. Possible Reasons for the Productivity Increase after 1965

(i) S.E.T.

Perhaps the most obvious candidate in this context is S.E.T. which was introduced in September 1966, at the rate of 25 shillings per male employee, increased by 50 per cent in September 1968 and by a further 28 per cent in July 1969. A primary

---

1 This is not so say, however, that either view is necessarily correct to the exclusion of the other; there may be in fact at least some element of truth in both.

object, was to encourage economy in the use of labour in services,[1] and at its initial level the tax typically raised the cost of employing assistants in the retail sector by about 7 per cent. However despite the widely held opinion that S.E.T. was a major factor behind the exceptional reduction in employment per unit of sales which occurred in retailing after its introduction, there is continuing controversy over the way in which this end was achieved, which in some degree is a reflection of the different views as to the primary source of productivity growth in retailing. This being so, our concern here is not only to assess the plausibility of attributing the productivity growth in distribution to the imposition of S.E.T., but also to consider the opposing arguments as to the mechanism underlying its effect in this regard. Both aims can be accomplished by examining the explanations advanced by two eminent economists, Professors Kaldor and Reddaway, who have been closely associated, at different stages, with the tax. At the same time, consideration of their arguments provides a convenient opportunity for a closer assessment of the alternative hypotheses as to the main source of productivity growth in retailing, which were referred to in our introductory chapter.

The Kaldor philosophy which underlies the intentions expressed in the S.E.T. White Paper is that, in respect of distribution at least, the incidence of the tax was likely to fall on traders rather than consumers. This follows directly from his view of this particular market and of the retail pricing procedure, which was described in some detail in the previous chapter. Thus, in terms of the exposition there, a tax on employment in distribution but not in manufacturing tends to increase overhead costs in retailing but does not affect the wholesale or ex-factory price. As is illustrated in Figure I.2, this will therefore leave the retail selling price, gross margin and output unaltered, but will reduce, in the first instance at least, the maximum profit that retailers are able to earn. The result is that marginal outlets are forced out of business and potential new entrants are deterred from so doing, giving rise to an expansion of sales for surviving traders, which serves to reduce average overhead costs per unit of turnover and thus to offset their S.E.T. payments. The productivity of the sector is therefore increased both through the elimination of the less efficient shops and through the rise in sales per person engaged in those shops that remain. The latter follows, of course, from the nature of equilibrium in a monopolistically competitive market, under which individual units operate at a less than optimal sales-size, in the sense that an increase in sales would be associated with a reduction in average cost or, in terms of Figure I.1, with a movement towards the minimum point on the average total cost curve. The imposition of S.E.T. with respect to distribution can therefore be seen as a means of reducing excess capacity, or, in other words, of increasing the scale of individual outlets nearer to the size they would be in a perfectly competitive market.

While this hypothesis, as any other, can only legitimately be tested on the basis of the empirical evidence, a number of comments can be made on the theoretical reasoning. Firstly, both the application of monopolistic competition theory to the distributive sector and the behavioural assumptions embodied in the model are open to criticism. For example, it is possible to argue, although difficult to verify, that oligopoly situations, whether explicit or implicit, frequently obtain — especially in

1 White Paper on *Selective Employment Tax*, Cmnd. 2986, H.M.S.O., May, 1966.

town centres — in respect of the sale of certain goods. Alternatively more recent theories of the firm have questioned whether profit maximisation is likely to be the sole object of management. Thus while the retail market still tends to be characterised by a large number of small retailers and easy entry conditions, nevertheless, as we indicate in the next chapter, large organisations are increasingly expanding their share of sales, and this is likely to be associated with a greater potential for collusion, the raising of entry barriers and with more opportunity for management to pursue goals other than the maximisation of profit.

Some comment is called for in this context on the 'excess capacity' implication of the monopolistic competition model. As we pointed out in the previous chapter this has been criticised along the lines that once selling costs are allowed to vary, equilibrium just might prevail at that point where average *production* costs are at a minimum. A more fundamental point is that the 'tangency' solution — on which the prediction of excess capacity is based — follows from the argument that new entrants will compete away any abnormal profits earned, thus causing a contraction in the demand for any individual retailer's output. In diagramatic terms, new entry will shift the demand curve to the left until it is tangential to the average cost curve and no abnormal profits prevail. However this argument rests on the assumption that potential entrants are able to duplicate the service offered by existing stores, which for a variety of reasons may not be true of the retail sector. For example, some locations are clearly more favourable than others, while restrictions on the development of new stores in particular areas may prevent potential competitors from setting up business, both of which might enable abnormal profits to persist. As the 'tangency solution' is not necessarily a feature of the model, neither is the prediction of excess capacity. The extent of the latter, or the ability of surviving shops to accommodate trade arising from the disappearance of marginal outlets, therefore depends to some extent on the importance of monopoly elements in the retail market, which may clearly vary between areas and between trades.[1]

Secondly, the view that labour in distribution is an overhead rather than a variable cost can be countered with the fact that a high proportion of the labour force is employed on a part-time basis, specifically to deal with demand at peak periods. However, while part-time working is undoubtedly of great importance, Kaldor emphasizes that labour tends to be treated *as if* it were an overhead, and therefore in practice does not affect price determination.

Thirdly, the model in common with comparative static theories in general ignores the time element. In other words there is nothing in the theory which tells us how long it is likely to take for marginal outlets to be eliminated and for the gain in labour productivity to materialise. This clearly makes empirical verification difficult and means that there are problems involved in discerning whether the pattern of events consequent on the introduction of S.E.T. is consistent with the hypothesis.

However before looking at the empirical evidence, it is as well to compare the Reddaway view of the tax with the Kaldorian arguments. The former essentially adopts a more pragmatic approach, starting from the presumption that indirect taxes tend to be passed on and then asking whether any features of S.E.T. are likely to disturb this presumption. Reddaway cites two features, one of which might imply

1   On this point see E.H. Chamberlin, *The Theory of Monopolistic Competition*, pp. 110–113.

that the tax was not fully passed on, the other of which might have served to 'slow down the passing on process'.[1] Thus firstly, S.E.T. was not a uniform influence but represented a smaller cost in relation to sales in respect of the more 'efficient' retailers, with relatively few employees per unit of turnover. To the extent that these happened to be the price-leaders — or margin-setters — the retail price might possibly have been increased by an amount equivalent to their rise in costs rather than to the average rise for the trade in question.

The second possibility is that, as S.E.T. is not levied on the goods themselves, the passing on process may be delayed, 'because it is not obvious . . . what the addition to price should be'.[2] This is especially so as distributive margins tend to be specified in percentage rather than cash terms, which according to Reddaway, has helped to promote stability, or 'stickiness', over the years. Thus '. . . often a conventional percentage mark-up has played a key role as the traders' yard-stick: departures from the traditional figure have been regarded as a major undertaking, on which each retailer would be reluctant to embark without ensuring that simultaneous action was being taken by his rivals'.[3] This seems to imply that Reddaway is thinking of the retail market more in terms of oligopoly than the polypoly structure of the Kaldor model, in the sense that he sees the behaviour of individual retailers as being influenced by the anticipated reaction of other traders. In other words, implicit collusion between retailers is regarded as a factor maintaining price stability.

Perhaps an equally relevant consideration in this context, which is not explicitly referred to by Reddaway (or indeed by Kaldor), is the part played by manufacturers in the determination of retail prices. Thus it is they rather than the retailers them-selves who, in the majority of cases, specify what the price to the consumer should be. Under a regime of retail price maintenance (r.p.m.) of course, retailers cannot but charge this price — and it is important to remember that r.p.m. was still of some significance at the time of the introduction of S.E.T. — and even where no such commitment obtains, there is a widespread tendency for retailers to follow the manufacturers' recommendations. Certainly there are relatively few instances where a price *higher* than that recommended by the manufacturer is charged.[4] This being so, the manufacturer exercises a large measure of control over the gross margin earned by retailers, which tends to vary with the ex-factory price or the recommended retail price — depending on the precise method of pricing adopted by the manufac-turer in question — rather than with retail operating costs.[5] It therefore follows that the incidence of S.E.T. depends to an important extent on the action taken by manufacturers, and it can be argued that unless distributors were able to persuade these to raise the margin allowed, the tax is likely to have fallen on distributors rather than consumers.

1   W.B. Reddaway, *Effects of the Selective Employment Tax, First Report*, p. 73.

2   *ibid.*

3   *ibid.*

4   See Monopolies Commission, *Recommended Resale Prices*, H.M.S.O. February, 1969.

5   See N.B.P.I. Report No. 55, *Distributors' Margins in Relation to Manufacturers Recom-mended Prices*, H.M.S.O. 1968.

In this regard it is worth recalling that S.E.T. was imposed at a time when Government policy was directed at restraining inflation and indeed that its introduction came in the middle of a freeze on prices and incomes, which was followed by a period of 'severe restraint' lasting until mid-1967. It therefore does not seem unreasonable to suppose that retailers would have found some difficulty in increasing their margins, since this would have tended to involve either a rise in recommended prices or an improvement in their buying terms, both of which may have encountered opposition on the part of government or manufacturers.

To sum up on the likely incidence of S.E.T., therefore, while the Kaldor hypothesis is open to dispute as an appropriate description of the retail pricing procedure, there are, nevertheless, a number of other possible reasons why the tax may have caused an initial reduction in retailers' net profits rather than a rise in retail prices. Thus although Reddaway does not embrace the Kaldor model of the retail market, he does recognise the possibility that at least part of the tax may not have been passed on or that there may have been delays in the passing on process. In other words, despite their different views of retailers' behaviour, in this particular case, and under the conditions prevailing at the time, their predictions as to the initial effect at least are not too dissimilar.[1]

More important differences between the two are involved in what they believe the main reaction to the reduction in profits is likely to have been. As we have seen, the Kaldor model predicts a closure of marginal shops and a consequent concentration of sales on fewer stores. Reddaway on the other hand emphasizes increases in sales per person engaged at the establishment level, and attaches a great deal of importance to what he terms the 'shock' effect of S.E.T. In his words, '(a) profit squeeze on retailers produces an incentive to reduce costs . . . which will not be confined to attempts to secure economy of labour, but the fact that the squeeze was produced through labour becoming more expensive may tend to concentrate efforts disproportionately in that direction, through a sort of 'shock effect".[2] Moreover, there is the acknowledgement that the more economical use of labour might well have been associated with a deterioration in service, taking the form, for example, of longer queues or less personal attention, although at the same time it is recognised that basic changes in methods of operation may have occurred. In particular, the evidence collected from retailers during his enquiry was that S.E.T. had accelerated the process of conversion to self-service or self-selection.

The recognition by Reddaway of the difficulty, if not impossibility, of differentiating between increases in sales per person engaged which are achieved through a deterioration in service and those which stem from 'genuine' improvements in the use made of labour, provides an insight into why Kaldor believes it crucial to examine the effect of S.E.T. on the number of shops. Thus in his view an implication of the excess capacity theorem is that the same level of retail output, in terms of the goods—service mix, could potentially be supplied with fewer resources. In other words, the

1 It is perhaps worth noting that the sample of retailers from which financial data were collected during the course of the Reddaway enquiry, revealed a tendency for net profits (including rent and interest) to decline as a percentage of sales between 1965/6 and 1967/8, the average fall being between eight and nine per cent. See W.B. Reddaway, *op. cit.* Chapter VIII.

2 *ibid.*, p. 74.

existence of market imperfections necessarily means that resources are not being optimally employed and that a reduction in the number of shops would constitute a move towards optimality. The question of whether individual retailers choose to offer less (or more) service with the goods sold is regarded as a separate issue, and as ancillary to this central point. Emphasis is therefore placed on the potential ability of the smaller number of retailers to offer the same goods—service package after the imposition of the tax as before; whether they actually decide to do so or not is considered to be a separate matter.

This attempt to overcome the problem of allowing for the effect of S.E.T. on the standard of service seems, however, to neglect the point that the total number of retail outlets can equally be regarded as an element of the service provided by the retail sector as the activities performed within individual shops. Thus the very fact that the demand curves facing individual traders are downward sloping implies that consumers are not indifferent as between shopping at one store as opposed to another. Fewer shops would seem to entail certain consumers being in a less preferred position — because they have to travel further to make their purchases for example. For these the service provided by the retail sector would be reduced, and for this reason it is not possible to conclude with complete certainty, unless various well-known assumptions are made, that the productivity of the sector in the 'welfare' sense had been increased. In other words the composition of the output of retail trades is necessarily different after the reduction in shops than before and there is no unambiguous way of comparing the two situations. In this sense the repercussions of S.E.T. on retail service cannot be satisfactorily isolated.

However it is true to say that a reduction in the number of shops is as much an implication of the Reddaway view of the retail market as of the Kaldor view. Equally the Kaldor hypothesis is not essentially inconsistent with gains in labour efficiency occurring at the establishment level, although the introduction of this possibility would prompt the question of why such gains had not been realised before S.E.T.[1] Both would probably accept the likelihood of both types of change occurring, the difference being in the relative importance attached to each. Thus Reddaway argues that the effect of S.E.T. on the number of shops would tend to be a long-term process and that 'any attempt to test the proposition directly comes up against a formidable collection of practical difficulties'.[2] Apart from the time-period involved and data problems, he cites the difficulty of allowing for size differences between shops and more specifically for the tendency for outlets to get bigger, in terms of floorspace, over time. In addition, the fact that S.E.T. did not apply to the self-employed is regarded as weakening 'the likelihood of S.E.T. having a speedy effect on the number of shops'.[3]

---

1 It is, of course, difficult to introduce the (entirely reasonable) possibility that labour is not being used at optimal efficiency into a comparative static model, especially one which assumes perfect knowledge. Reddaway for his part attempts to get round this type of difficulty by emphasizing the 'shock' effect of S.E.T. in inducing changes that were desirable anyway.

2 *ibid*. p. 76.

3 *ibid*.

The latter proposition is undoubtedly relevant, especially if account is also taken of the fact that a large part of the labour force in small shops tends to consist of unpaid family helpers, who by definition cannot have been affected by the tax — except in so far as there was an incentive to increase their importance. However, it should be noted in this context that 'marginal' shops are not necessarily 'small' shops. There is a common tendency, of which Reddaway is guilty at certain points, to equate the two, whereas marginal outlets may equally be of some importance at the larger end of the scale. For example, it is not obvious that a department store is necessarily more efficient than a much smaller 'specialist' shop.

Moreover it is by no means certain that the lag involved in S.E.T. affecting the number of shops was necessarily as long as envisaged by Reddaway — 'little effect would have been produced by 1968'.[1] Indeed it is quite conceivable that S.E.T. might have represented 'the final straw' to retailers who had been 'at the margin' for a period of time and prompted a fairly rapid closure of such outlets.[2]

Furthermore while Reddaway is undoubtedly correct in drawing attention to the importance of taking account of differences in shop size, it does not follow that the relevant concept to consider is the change in capacity or total floorspace, to the exclusion of changes in the number of shops. Thus in the light of economies of scale and the likely advantages accruing from specialisation, it is highly plausible that for any given level of total capacity, measured in terms of the total floorspace devoted to retailing, sales per person engaged would tend to be inversely related to the number of retail outlets. In other words, a reduction in the number of individual shops is likely to be associated with a rise in sales per person engaged even if capacity as measured were to remain unchanged. Consequently, it is possible to argue that the 'excess capacity' implication of the monopolistic competition model is, in this case, more appropriately interpreted in terms of 'too many shops', rather than 'too much floorspace'. Indeed there may well be a long-term tendency for these two factors to diverge, as a result of innovations in methods of retailing and of increases in labour costs relative to those in manufacturing, both of which are likely to encourage the construction of larger stores. An implication of this reasoning is therefore that the imposition of S.E.T. may have been associated with an increase in shop size as well as a reduction in shop numbers. It should be recognised, furthermore, that the former effect would not necessarily involve a long time lag before showing itself, in the sense that it may be relatively easy, for example, to convert two adjacent properties into one shop.

However, as Reddaway says, there are immense difficulties in testing the Kaldor hypothesis. If we consider the empirical evidence, it becomes clear that it really does not allow us to come to any firm conclusion one way or the other. Largely on the basis of valuation figures derived from Inland Revenue statistics, Reddaway estimates that there was a slight increase in 'capacity-in-use' of about two to three per cent over the period 1966 to 1970, which was less than over the previous four years but which was associated with a much lower rise in retail sales. From this he

1 *ibid.*

2 This is not to deny, however, as we remarked earlier, that the time element is an important omission from the type of model advanced by Kaldor.

concludes that there is little sign of S.E.T. exerting any influence in this direction. However as we have argued, his emphasis on capacity may be misplaced, in the sense that it is difficult to predict just what the influence of S.E.T. on this factor is likely to be. Moreover the statistics for rateable values cover banks in shopping areas and cafes as well as shops, and while these too were affected by S.E.T., the effect was not necessarily, or even likely to have been, similar in kind. A comparison with Census of Distribution figures casts considerable doubt on whether the broad series used by Reddaway is representative, in terms of movement, of what happened to the number of shops over the period. Thus the former shows a reduction of 7 per cent in the number of shops between 1961 and 1966 which compares with a decline of about 2·4 per cent shown by the Reddaway series (that is, his series for shop numbers rather than their rateable values).[1]

Nevertheless even if we take Census of Distribution figures and look at the *number* of shops, Reddaway's conclusion remains unaltered. Thus the provisional results of the 1971 Census indicate a much slower rate of decline in shop numbers — especially when considered against the slower rate of sales growth — over the period 1966 to 1971 than over the period 1961 to 1966, the actual decline being 3·8 per cent as compared with 7·0 per cent.[2]

In the light of these figures, it seems difficult to hold onto the belief that the main effect of S.E.T. was on the number of shops. However, the first and most obvious point to make is that there is room for some doubt about the accuracy of the figures. Thus, quite apart from the fact that the 1971 results are liable to be changed at a later date, the 1966 Census of Distribution was conducted on a sample basis, in the sense that returns were collected from small independents and new shops (established since 1961) only in sample areas. This means that the total for the number of shops is subject to a margin of error which is wider than for the other Census magnitudes. Nevertheless, according to the Census, the standard error of the estimate for total shops is one per cent, which implies that there is only about one chance in twenty that the 1966 figure is sufficiently wrong to make the actual fall in shops between 1966 and 1971 equal to that between 1961 and 1966. A reversal of the trend is therefore extremely unlikely.

Even if the figures are accepted, however, there are a number of possible ways in which the evidence might be rationalised to give a different interpretation. Firstly, it has been suggested that while the fall in shops may have been smaller in the five years after 1966 than in the five years before, nevertheless, it might still be true that it was greater than it otherwise would have been in the absence of S.E.T. In particular, it can be argued that as the decline was especially large between 1961 and 1966 there was some reason for expecting a slowing down in subsequent years. If this argument is accepted, however, it merely serves to highlight the question of why the time pattern of productivity increase was as it was. In other words, it is necessary to explain why productivity growth was higher after 1966 than before.

A second possibility is that a larger number of relatively small shops were opened in the period 1966 to 1971 than was the case over the previous five years, while, at

1 This is assuming that the Census of Distribution statistics are correct which is not necessarily so, as is pointed out below. Even so it is hardly conceivable that the margin of error is sufficient to close the gap between the two figures to any significant extent.

2 See *Trade and Industry*, 21st December, 1972.

the same time perhaps, a larger number of relatively large stores were closed down. This of course is the Reddaway argument in reverse and can be related to our earlier remark that there is no necessary reason why the marginal outlets should be small shops. The available evidence is therefore consistent with a closure of marginal stores which happened to be larger than average — and larger than those closed down in the preceding Census period — and with an opening of small shops, perhaps encouraged by the exclusion of the self-employed from the S.E.T. base. A full investigation of this possibility is not yet possible.

Thirdly attention might be drawn to the fact that the 1966 Census forms were actually sent out at the beginning of 1967, so that the number of shops refers to those existing at a time four months after the introduction of S.E.T. While this might be of some relevance, it seems hardly plausible that S.E.T. would have forced the closure of many shops in such a brief period. It may be more relevant to note, however, that the rate of S.E.T. was halved as from July 1971 and the intention of the Government to abolish the tax was widely known sometime before then. This gives rise to the possibility that the number of shops enumerated by the 1971 Census was greater than would have been the case had the rate of S.E.T. been maintained or had not the change in Government occurred in 1970. A stronger view is that the impending abolition of S.E.T. may have stimulated an expansion of shop construction towards the end of the period covered by the Census comparison.

For this type of reason, therefore, the conclusion that S.E.T. did not affect the number of shops, or rather did not raise productivity primarily through the mechanism of concentrating sales on fewer outlets, must remain tentative.

As a final reflection on the controversy, the debate on whether S.E.T. affected the number of retail *outlets* seems to have diverted attention away from the potential effect of the tax on the number of retail *organisations*, a reduction in which may have equally important implications for the productivity of the sector as a decline in shops. Thus it might well be that economies of scale and gains from specialisation are at least as significant at the organisation level as at the establishment level, and the argument can be advanced that S.E.T. may have been associated with a concentration of sales on fewer organisations, rather than — or perhaps as well as — on fewer shops, through its effect on net profits. Again, however, the available evidence does not allow this proposition to be adequately tested. The provisional results of the 1971 Census indicate in fact that multiple retailers — those owning ten or more retail establishments — increased their share of overall sales by exactly the same amount between 1966 and 1971 as over the previous five year period (by 5·3 percentage points in both cases), but there is no information as yet on the change in concentration among multiples.

To sum up the discussion, we can say that a number of different hypotheses predict that the imposition of S.E.T. was likely to have induced an increase in sales per person engaged in retailing. Thus it is extremely plausible that the tax should have been associated, at least in the first instance, with a reduction in retail profits, especially in view of the timing of its introduction. If this is accepted, it is likely that their restoration would have involved a rise in retail productivity as measured, whether this was achieved through internal measures or through a reduction in the number of retailers. As we have seen, the empirical evidence available does not enable us to determine conclusively which of these was the more important, but it is fair to add that there is certainly no indication of an acceleration in the rate of decline in the number of outlets since the introduction of S.E.T.

(ii) The End of R.p.m.

The progressive disappearance of resale price maintenance (r.p.m.) following the Resale Prices Act of 1964 provides a second possible explanation for the abnormally high productivity growth in retailing occurring after 1965. The argument here is that the freedom to vary their selling prices enables the more efficient traders to expand their turnover more effectively than had previously been the case. In the same way as S.E.T. therefore, the end of r.p.m. may have been associated with a diversion of sales from the less efficient to the more efficient retailers, and hence with an overall rise in the labour productivity of the sector.

However, it is as well to emphasize, firstly, that probably only about a third of consumer expenditure on goods was still subject to r.p.m. at the time of the passing of the 1964 Act.[1] Secondly, some debate is possible on whether the probable time-scale involved in respect of this influence is consistent with the pattern of events. Thus r.p.m. only really began to disappear from a significant proportion of consumer expenditure – excluding those goods on which r.p.m. had ended prior to 1964 – after the beginning of 1967 and still existed on many products at the end of that year, although it is reasonable to suppose that it was not applied as stringently in some cases after the passing of the 1964 Act.[2] At the same time, it is likely that there was some delay before the emergence of any substantial productivity gain resulting from the abolition of the practice, insofar as the diversion of sales would almost certainly not have had an immediate impact on the less efficient retailers. In other words, there might well have been a (perhaps lengthy) time-lag before such traders realised that they had permanently lost part of their turnover and adjusted their employment policy accordingly or went out of business. This is especially so in the case of one-man or family concerns, as the owners tend to be reluctant to sell out, and bankruptcy takes time to materialise. However it is worth repeating two points in this context. As we mentioned in connection with S.E.T., the less efficient outlets are not necessarily small businesses and, secondly, the end of r.p.m. may have represented the 'final straw' to a shop already in a precarious financial position.

On the other hand, the progressive abolition of r.p.m. following the 1964 Act began to occur at about the same time as S.E.T. was introduced, and may have increased the potentially beneficial effect of the tax on productivity. In particular, to the extent that it intensified competition at the retail level, it is likely to have

---

1 See J.F. Pickering, *Resale Price Maintenance in Practice*, Allen and Unwin, 1966, p. 226.

2 A very limited number of manufacturers voluntarily abandoned r.p.m. following the 1964 Act, while a few categories of product on which r.p.m. had previously been enforced were not registered for exemption under the provisions of the Act. The main goods passing through retail shops that were affected were wallpaper and paint, razor blades, sports goods, wines and spirits and 'Hoover' and 'Pyrex' products. See J.F. Pickering, *op. cit.*, pp. 225–226.

made it more difficult for traders to pass on S.E.T. to customers.[1] Indeed it is impossible in practice to distinguish between the effects of the two measures, and perhaps the most sensible conclusion is that the two factors in combination probably represented a more powerful stimulus to raising labour efficiency than either in isolation.

(iii) Other Factors

There is a tendency for other explanations of the 'jump' in productivity to dispute the size of the S.E.T. and/or r.p.m. effects rather than to deny their existence at all. In other words, it is widely accepted that these two measures contributed to the increase that occurred, but there is some debate as to whether they were the most important factors involved. Thus it has been suggested, for example, that at least part of the increase may be explicable in terms of the delayed impact of the rise in investment which took place in the period 1962 to 1964, when gross fixed capital formation expanded by about 25 per cent in value terms.[2] Quite apart from the questionable assumption that changes in the latter reflect similar changes in investment with respect to retailing – account has to be taken of the importance of rented property – what needs to be explained if the hypothesis is to be accepted is why the even bigger increase in capital formation in the period 1958 to 1960 (of almost 36 per cent) was not followed by a similar abnormal growth in productivity.[3] Clearly the form which the rise in investment took is a crucial consideration here. If it were largely associated with conversions to self-service, for example, then it is likely to have had a greater effect on labour productivity than if it took the form of the construction of more luxurious shopping facilities.

In fact there is evidence that self-service trading showed a marked increase in the years prior to 1966. According to the Census of Distribution, however, it was almost entirely confined to the grocery trade. Thus in 1966, the Census estimates that 95 per cent of all self-service sales took place in grocery stores, which was much the same proportion as in 1961.[4] But the Census definition of self-service excludes all self-selection methods of selling other than those 'where the customer collects the goods required and pays for them at a check-out point'.[5] In other words, it excludes the less 'extreme' forms of self-service which are prevalent in non-food trades and which have undoubtedly shown a substantial increase in importance over

---

1   An alternative but less likely thesis is that the freedom granted to retailers to vary their selling prices in fact enabled them to pass on the tax. In most cases, as we show in the second part of the study, manufacturers continued to suggest resale prices after r.p.m. was prohibited and these usually represented the effective maximum that could be charged.

2   See Lady Margaret Hall's review of Reddaway, *op. cit.*, in *The Times*, March 16, 1970.

3   This point is taken from K.D. George, *Industrial Organization*, Allen and Unwin, 1971, p. 184.

4   See *Report on the Census of Distribution and Other Services, 1966*, Volume 2. H.M.S.O., 1971.

5   *ibid.*, p. 108.

recent years.[1] Moreover the information for the grocery sector indicates that the most rapid rate of self-service development occurred sometime during the period 1961 to 1968, which is clearly consistent with an acceleration in productivity growth in the period after 1965 — assuming some time-lags. Thus the proportion of grocery sales made by self-service outlets increased from an estimated 21 per cent in 1961 to about 45 per cent in 1966 and to about 55 per cent in 1968.[2]

At the same time, it should be recognized, as we have pointed out, that the development of new methods of retail operation may itself be a consequence of the imposition of S.E.T. and/or the end of r.p.m., and may therefore be regarded as one medium through which these measures affected the growth of productivity. On the other hand, if we accept the figures quoted above, then much of the period of rapid self-service development in the case of groceries had elapsed before the tax was introduced, although it may have been partially responsible for the increase in 1967 and 1968. It seems more plausible to pinpoint the disappearance of r.p.m. from the grocery trade in the late 1950's as a critical factor, but of course it may be that the spread of self-service in other trades was accelerated by S.E.T.

Yet a further view links the abnormally high increase in retail productivity with the performance of the manufacturing sector over the same period of time.[3] Both sectors, it is argued, show similar deviations from 'trend' productivity after 1965. This is held to imply that a common factor (or factors) may have been at work in both cases, which would clearly rule out S.E.T. as being responsible, or at least reduce the importance of its contribution. The progressive abolition of r.p.m. would still be a candidate, but there is some difficulty in making out a convincing case in support of such a possibility. The advocates of this view have, however, stopped short of identifying just what common factor was involved, making out a case in its favour and estimating its likely impact on retailing. All three are crucial steps if their hypothesis is to gain acceptance. In other words, the similarity of the experience of the two sectors might suggest a search for a common factor, but it does not demonstrate that a common factor must exist.

What are the candidates for the role of common factor? One suggestion is that the employment policy of both manufacturers and retailers was affected by the measures taken in July 1966 and subsequently, and that these caused a 'shake-out' of labour through their influence on business expectations.[4] More precisely, it might

1   If we take chemist shops as an example, it is estimated that in 1968 half of all outlets incorporated some self-service facilities; by 1971 the proportion had increased to almost two-thirds. See *Nielsen Researcher*, November—December, 1971.

2   See Board of Trade Journal, 20 December 1963; *Report on the Census of Distribution, 1966*; and *Nielsen Researcher*, March—April, 1971. Between 1957 and 1961, the self-service proportion rose by only 12 percentage points and between 1968 and 1970 by only about five percentage points.

3   See, in particular, J.D. Whitley and G.D.N. Worswick, 'The Productivity Effects of Selective Employment Tax', *National Institute Economic Review*, May 1971.

4   Whitley and Worswick, *op. cit.* The authors in fact do not specify what they mean by 'shake-out', but this seems the only sensible interpretation in this context. See R.D. Sleeper, 'S.E.T. and the Shake-Out: A Note on the Productivity Effects of the Selective Employment Tax', *Oxford Economic Papers*, July, 1972, pp. 197–211. The discussion in the text on this issue owes much to this particular article.

be that there was '(a) change in the speed of adjustment of employment to variations in output requirements reflecting changes in entrepreneurial expectations about future manning requirements'.[1] However on *a priori* grounds one would expect labour hoarding – and hence the scope for a 'shake-out' – to be much less prevalent in distribution than in manufacturing, and this is supported by the empirical evidence for the period in question. Thus there are a number of reasons why retailers should find it less attractive than manufacturers – in terms of future cost considerations – to operate with more labour than is required in the short-term. For example, less skill is attached to jobs in retailing than tends to be the case in manufacturing, and hence the amount of training needed is also less – often considerably so. In addition, there is a marked difference in the speed of labour turnover, an annual rate of between 25 and 40 per cent among female staff having been mentioned in respect of retailing,[2] while the same is true with regard to cyclical fluctuations in demand, these being of a greater amplitude in manufacturing. More-over the empirical evidence shows that distribution, typically a source of manpower for other sectors, experienced unusually high losses of labour in the year preceding the July, 1966 measures and also faced recruitment difficulties at the same time. By contrast, manufacturers appear to have retained labour during this period despite the slow growth of output.[3] The evidence therefore suggests that there was some scope for labour-shedding in manufacturing after July, 1966, but fails to reveal any at all in distribution.

Other potential candidates for the role are also associated with government policy to restrain inflation in the period 1966 to 1968. These include, for instance, the 'squeeze' on credit and prices and incomes policy. The effect of the former was to make it more costly for retailers, and firms generally, to borrow from the financial sector, but also more difficult to obtain trade credit from suppliers, as a result of higher interest rates and a shortage of loanable funds. Allied to the increased cost of borrowing and financing the holding of stock, retailers also experienced a general, though by no means uniform, rise in the cost of renting property, while at the same time there was a tendency for local authority rates to increase, although there is no firm evidence of any acceleration in these two items.[4] It is plausible to argue therefore that rising costs in this area represented an incentive for businesses to look for ways of reducing operating costs as a whole, with consequent impli-cations for labour productivity; alternatively (or additionally) they may have led to the disappearance of marginal shops. This was particularly likely as other govern-ment measures were intended to make it more difficult for traders to pass on cost increases to customers, as we have mentioned.

Such measures included the policy on prices and incomes, which seems at least to have encouraged firms to give greater consideration to proposed price increases

---

1 R.D. Sleeper, *op. cit.*, p. 198.

2 See Christina Fulop, *Competition for Consumers*, Andre Deutsch, 1964, p. 179.

3 Employment in manufacturing remained virtually constant between 1965 and 1966 although output increased by only 1·6 per cent.

4 There has, however, been a tendency towards more frequent rent reviews.

and their justification.[1] In addition, the policy can be regarded as a manifestation of the higher official priority attached, in the period in question, to raising productivity, which in itself may conceivably have had some influence on business policy, although it is hardly credible that this factor alone could have given rise to the productivity gain being considered.

It is arguable that the depressed state of demand at the time represented a more important factor in restraining price increases than prices and incomes policy. If we look back at Table II.1, it will be seen that retail sales increased by little more than six per cent in volume terms between 1965 and 1970, which is a marked departure from the experience of earlier years. Indeed it represents an average rate of growth of less than half that of the previous ten-year period. This raises a question-mark over the validity of basing predictions of productivity change for the period after 1965 on the relationships which held prior to 1965. Thus it might well be that the influence on productivity of a sustained period of slow growth is very different from the effect of the shorter cyclical recessions which were a feature of the years between 1954 and 1965. In particular the ease with which marginal businesses are able to survive is likely to be positively related to the rate of expansion of the market. The longer the period of slow growth, the greater is likely to be the closure of such businesses. In other words, marginal units may well experience an absolute contraction in demand as a result of the attempt by intra-marginal units to maintain their previous rate of growth. Such a contraction implies that they will no longer be able to cover their fixed costs, and although many may be able to finance losses for a period of time, the longer this persists, the greater the exit of marginal concerns is likely to be. Moreover there is little inducement during such periods for new entry, so that the outcome may be that sales are concentrated on fewer units of relatively high efficiency. In terms of the monopolistic competition model, therefore, a period of recession can be regarded as analogous to a rise in real wages in its effect on overall productivity. Having said that, however, we should mention again that there is little evidence that any acceleration in the rate of shop closure actually took place during the period being considered.

(iv) Concluding Remarks

The above discussion indicates that there are a large number of special factors which may conceivably have affected productivity growth in retailing over the period 1965 to 1970. At the same time, the difference in underlying conditions between this period and earlier years might be taken to imply that relationships formulated on the basis of the latter may give a poor indication of the 'ceteris paribus' pattern of events after 1965. Thus it is possible that the slow growth of output had a positive effect on productivity rather than the dampening effect predicted. Moreover the trend rate of productivity increase may have been higher in the years after 1965 as a result of the faster development of self-service stores, although such an

---

1 It may be relevant to note that one report of the National Board for Prices and Incomes (N.B.P.I.) was specifically aimed at disrupting the automatic tendency for retail prices to vary with production costs through the application of conventional percentage retail (and wholesale) mark-ups. See Report No. 55, *Distributors' Margins in Relation to Manufacturers' Recommended Prices*, H.M.S.O., February, 1968.

acceleration may be attributable to the imposition of S.E.T. or the end of r.p.m. for example.

All things considered, it seems naive to select one factor as being *solely* responsible for the extremely large rise in retail productivity that occurred over the period 1965 to 1970. Indeed as we have indicated there is likely to have been a high degree of interaction between a number of elements, with the possible result that the total effect was greater than the sum of the influence of each considered in isolation. Thus, for example, it is difficult to deny that S.E.T. made an important contribution to the gain in productivity, but this would almost certainly have been less, had the introduction of the tax not coincided with the end of r.p.m. and a period of slow growth in retail sales.

Finally, we should repeat that the rise in the volume of retail sales per person engaged may have been achieved in part through a reduction in service. One point to emphasize in this connection is that we would expect to have observed some decline in service during the period in question, as a consequence of the abolition of r.p.m. A decline stemming from this source, however, is not indicative of a decrease in consumer welfare, insofar as it merely served to correct the previous over-expansion of services arising from the prohibition on price competition at the retail level. In other words, the maintenance of resale prices would be expected to be associated with competition in terms of service rather than price, and consequently with the amount of service provided by the retail sector being greater than that demanded by customers, given the choice. If this was in fact so, the likely response of some retailers to the end of r.p.m. would have been to substitute lower prices for some element of service. The reduction in retail service may therefore have actually increased the welfare of retail customers, in the sense that it made some people better off — those who preferred lower prices to more service — without making anyone worse off — as long as those people who preferred 'more' service could still get it. This being so, it seems more justifiable to regard the decline in service as a factor increasing retail output rather than as one tending to reduce it.

This is not to imply, of course, that any deterioration in retail service that may have occurred was necessarily a result of the abolition of r.p.m. But it does represent a counter-argument to those who tend to attribute any observed decline in service to the imposition of S.E.T. and use such observations to support the claim that the rise in productivity as measured, which has taken place since the introduction of the tax, is largely spurious.

5. Summary of Main Points

Over the period for which reasonably reliable figures on output and employment changes are available for retailing (1954 to 1970), the labour productivity of this sector increased as much the same rate as in manufacturing, and at a faster rate between 1965 and 1970. The acceleration in this latter period represents a marked departure from previous experience, in the sense that there is a significant difference between actual productivity growth and that expected on the basis of the relationship between employment and other factors over the previous 11 years. Thus for each of the years 1954 to 1965 a good explanation of employment in retailing is obtained by postulating that this is a positive function of the volume of sales and an inverse function of the number of unfilled vacancies, expressed as a percentage of the total labour force, and time, there being an upward trend in productivity over this period.

Many reasons have been advanced for the acceleration in productivity after 1965, the most notable being the imposition of S.E.T. An examination of the controversy surrounding this measure pointed to the conclusion that it was extremely likely to have reduced employment per unit of sales, but that it is not possible to identify with certainty the main way in which this end was achieved. However there is no evidence to hand that the tax raised productivity by forcing marginal shops out of business and inducing a concentration of sales on fewer outlets, which is the Kaldor view. Other possible reasons include the progressive abolition of r.p.m. after the 1964 Resale Prices Act, the effects of which are difficult to separate from those of S.E.T., the increase in capital expenditure between 1962 and 1964, the development of self-service trading, the squeeze on credit, prices and incomes policy and a general 'shake-out' of labour after July, 1966. In each case there is room for debate on whether the magnitude of the likely effects of such factors and the time-scale involved are consistent with the evidence. An additional consideration concerns the appropriateness of applying an equation formulated on the basis of the years 1954 to 1965 to explain employment in the years 1965 to 1970, which was a sustained period of slow output growth without precedent in the post-war period.

The most probable explanation of events is that a number of different factors were each at least partly responsible for the increase in the rate of productivity growth after 1965, and that there was a good deal of interaction between these. While this increase may have involved some deterioration in retail service, it is as well to bear in mind that, because of the existence of r.p.m., the amount of service provided with the goods sold before 1965 may have been greater than demanded by retail customers.

III

The National Picture – Changes within the Retail Sector, 1957 to 1966

In the previous chapter, it was seen among other things that the number engaged in retailing in the years 1954 to 1965 was a function of the volume of sales, the degree of tightness in the labour market and a time factor reflecting the underlying upward trend in productivity. The remainder of Part One of the study adopts a cross-sectional approach to the problem of identifying those factors influencing retail productivity growth over the long-term. In this chapter we use the data on different categories of retail business from three Censuses of Distribution – 1957, 1961 and 1966 – to examine the association between movements in the volume of sales per person engaged and changes in sales volume, the number of shops and sales per shop over the period 1957 to 1966. In addition, we look at the relationship between productivity growth and changes in gross margin and attempt to assess the effect on the former of structural changes and the development of self-service.

1. Productivity Change by Kind of Business

Given the diverse composition of the retail trades, it is to be expected that the aggregate figures for movements in labour productivity, sales and numbers of shops over any period of time would conceal significant variations between different kinds of business. The scope for introducing more efficient methods of labour utilisation, the rate of growth of consumer expenditure and the advantages attained from constructing larger stores are in each case most unlikely to be the same in respect of all commodity groups. Such variations are immediately evident in Table III.1. This shows the various kinds of business defined by the Census of Distribution (excluding the two categories mentioned in the notes to the table), arranged according to the percentage increase in the volume of sales per person engaged, and the corresponding changes in sales volume, the number of shops, sales per shop and gross margin per unit of sales.

Looking firstly at the first two columns, substantial differences are apparent in the increase in productivity as measured, which varied from over 50 per cent in the case of 'Jewellery, leather and sports goods' shops to under two per cent in the case of 'Bread and flour confectioners' and 'Greengrocers and fruiterers'. The disparity, however, is even greater in respect of sales growth. At the same time, there is a marked tendency for these two variables to be positively associated: those businesses which showed relatively large increases in productivity also typically experienced high rates of sales increase, and vice versa. Thus the average productivity gain for the first five trades in the table was 40·4 per cent and their average sales rise was

Table III.1 *Percentage Changes in Sales per Person Engaged, Sales, Sales per Shop and Number of Shops, by Kind of Business: 1957 to 1966*

Kind of Business	Percentage Changes in:				
	Sales per person engaged	Sales	Number of shops	Sales per shop	Gross margin per unit of sales
1. Jewellery, Leather, Sports Goods	52·4	70·6	7·7	58·4	9·9
2. Radio and Electrical Goods	45·4	57·7	24·1	27·1	14·8
3. Women's and Girls' Wear	38·0	36·9	−6·6	46·6	24·4
4. Grocers and Provision Dealers	33·7	20·1	−17·6	45·8	24·7
5. Hardware, Wallpaper and Paint	32·6	44·8	13·0	28·1	25·3
6. Chemists, Photographic Dealers	31·8	48·9	0·1	48·7	24·7
7. Off-Licences	28·6	55·5	23·0	26·5	21·0
8. Department Stores	26·2	26·6	5·8	19·6	21·9
9. Dairymen	25·3	18·1	−40·7	99·2	37·5
10. Furniture and Allied	25·0	52·5	27·6	19·6	23·3
11. Other Non-Food	24·0	38·0	10·7	24·6	12·6
12. Book-Shops and Stationers	23·4	12·0	−8·6	22·5	33·8
13. Men's and Boys' Wear	19·3	25·8	8·3	16·2	38·7
14. Boots and Shoes	15·8	18·0	−1·7	20·0	56·4
15. Variety and Other General Stores	15·0	7·3	−30·0	53·2	64·3
16. Butchers	5·4	−2·9	−7·0	4·4	51·0
17. Fishmongers, Poulterers	5·4	−12·7	−18·6	7·3	56·8
18. Confectioners, Tobacconists, Newsagents	4·9	4·5	−17·6	26·8	52·3
19. Greengrocers, Fruiterers	1·7	−5·9	−16·0	12·0	57·7
20. Bread and Flour Confectioners	1·3	−0·5	3·4	−3·7	70·0

Source: Census of Distribution, 1966.
Notes: The figures are derived primarily from Table E of the 1966 Census and relate to changes excluding market traders, which were not covered in 1966. In each case, the changes in sales have been deflated by price indices supplied by the D.T.I. (previously Board of Trade), while persons engaged are in terms of full-time equivalents − counting two part-time workers equal to one full-time worker. 'Radio and television hire' shops and 'Cycle and perambulator' shops are excluded − the former because they represent a rather special area of the trade; the latter, because of the lack of a suitable price deflator. (They accounted for 2·9 per cent and 1·2 per cent of retail turnover, respectively, in 1966).

The change in the 'gross margin per unit of sales' represents the change in the cash margin earned from selling a given volume of sales and is calculated by comparing the percentage gross margin in 1966 − derived from 'organisation' rather than 'establishment' data − multiplied by the price index for the category in question (with 1957 = 100), with the percentage gross margin in 1957.

46·0 per cent, while the corresponding averages for the bottom five trades were an increase of 3·7 per cent and a fall of 3·5 per cent, respectively. Moreover of the top seven trades in terms of productivity growth, five were in the top seven in terms of sales growth, and of the seven trades listed at the bottom of the table, six were similarly placed in terms of sales growth.

The close association between the two variables is summarized by the regression equation:

$$P = 9·2 + 0·526T \qquad r^2 = 0·77$$
$$(0·068)$$

where P equals the percentage increase in productivity and T is the percentage change in the volume of sales over the period 1957 to 1966 for the twenty business categories of Table III.1. The equation indicates that a retail trade which experienced a rise in sales of ten percentage points above average would tend to have shown an increase in productivity of over five percentage points above average.

This result may be taken to reveal the 'long period' influence of sales growth on productivity in retailing. There are, however, a number of objections which might be raised against such an interpretation. Firstly, it might be argued that lag effects may have some bearing on the relationship even over a nine-year period, in the sense that expanding trades may have been a little more behind with their recruitment in 1966 than in 1957 than was the case for slow growing or declining trades. Secondly, it is possible that errors in estimating the price indices used to deflate sales movements may affect the result as they enter into the measure of both productivity and output changes. An underestimate of the price deflator, for example, will therefore raise the change in both sales and productivity. Thirdly, it has to be admitted that the regression equation cannot be held to imply that it is exceptionally large rises in sales which *cause* high rates of productivity growth. The reverse direction of causation is, of course, fully consistent with the evidence.

With regard to the first objection, we have to recognise that it is not possible to eliminate short-term factors from the analysis, but at the same time, it seems difficult to attach much importance to their influence. A good deal depends, of course, on the timing of the rises (or falls) in sales over the period; the more they are concentrated in the later years, the more important are adjustment lags likely to be. The overall sales figures for individual years, however, do not suggest that such a concentration in fact obtained.

As far as the second objection is concerned, there is no real answer. All we can do is acknowledge that such a possibility might have occurred, while pointing out that the estimation errors would need to be very large indeed in order for this to represent a major part of the explanation for the finding.

Finally, there does seem to be a convincing answer to the third objection. Thus with regard to retailing, there is some difficulty in making out a case in support of the direction of causation running from productivity gains to increases in sales. In particular, the retail value-added generally represents a minor part of the total selling price of any product, with the implication that variations in efficiency at the retail level are likely to be much less important than variations at the production stage in their impact on relative prices and hence on the pattern of demand.[1]

Consequently, it would seem that a sustained period of high sales growth does tend to exert a positive influence on productivity. The possible reasons for this were outlined in our introductory discussion. Thus it might be that a rapid rate of sales expansion raises productivity through its effect on the introduction and spread of innovations in retail techniques. Specifically, the faster the rate of growth of demand for any product, the greater is the expansion of retail capacity likely to be, and the greater, *ceteris paribus*, is therefore the proportion of sales

---

1 A counter-argument is that variations in retail efficiency have caused shifts in consumer expenditure on a *given* product between kinds of business. To our mind, changes in consumer attitudes and habits — such as the trend towards 'one-stop' shopping — have probably been more significant here than efficiency differences.

made by new shops. These shops by the very fact of their newness can be expected to incorporate the latest and most efficient methods of selling, which probably means that they will tend to have a higher level of sales per person engaged than older stores. Alternatively, it may be that relative rates of sales increase reflect either 'the changing incidence of excess capacity'[1] as between business categories or relative increases in the average value of transactions per customer. The implication of the latter possibility may be that the amount of 'service' per pound's worth of sales showed a greater tendency to decline in respect of rapidly expanding trades. In other words, the change in the number of persons needed to retail a given volume of goods is likely to be a function of the change in transaction size. To take an extreme example, the extra selling effort involved in retailing a colour television set as opposed to a monochrome set is, on average, considerably less than the difference in price.

At the same time, it is also possible to argue that even where the rise in sales took the form of more customers, or more shop visits, rather than an increase in purchases per customer, this also may have had beneficial repercussions on sales per person engaged. In particular, it may have enabled staff to be more fully employed in existing stores. This is not necessarily because staff were previously used inefficiently, in the usual sense of the term — although the concept of optimal efficiency probably has little practical application[2] — but possibly because of the nature of the demand for retail services. Thus the level of retail sales varies markedly over the shopping week, demand at the peak determining in large measure the amount of resources employed in retailing.[3] To the extent, therefore, that demand increases during off-peak periods, little addition to staff, or shopping facilities generally, may be necessary.

Turning our attention to the third and fourth columns of Table III.1, it can be seen that, firstly, there was a tendency for the number of shops to increase in those kinds of business which experienced a relatively high growth of sales and made large gains in productivity, the reverse being true for slow-growing or declining businesses. This feature is clearly consistent with the hypothesis which emphasizes the spread of innovations through the construction of new capacity. Secondly, it is evident that the number of shops generally changed much less than in proportion to the change in sales, and that those kinds of business which experienced a relatively high rate of sales increase also tended to show an above average rise in sales per shop. In other words, there was a rise in sales per shop in all trades — with the exception of 'Bread and flour confectioners' — but the amount of the increase was positively related to the rise in sales,[4] and therefore to the gain in productivity. It should be noted that this relationship becomes much closer if we exclude 'Dairymen' and

---

1 Kaldor, *op. cit.*

2 By this we mean that it is probably possible in most cases to raise output without increasing inputs, or in other words that an element of 'organisational slack' will usually exist. For a discussion of this concept, see, R.M. Cyert and J.G. March, *A Behavioural Theory of the Firm*, Prentice-Hall, 1963.

3 It has been estimated that about 60 per cent of retail sales typically take place on Fridays and Saturdays; see, for example, Christina Fulop, *Competition for Consumers*, pp. 236–238.

4 The correlation coefficient between these two variables is 0·68, when the two kinds of business mentioned subsequently are omitted.

'Variety and other general stores' both of which were subject to significant changes in composition between 1957 and 1966.[1]

The association between changes in sales per shop and productivity is summarized by the regression equation,

$$P = 4 \cdot 1 + 0 \cdot 757X \qquad r^2 = 0 \cdot 67$$
$$(0 \cdot 134)$$

where P equals the percentage increase in sales per person engaged and X is the percentage change in sales per shop, for the kinds of business listed in Table III.1, excluding the two mentioned above. This indicates a tendency for a rise in sales per shop of ten percentage points above average to be associated with an increase in productivity of more than seven percentage points above average.

This finding is clearly consistent with hypotheses which emphasize the realisation of productivity gains through the fuller use of retail staff or through the elimination of marginal outlets and the consequent concentration of sales on fewer shops.

It must be recognised at this point, however, that we cannot necessarily identify changes in the number of outlets with similar changes in retail capacity, or the amount of floorspace devoted to retailing. Thus the replacement of small shops by fewer stores of greater size has been a significant feature of a number of businesses, particularly of the grocery trade. Indeed it may well be that the total floorspace devoted to the sale of groceries increased between 1957 and 1966, even though the table indicates that the number of establishments declined significantly over the period. Furthermore, as the net change in shop numbers conceals the number of 'births' and 'deaths', we cannot necessarily conclude, for example, that a business which shows a large rise in outlets is liable to have gained more from innovations than a business which shows no change or even a decline.

On the other hand, there is some evidence that economies of scale are a feature of the retail trades, in the sense that larger stores tend to have a higher level of sales per person engaged — and hence lower labour costs per unit of turnover — than smaller shops.[2] The construction of larger stores, therefore, is itself likely to raise productivity. In consequence, a decline in the number of shops relative to sales may

1 To be specific, both experienced substantial increases in sales per shop as a result of the rise in importance of organisations which typically operated considerably larger establishments than others in the trade. For example, multiple dairies owned depots which in 1966 were, on average, more than ten times the size of independent establishments in terms of turnover, and the rise in their importance was responsible for more than half of the total increase in average sales per 'shop'. At the same time, the change in the relative importance of the different types of organisation contributed in only a minor way to the overall growth in productivity (see Table III.4 below), the level of sales per person engaged of multiples being less than a third higher than that of independents in 1966. Similarly with respect to 'variety and other general stores', there was a demise in the 'other general stores' sector and an expansion of 'variety stores', which carried with it a large increase in average shop size.

2 The 1966 Census of Distribution shows, for instance, that turnover per person engaged was, on average, over £9,000 for grocery outlets with annual sales of more than £200,000, as opposed to less than £6,000 for sales under £20,000. However, while in the case of this trade sales per person engaged increase progressively with shop size, with respect to some other businesses, the attainment of most economies of scale seems to be possible at relatively low levels of annual turnover. For example, in the case of 'Men's and boys' wear' shops, the level of productivity was much the same in outlets with an annual turnover of between £20,000 and £50,000 as in those with an annual turnover exceeding £200,000.

be associated with both the concentration of sales on less retail capacity and the substitution of larger stores for smaller shops. Both can be expected to influence productivity in the same direction, the former through the elimination of marginal outlets and the fuller use of staff in remaining stores, the latter through the realisation of economies of scale and the attainment of a higher degree of specialisation.

To sum up the points made earlier, a rise in sales has a beneficial effect on labour productivity, which operates through increasing sales per shop, but partly, it would appear, through other means, such as through the construction of more modern facilities. Thus taking account of both changes in sales and changes in numbers of shops increases the degree of explanation of variations in productivity growth between kinds of business. The regression equation is:

$$P = 3 \cdot 5 + 0 \cdot 747T - 0 \cdot 467S \qquad \overline{R}^2 = 0 \cdot 84$$
$$(0 \cdot 089) \quad (0 \cdot 150)$$

where P and T are as above and S is the change in the number of shops, for the 18 business categories.

The equation indicates therefore that an increase in the number of shops with sales remaining constant tends to reduce the rise in productivity, but also that an increase in sales which is associated with an equivalent rise in the number of shops tends nevertheless to have a beneficial effect on productivity. In other words, a rapid rate of sales growth has a positive influence on the rate of productivity growth other than through raising the sales-size of shop.

Turning finally to the last column in Table III.1, this shows the change over the period in the gross margin per unit of sales, or, in other words, in the cash margin earned by retailers from selling a given volume of goods. It is derived by taking the change in gross margin as a percentage of turnover between the two years and adjusting for the movement in the price of the goods sold, which varied substantially between products. Thus an allowance is made for the fact that retailers of electrical appliances, for example, experienced a reduction in unit price — because of productivity gains made at the manufacturing stage — while off-licences enjoyed an increase in unit price. A constant gross margin as a percentage of turnover would have therefore been associated with a decline in the cash margin per unit of sales in the first case and an increase in the second case, which means that a comparison of changes in percentage margins gives no indication of relative changes in gross profit (defined as the value of sales minus the cost of goods bought). For the two examples given, we might expect to find, in other words, a greater rise in the percentage gross margin earned by electrical goods retailers than by off-licences, other things being equal.

To some extent we can regard changes in gross margin per unit of sales as reflecting relative changes in the price of retail service, assuming that the amount of service included with the goods sold remained more or less constant over the period as between kinds of business, or even that it changed in a random way.[1] This being so, it enables us to examine the question of whether gains in retail productivity were

1 Further difficulties here include possible changes in the composition of goods and the fact that retail operating costs are not invariant to the price of goods sold. In particular, the cost of holding stock varies directly with unit price and ideally some allowance should be made for this. However it is not possible for us to estimate how important stock-holding costs are as a proportion of the total.

passed on to customers in the form of lower prices or whether they led to increases in net profit — on the assumption, of course, that relative wages in different kinds of business remained unchanged, which seems highly plausible. It is immediately apparent that an inverse relationship exists between movements in sales per person engaged and in gross margin per unit of sales in Table III.1, there being a marked tendency for the latter to increase as we read down the table. The correlation coefficient between the two variables is in fact -0.87. The conclusion therefore emerges that retailers making relatively large gains in productivity tended to show relatively small increases in the cash margin earned per unit of sales.

However we cannot necessarily interpret this result as demonstrating that gains in productivity were passed on in the form of lower prices. Quite apart from the problem concerning the amount of service supplied, a plausible case can be made out in support of the possibility that the direction of causation runs in the opposite direction. Thus it might be argued that low increases in margin encouraged a search for ways of reducing operating costs and hence stimulated increases in sales per person engaged, or alternatively that an inability to raise margins led to the elimination of marginal shops, which would be consistent with the Kaldor hypothesis.[1]

2. Productivity Change by Form of Organisation

With a little manipulation of the Census figures, it is possible to disaggregate still further and compare the experience of the three major forms of retail organisation by kind of business. The main points of interest here are, firstly, whether multiple retailers have tended to show larger gains in productivity than independents or cooperative societies, as perhaps is widely supposed, and if so the extent of the difference; secondly, whether a similar pattern to that for all retailers emerges at this level of disaggregation.

Table III.2 shows the changes in productivity for multiple organisations, independent retailers and cooperative societies between 1957 and 1966 with respect to the 20 kinds of business of Table III.1. The corresponding changes in the volume of sales and in sales per shop are also shown. Although the figures involve a certain amount of estimation, insofar as it was necessary to adjust the 1957 Census data for a number of trades to make them consistent with the statistics published in the

---

1 Assuming demand conditions remain unchanged, the Kaldor hypothesis predicts that the percentage gross margin should also remain unchanged, apart from changes in the cost of holding stock, as a result of movements in interest rates, and changes in the composition of turnover. All three items are liable to change over time, however, and may have a differential effect as between retailers. Percentage gross margins in fact generally increased over the period 1957 to 1966, but not in any apparent systematic way.

Table III.2   *Percentage Change in Sales per Person Engaged, Sales and Sales per Shop, by Form of Organisation: 1957 to 1966*

Kind of Business	Multiples			Independents			Coops		
	(1)	(2)	(3)	(1)	(2)	(3)	(1)	(2)	(3)
Jewellery, etc.	29·1	147·5	32·2	52·6	61·6	54·2	17·6	49·1	23·8
Radio and Electrical	53·0	239·9	17·0	45·1	38·1	25·4	20·2	200·2	14·6
Womenswear	28·9	90·1	16·2	28·2	11·0	25·3	12·1	−9·0	3·7
Grocers	48·4	95·6	119·9	28·6	3·1	29·1	15·3	−12·6	−11·0
Hardware	21·3	44·5	5·9	34·6	45·8	31·0	24·6	14·2	15·7
Chemists	33·6	60·8	54·2	33·0	45·7	45·9	12·7	11·7	18·6
Off-licences	14·0	134·8	20·7	25·2	2·0	21·7	36·4	878·6	22·7
Department Stores	32·5	99·1	44·2	23·6	6·6	29·1	20·2	42·3	13·6
Dairymen	22·0	76·5	60·9	25·4	−24·2	45·4	13·7	12·7	69·5
Furniture and Allied	11·7	60·0	− 9·2	30·7	52·2	23·8	3·6	25·8	−5·9
Other Non-Food	13·3	25·0	20·3	28·8	48·4	30·7	7·0	76·3	46·2
Book-Shops	38·8	70·1	66·1	18·1	−5·0	5·6	−16·3	29·8	42·7
Menswear	13·0	46·5	16·3	19·2	11·9	9·5	9·7	−17·8	−14·3
Boots and Shoes	12·0	29·4	14·2	19·6	3·2	18·3	2·2	−15·9	−3·7
Variety Stores	18·4	21·3	32·0	5·3	−66·2	33·5	−2·6	−22·2	40·4
Butchers	8·4	15·9	12·0	5·9	−1·4	6·6	−3·8	−31·7	−22·5
Fishmongers	26·5	−24·7	37·3	3·9	−9·6	7·2	0·5	−37·0	7·1
C.T.N.'s	13·5	31·6	32·9	3·0	1·0	24·9	43·7	−13·6	24·4
Greengrocers	−1·3	49·7	8·3	1·5	−6·9	12·1	−0·5	−47·1	−23·1
Bread	1·9	84·1	−11·0	0	−15·5	2·0	−13·2	−37·4	−12·9

Source: Census of Distribution, 1957, 1961, 1966.

Notes: Column (1) is the percentage change in the volume of sales per person engaged. Column (2) is the percentage change in the volume of retail sales. Column (3) is the percentage change in the volume of sales per shop.

For each trade, volume changes are derived on the assumption that the change in price was the same for all three forms of organisation. Market traders have been excluded in each case, and adjustments have been made to the figures published in the 1957 and 1961 Census to take account of classification changes. This involved some element of estimation for the employment figures for the earlier year, with regard to a number of trades, but the margin of error arising from this source is relatively low.

Multiples are defined as those organisations owning ten or more retail outlets.

1966 Census, the possible errors arising from this source are very minor.[1]

It is apparent that there was a considerable degree of variation between the productivity performance of the three forms of organisation over the period. The only clear tendency to emerge is for multiples and independents to have increased

1   Specifically, for eight of the trades, changes were made in classification between the 1957 and 1961 Censuses, which are not fully documented with regard to their effect on employment by form of organisation. For three of the eight, however, the *total* change involved a transfer of less than one per cent of persons engaged. In all cases, the implications of the changes for employment were estimated on the basis of their effect on turnover. In addition, 'soft furnishings' shops were transferred from 'Furniture' to 'Women's wear' in 1966. Estimates for 1957 of the division in turnover and persons engaged between forms of organisation for such shops were based on the figures for 1961, and the 1957 figures for the two kinds of business were adjusted accordingly. Moreover 'Radio and television hire' shops are separately distinguished from 'Radio and electrical goods' shops in 1966 but not in earlier years. These are excluded from the change shown in the table for the latter category, estimates for 1957 being again based on the 1961 division between forms of organisation.

productivity by far more than coops. The exceptions are 'Confectioners, tobacconists and newsagents' (C.T.N.'s) and 'Off-licences' but coops were responsible for less than one per cent of the sales of these two categories in 1957. Only in three other kinds of business ('Hardware', 'Department stores' and 'Greengrocers'), was their performance at all comparable to that of either multiples or independents. It is of interest to note that these five kinds of business were the only ones in which the sales record of coops was not inferior to that of the other two forms of organisation.

Comparing multiples and independents, we find in aggregate that the former showed a greater gain in labour productivity than the latter over the period, the overall percentage increase being 28·6 per cent as against 20·8 per cent, if allowance is made for the difference in business composition between the two forms of organisation.[1] There is, however, no general tendency in Table III.2 for multiples to have increased their volume of sales per person engaged by more in individual business categories than independents − or, indeed, vice versa. Thus in eleven of the twenty kinds of business, the productivity gain of multiples exceeded that of independents, but in only seven trades was the difference more than three percentage points. On the other hand, a tendency emerges for the productivity of multiples and independents to have increased at a relatively high (or low) rate in the same kinds of business, the (Spearman's) rank correlation coefficient between the kinds of business ranked according to the growth in productivity shown by multiples and ranked according to the productivity growth of independents being 0·52.

Moreover if we look at the other columns of Table III.2, little association is discernible between the relative productivity performance of multiples and independents by kind of business and the relative changes in sales and sales per shop. In other words, it does not appear possible to explain, for example, the superior productivity gain made by one form of organisation in a particular trade by reference to higher sales growth or greater sales per shop. Thus in all trades apart from three, multiples experienced a much larger rise in sales volume than independents, but in only six cases was their productivity growth significantly greater. In eleven of the twenty businesses, the rise in the average sales-size of independent shop exceeded that of multiple outlets, but in four of the eleven, the productivity growth of independents was less than that of multiples.

However if we look at multiples and independents separately, and relate changes in productivity to changes in sales and sales per shop by kind of business, it is evident that a similar pattern exists as for all retailers. This is indicated in Table III.3, which shows the results of regressing productivity growth on the latter two variables for these two forms of organisation over the period 1957 to 1966.

Again variations between businesses in sales growth and the rise in sales per shop statistically explain much of the variation in productivity change ($\overline{R}^2$ equalling 0·71 in the case of independents and 0·62 in the case of multiples), although less than when all retailers are considered together.

---

1 The effect of allowing for differences in business composition is, in fact, only to slightly change the increase in total sales per person engaged for both forms of organisation, which was 27·8 per cent for multiples and 21·8 per cent for independents.

Table III.3 *Regressions of Productivity Change on the Change in Sales and Sales per Shop, by Form of Organisation: 1957 to 1966*

Form of Organisation	Equation	Constant	Regression Coefficients of:			
			Δ Sales	Δ Sales per Shop	r^2	$\overline{R}^2$
Multiples	(1)	12·5	0·135 (0·050)		0·29	
	(2)	12·5		0·320 (0·086)	0·43	
	(3)	4·2	0·125 (0·035)	0·304 (0·067)		0·62
Independents	(1)	18·0	0·356 (0·075)		0·56	
	(2)	4·9		0·697 (0·179)	0·46	
	(3)	7·1	0·277 (0·062)	0·486 (0·133)		0·71

Note: The equations are based on the data contained in Table III.2 for the twenty kinds of business.

Δ Sales represents the percentage change in the volume of sales.

3. Structural Changes

Our concern in this section is: firstly, to examine the changes over the period 1957 to 1966 in the market share of multiples, independents and cooperative societies; secondly, to see whether such changes are explicable in terms of productivity differences; and thirdly, to estimate the contribution made by such changes to the productivity performance of the sector and its constituent trades.

As we noted above, there were marked differences over the period in question in the sales growth experienced by the three major forms of organisation, which of course means that the structure of the retail trades altered a good deal between these two years. Specifically multiple organisations increased their share of the market at the expense of both cooperative societies and independent retailers. Thus multiples were responsible for 34·5 per cent of total retail sales in 1966 as opposed to 25·1 per cent in 1957. By contrast, the share of coops fell from 12·1 per cent in 1957 to 9·1 per cent in 1966, while the share of independents declined from 62·8 per cent to 56·4 per cent over the same period.

This pattern of change has, as we have remarked, been associated with a rise in average sales per shop, 'Dairymen' and 'Variety and other general stores', providing extreme examples. It has also produced some overall gain in the productivity of the sector, insofar as it represents a diversion of sales away from shops with a relatively low average value of turnover per person engaged to those with a relatively high value. Thus in 1966 total sales per person engaged in multiple stores amounted to £6,173 whereas the corresponding figure for independent shops was £4,623.[1]

However there is a good deal of variation between kinds of business both with respect to the relative growth of the multiple form of organisation over the period 1957 to 1966 and with respect to the difference in the level of labour productivity between multiples and other retailers. These two elements of variation are indicated

---

1 The two figures are not strictly comparable as they do not take account of the differing proportion of sales made in individual kinds of business.

Table III.4   *Structural Change 1957 to 1966 and its Effect on Productivity Growth*

Kind of Business	% Share of multiples in 1966	Change in share of multiples 1957–66[a]	% Productivity difference in 1966, between multiples and non multiples	Increase in sales per person engaged	Effect of structural change[b]
1. Jewellery, Leather Sports Goods	15·3	4·4	34·3	52·4	1·2
2. Radio and Electrical Goods	27·0	14·5	48·1	45·4	5·6
3. Women's and Girls' Wear	47·3	13·3	94·6	38·0	8·1
4. Grocers and Provision Dealers	36·3	14·0+	34·8	33·7	3·3
5. Hardware, Wallpaper and Paint	12·1	0	−0·4	32·6	−0·1
6. Chemists, Photographic Dealers	37·5	2·8	−6·8	31·8	−1·5
7. Off-Licences	57·4	19·3	24·6	28·6	3·0
8. Department Stores	24·3	8·9	0·6	26·2	1·4
9. Dairymen	43·7	14·5	22·6	25·3	4·0
10. Furniture	25·5	1·2	9·8	25·0	−0·2
11. Other Non-Food	7·8	−6·5	60·4	24·0	−2·5
12. Book-shops and Stationers	34·3	11·7	6·6	23·4	0·7
13. Men's and Boys' Wear	51·0	7·2	41·8	19·3	2·3
14. Boots and Shoes	66·4	5·8	25·2	15·8	1·2
15. Variety and Other General	91·5	10·6	−19·2	15·0	−0·8
16. Butchers	15·8	2·5*	16·7	5·4	0·6
17. Fishmongers, Poulterers	14·5	−1·3	57·2	5·4	−0·9
18. Confectioners, Tobacconists etc.	14·5	3·0	47·8	4·9	1·0
19. Greengrocers, Fruiterers	9·8	3·7*	22·1	1·7	0·4
20. Bread and Flour	35·9	16·5+	36·1	1·3	3·0

Source: Census of Distribution 1966.
Notes: The figures are adjusted to exclude market traders in 1957 and 1961.

a The percentage of turnover accounted for by multiples in 1966 minus their percentage share in 1957. The gain was mainly at the expense of independent retailers, except for the two kinds of business marked with *, where the gain was almost wholly at the expense of coops, and the two marked with +, where both coops and independents suffered a similar loss of sales.

b This represents the percentage by which productivity would have increased between 1957 and 1966, if sales per person engaged had remained constant for each individual form of organisation. For each kind of business, it is obtained by weighting the respective numbers engaged per £100,000 turnover in multiples, independents and coops in 1966, by the respective percentage shares of turnover of these in 1957. The resultant 'weighted average' figure is then inverted to give an adjusted value for sales per person engaged for 1966. The percentage by which actual sales per person engaged in 1966 exceed this adjusted value is what is shown in this column.

in the second and third columns of Table III.4, the first column showing the proportion of sales made by multiples in 1966. Thus the change in the multiple share of trade varied from an increase of 19·3 percentage points in the case of 'Off-licences' and one of 16·5 per cent in that of 'Bread and flour confectioners', to a decline of

6·5 per cent in the case of 'Other non-food' shops and 1·3 per cent in that of 'Fishmongers and poulterers'.

In most instances, the growth of multiples has been associated with a decline in the proportion of trade going through independent outlets, but these were still responsible for over half of the sales of 13 kinds of business in 1966 and in only three cases was their share less than 40 per cent ('Dairymen', 'Boots and shoes' and 'Variety stores'). Cooperative societies generally accounted for a very minor part of the sales of each category, partially because they tend to concentrate on the department and grocery store type of operation, selling durable goods through the former and non-durable goods through the latter. Apart from these two kinds of business and 'Dairymen', 'Butchers' and 'Bread' shops, less than five per cent of the sales of each business went through outlets owned by coops. Moreover there was a decline in the coop share of trade in each case, with the exception of 'Off-licences', 'Radio and electrical goods' shops and 'Department stores', where their gain was minimal.

The third column reveals an even greater degree of diversity than the second, the level of sales per person engaged of multiple outlets in 1966 exceeding that in other retailers by 94·6 per cent in respect of 'Woman's and girls' wear', while being 19·2 per cent below that of other retailers in respect of 'Variety and other general stores'.

A comparison of columns 2 and 3 shows no systematic tendency for multiples to have increased their share of business by more in those trades in which their relative superiority in terms of sales per person engaged was greatest — the difference in labour productivity between multiples and other retailers being in most cases similar in 1957 to that shown for 1966. A positive association might have been expected insofar as the inverse of sales per person engaged reflects labour costs per unit of turnover, the hypothesis being that where these are relatively low, multiples are potentially in a better position to expand sales at the expense of their competitors. However there are a number of reasons why this might not be so. For example, the existence of r.p.m., whether *de jure* or *de facto*, may have restricted the ability of multiples to attract additional custom over this period, or the nature of the trade may have imposed a limit on their growth, or the composition of multiples' turnover may differ from that of other retailers, making comparisons of labour costs invalid. Alternatively, other circumstances may have outweighed any discernible tendency for differences in labour costs to affect relative growth rates. This is particularly relevant with regard to the food trade, where there has been a diversion of sales from specialist retailers, such as 'Fishmongers and poulterers' and 'Greengrocers and fruiterers' to 'Grocers and provision dealers'. In more general terms, it should be remembered that the figures in the table relate to business categories rather than to commodities and therefore may conceal a shift in the sale of certain product groups to multiples, if these happen to be classified to trades other than those specialising in their sale.

The final column of Table III.4 shows the contribution to the overall rise in productivity — reproduced in column 4 — of the switch in sales between forms of organisation that occurred over the period in question. The figures are derived by assuming that the respective percentage market shares of multiples, independents and coops were the same in 1966 as they had been in 1957, and show, in fact, the percentage by which actual turnover per person engaged in 1966 exceeded that which would have obtained, had this assumption been realised. Fuller details on the method of calculation are contained in the notes to the table. To take 'Radio and electrical goods' as an example, the overall productivity gain was 5·6 per cent higher than it would have been − 45·4 per cent as opposed to 37·7 per cent − if multiples, and, to a far lesser extent, coops, had not increased their share of sales.

In absolute terms, the contribution to overall productivity growth of this structural component tends, of course, to be greatest where the increase in the market share of multiples and the excess of their level of productivity over that of other retailers were both large, the most prominent example being that of 'Women's and girls' wear' shops. In certain instances, however, the effect on overall productivity of the increasing importance of multiples was partly offset by the declining proportion of sales going through cooperative societies, which also generally had a higher level of turnover per person engaged than independents. This was most notable in respect of 'Grocers and provision dealers', where coops suffered almost the same decline in their market share as independents, while their level of labour productivity in 1957 actually exceeded that of multiples (by over 17 per cent).[1]

Although Table III.4 indicates that structural changes generally contributed to productivity growth over this period, it is apparent that, with a few exceptions, they represented a relatively minor factor and that by far the greater part of the increase in productivity occurred as a result of increases *within* forms of organisation. Thus, in overall terms, the productivity of the twenty trades included in the table increased by 24 per cent between 1957 and 1966, but only two percentage points of this increase arose as a direct result of switches in consumer expenditure between forms of organisation.

One final point which deserves mention in this connection, is that the data on which the above analysis is based refer to retail establishments rather than retail organisations. This means that they exclude the people working in the central offices and warehouses of multiple retailers and cooperative societies, together with the very small amount of turnover for which these are directly responsible. It follows from this that we would expect the value of sales per person engaged to be higher in respect of multiples and coops than for independents, if only because part of the labour force responsible for the output of the former two are excluded from the employment figures we have used, whereas people performing similar functions are to some extent included in the employment figures for independents.[2] The 1966 Census of Distribution indicates that almost 16 per cent of the total persons employed by multiple organisations in their retail activities were engaged in central offices and warehouses, and hence do not appear in our employment figures.[3] If we adopt the extreme assumption that all such persons were employed full-time, this would reduce overall sales per person engaged, on a full-time equivalent basis, for multiples from £6,173 to £5,141, which still remains greater than the corresponding value for

1 By 1966, the position had been reversed, the level of labour productivity in multiples exceeding that in coops by about ten per cent.

2 More realistically, some of the persons engaged in independent stores will spend some of their time on matters which in the case of multiples are handled by the central office.

3 The proportion was even larger with respect to coops at over 20 per cent.

independents of £4,623.

However such a revised comparison neglects the point that the activities performed by multiple retailers tend to be more extensive than those undertaken by independents. In particular, the latter usually purchase a much higher proportion of their stocks from wholesalers than do multiples, which, in many cases, carry out the necessary wholesaling functions by taking deliveries direct from manufacturers at central warehouses and supplying their individual branches from these. Consequently, if we wish to compare productivity in *retailing* between these two forms of organisation on the same basis, it is probably correct to exclude the staff employed by multiples in their central warehouses. Unfortunately, separate figures are not included in the Census. On the other hand, if we wish to estimate the effect on productivity in *the distributive trades* of the relative growth of multiple sales, we should take account of those persons engaged in the wholesale sector who are displaced by this change in the pattern of retailing.

The analysis undertaken in this chapter is therefore based on the turnover and employment of retail establishments or shops, and this is true of the remainder of this part of the study. The above discussion does, however, indicate that the relative growth in multiple turnover has led to an increase in productivity both in retailing and in the distributive trades as a whole, even though it is not possible from the information available to measure the precise magnitude of the gain in either case.

4. Changes in Methods of Selling

(i) The Impact of Self-Service on Grocery Productivity
As we remarked in the previous chapter, a marked feature of retailing in recent years has been the development of self-service methods of selling. In some form or other, this is now of some significance in most areas of retailing, but the Census of Distribution provides information only for the grocery trade. Nevertheless by using these details, it is possible to illustrate the potential influence that the adoption of self-service methods has on labour requirements. At the same time it should be recognized that the grocery trade lends itself most ideally to this form of operation, and we cannot therefore assume that its development, in some form, has similar consequences for other parts of the sector.

Table III.5 shows the development of self-service in the grocery trade over the period 1957 to 1966 and compares the changes in sales per person engaged and sales per shop in respect of self-service stores with those for other grocery outlets. Thus the proportion of grocery sales sold on a self-service basis increased from nine per cent in 1957 to 45 per cent in 1966. Over the same period, productivity in self-service stores rose by 24 per cent as compared with an average rise of 16 per cent in other shops. Both these increases are significantly lower than the gain for the trade as a whole, which was almost 33 per cent. We can therefore ascribe much of the overall gain in productivity to the growth in the proportion of grocery sales taking place in self-service stores, which had a markedly higher level of sales per person engaged than counter-service shops (49 per cent greater in 1966). Indeed if the same proportion of grocery sales had been sold on a self-service basis in 1966 as in 1957, the overall rise in the productivity of the trade would have been reduced from 33 per cent to less than 17 per cent.

Table III.5   *Self-Service Trading in Grocery Stores, 1957 to 1966*

	1957	1961	1966	% Change in real terms, 1957 to 1966
Self-Service Sales as % of Total	8·9	21·2	44·9	
Turnover per Person Engaged (£):				
Self-service	5672	6200	8413	+24·1
Other shops	4073	4634	5657	+16·2
All shops	4179	4896	6631	+32·8
Turnover per Establishment (£):				
Self-service	57260	54889	70369	+2·8
Other shops	12585	13449	14983	−0·4
All shops	13528	16016	23174	+43·4

Source: Board of Trade Journal, 20 December 1963 and *Report on the Census of Distribution, 1966, Volume 2.*
Notes: Market-traders are excluded in each case. The 1966 figures are based on a different method of estimating the totals from the sample of independents than in previous tables; the changes shown for all grocery shops therefore differ slightly from those shown in Table III.1.

The development of the self-service method of operation made an even greater contribution to productivity growth over the period 1961 to 1966. Thus if we assume that such sales accounted for the same percentage of grocery turnover in 1966 as was the case in 1961, and if we further assume that the rate of productivity growth of self-service stores over this period was the same as that of other grocery outlets,[1] the overall gain in productivity of the trade is reduced from 18 per cent to only six per cent.

Moreover if we look at the figures in the table for turnover per establishment, it is clear that the switch to self-service was entirely responsible for the large increase in the average sales-size of grocery outlet that occurred over the period. Thus in 1966 self-service stores were on average almost five times the size of counter-service shops in terms of annual turnover, and if they had not increased their share of grocery sales, sales per shop would have actually shown an overall decline between 1957 and 1966.

There is also evidence that multiple organisations have taken much fuller advantage of self-service than either cooperative societies or independent retailers, despite the coops' earlier adoption of this method of selling. In 1957, 24 per cent of cooperative grocery sales took place in self-service stores and 62 per cent by value of all grocery sold on this basis, were made by coops. The relevant figures for multiples were 11 per cent and 27 per cent, respectively. By 1966, 62 per cent of cooperative grocery sales took place in self-service stores, but these accounted for only 22 per cent of the total grocery sales sold on this basis. By contrast, the relevant figures for multiples

1   This 'extra' assumption is founded on the probability that the productivity growth achieved by self-service stores over the period was associated with this particular method of selling and would not have been realised had conversions not been made. In particular, it is likely that much of the gain accrued from improvements in self-service, which newly converted or constructed outlets could take advantage of.

had increased to 74 per cent and over 57 per cent, respectively.[1] Furthermore the average sales-size of self-service store rose by over 61 per cent over the period in respect of multiples, but fell by over 18 per cent in respect of coops. In consequence, the benefits attained by multiples from economies of scale, which are a significant feature of this method of operating were considerably greater than those attained by coops.[2]

Of course, it may be argued that the gain in productivity resulting from conversion to self-service is more apparent than real, in the sense that it merely involves a transfer of part of the retail function from the retail sector to the 'household' sector, which is thus associated with a tendency to understate the number of manhours devoted to retailing. Alternatively this might be regarded as a reduction in the service provided by the retail trades. However it is as well to recognise that shoppers do have a choice as to where to purchase their groceries — 85 per cent of grocery shops did *not* operate on a self-service basis in 1966 — and have shown in aggregate a marked preference for self-service stores. Presumably therefore the 'disutility' of undertaking part of the retail function is more than compensated by the improvement in the price—service package obtained.

(ii) Impact of Self-service on Overall Productivity Growth

As a further step, we can estimate the approximate contribution made by the increase in the relative importance of self-service stores in the grocery trade to the rise in productivity that occurred in retailing as a whole between 1961 and 1966. Thus in view of the central role attached to this development by a number of commentators, it is clearly of some interest to have an idea of its impact on overall efficiency over this particular period, when its contribution to the gain in productivity made by grocery stores was especially large.[3]

Our estimate of the contribution is based on the assumption that the effect of introducing self-service was to reduce the number of persons engaged per unit of turnover but that it did not affect total sales. Essentially we ask the question how many people would have been employed in retailing in 1966, had the proportion of self-service sales been the same in 1966 as in 1961 and had the rise in productivity been identical in self-service stores to that in counter-service shops. On this basis, we calculate that an additional 50,955 'full-time equivalent' persons would have been required to retail the amount of grocery sales in 1966, which represents an increase

---

1 As far as independents are concerned, less than 19 per cent of their grocery sales occurred in self-service outlets in 1966.

2 The 1966 Census shows average turnover per person engaged as less than £8,000 for self-service stores with annual sales of less than £100,000, but as around £10,000 for stores with sales of over £200,000. In 1966, 84 cooperative outlets — or under two per cent of all coop self-service shops — were included in the latter category, as opposed to 988 multiple outlets — or 15 per cent of all multiple self-service shops.

3 While the estimate may give some indication of whether it is plausible to suppose that the 'productivity jump' of the period 1965 to 1970, considered in the previous chapter, was a consequence of the switch to self-service, it has to be borne in mind that the impact on marginal outlets, possible lag-effects and the spread of self-service to other types of shop may be of considerable importance. Because of such factors, it is not possible at this time even to attempt an estimate of its likely impact on this later period.

of 12 per cent over those that were actually employed. This is equivalent to a rise
of 2·4 per cent in the total persons engaged in retailing as a whole, which implies
that the productivity growth of the retail trades over this period would have been
reduced from 10·0 per cent to 7·4 per cent.[1] In other words, of the total increase
in productivity that occurred over the period 1961 to 1966, 26 per cent can be
attributed to the growth of the self-service method of selling and to the more
efficient use of labour in such stores.

However, it should be repeated that we have only been able to assess the impact
made by the switch to self-service in the grocery trade. As we have mentioned, while
grocery stores were responsible in 1966 for virtually all the sales made by this method
as defined by the Census of Distribution, self-service techniques in some modified or
less 'extreme' form were employed in a great many shops in other trades. As such
techniques undoubtedly increased in importance between 1961 and 1966 a wider
definition of self-service would naturally yield a higher estimate of its contribution
to the overall gain in productivity.

On the other hand, it is almost certainly true that the development of self-service
in the grocery trade was a feature associated with the more efficient rather than the
less efficient organisations, the implication being that such retailers would have
tended to show a greater improvement in productivity over the period than others,
even if no conversion to self-service had been made. In other words, part of the
increase in productivity which we have attributed to self-service may not necessarily
have been a consequence of the adoption of this method of selling but perhaps can
more appropriately be regarded as stemming from the relative growth of the more
efficient retailers. Correspondingly, the contribution made by the switch to self-
service may be over-estimated in the above exercise.

5. Summary of Main Findings

The main points to emerge from the analysis of the experience of the different
kinds of retail business over the period 1957 to 1966 are as follows:—

1. There is a close association between the change in the volume of sales and
   the growth in sales per person engaged. The direction of causation most
   plausibly runs from the former to the latter, and can be explained in terms
   of a number of hypotheses, including, for example, those which emphasize
   the role of new capital investment or the effect of increasing transaction
   size.
2. The data also revealed a tendency for the change in the number of shops
   and sales per shop to be positively related to the expansion of trade. In
   addition, productivity growth was associated with increases in sales per shop.
   This, it was argued, might reflect, for instance, the fuller use made of staff
   in existing stores or the effect of the elimination of marginal outlets.
3. Changes in sales and changes in the number of shops, or in sales per shop,
   together provide a high degree of explanation of variations in productivity

---

1 The rise of 10·0 per cent, which is estimated to have occurred between 1961 and 1966,
   is calculated on the basis of Census of Distribution data for the twenty kinds of business
   listed in Table III.1; two part-timers are counted as equivalent to one full-timer and the
   1966 sales of each business are summed in terms of 1961 prices.

growth. This also applies if multiples and independents are considered separately, although the degree of explanation is slightly less.

4. A close inverse association emerged between productivity growth and changes in the gross cash margin earned by retailers per unit of sales. If the latter is taken as a proxy for changes in the relative price of retail service, the result indicates a tendency for productivity gains to be passed on to customers in the form of lower prices.

5. No tendency was found for the performance of multiple retailers, in terms of productivity growth, to be superior to that of independents in respect of individual business categories, but the performance of cooperative societies was generally far inferior to both.

6. Multiple retailers increased their share of retail sales, in same cases significantly, but although structural change contributed to the overall gain in productivity, this was generally a minor factor.

7. Self-service trading developed at a rapid rate over the period and between 1961 and 1966 was responsible for most of the increase in the sales per person engaged of the grocery trade. It was estimated that about 26 per cent of the overall rise in productivity of the retail trades between these two years could be attributed to the expansion of self-service grocery stores.

IV
Town Analysis – Introduction

1. Introduction

The analysis of the preceding two chapters has left a number of issues only partly considered. In particular, the data examined have not enabled us to explore the relationship between productivity growth and labour market conditions in any depth. Thus we have seen that employment in retailing in the years 1954 to 1965 was affected among other things by the degree of labour shortage, there being some reduction in numbers employed per unit of sales when unfilled vacancies were relatively high. It was argued however that any gains in output per person engaged from this source were likely to be short-term in nature, reflecting a temporary deterioration in retail service, and that more permanent gains would tend to be concealed in the trend factor. While the long-term association between the two variables might be pursued using time-series data, by taking comparisons over periods of a number of years at a stretch, for example, the variation in the degree of labour scarcity is likely to prove insufficient to give an adequate guide – at least over the comparatively recent period for which reasonably reliable figures are available. Furthermore the problem arises of allowing for the influence of special factors – S.E.T. for instance – which are peculiar to certain years.

The availability of statistics on retailing in individual towns for 1961 and 1966 allows a more satisfactory analysis to be made of the relationship between these two variables, and also provides an alternative method of investigating the association between productivity changes and sales growth. This is especially so as the experience of the towns which we are able to include in the analysis varied quite substantially, with regard to the movement in sales and labour market conditions, for instance, over this period. Our intention is therefore to examine the influence of differences in the feature of the towns on the productivity performance of the retailers located within their boundaries. Thus in some sense we take the towns as approximating to individual markets, the object being to look at the effect of variations in the characteristics of these markets on retailers' operations.

2. The Sample of Towns

The analysis is based primarily on a sample of fifty of the largest towns in Great Britain, outside the London area, data on retailing in which were compiled for 1966 and provided especially for the study by the Department of Trade and Industry. Use is made of the statistics published in the 1961 Census of Distribution to assess differences between these towns in both 1961 and 1966 and to compute the changes which occurred over this five-year period. In addition we draw on the findings of an

Table IV.1   *The Sample of 50 Towns by Value of Retail Sales, 1966*

Retail Sales, 1966 (£ million)	Number of Towns	Average Total Population 1966 ('000)
17 < 30	9	113
30 < 40	9	130
40 < 50	11	162
50 < 100	13	246
100 and over	8	652

Sources: The figures for retail sales are derived from information collected during the 1966 Census of Distribution and especially provided by the Department of Trade and Industry. Population figures are taken from the Sample Census of 1966.

analysis conducted on the basis of data from the 1961 Census for 160 towns — our fifty towns being included.[1]

As far as the sample of fifty towns is concerned, these range in size from Birmingham, with a population of over a million and retail sales of £261 million in 1966, to Wigan, with a population of less than 80 thousand and retail sales of £21 million, and South Shields with a population of 106 thousand and sales of less than £18 million. The majority of the towns had retail sales of below £50 million in 1966, while eight had sales exceeding £100 million. Fuller details are shown in Table IV.1.

Even the smallest towns included in the sample are therefore large by most standards, and it may be that the findings of the subsequent analysis are not applicable to 'small' towns. However the 1961 study of 160 towns revealed no discernible tendency for the results for the smallest towns included to differ in any systematic way from those formulated from the sample as a whole, although no towns with sales of less than £10 million or with a population of below 30 thousand were covered. At the same time, it should be recognized that if the size of towns is reduced to any great extent, they become less close approximations to individual retail markets, in the sense that they are likely to be situated close to larger centres of population and the operations of their retailers more influenced by the features of these than the characteristics of their own town.

Details of the sample of 160 towns in 1961 are reproduced in Table IV.2.

3. The Data

The data on which the analysis is based were collected during the 1961 and 1966 Censuses of Distribution. The former was a full census,[2] while the latter was conducted on a sample basis, which meant that multiples, coops and independents with a turnover exceeding £50 thousand in 1961 were covered in full, but returns were collected from only a sample of other traders. The sampling scheme used for our fifty towns (Wigan apart) was to cover small independents in a sample of streets, or segments of streets. This represents some qualification to the findings, insofar as it

1 See K.D. George, *Productivity in Distribution*, D.A.E. Occasional Papers No. 8, C.U.P. 1966.

2 Full in the sense that every known retailer was approached, but in fact the town figures cover only 'returns received', which represented an estimated 88 per cent of total retail establishments for the country as a whole and 93 per cent of total turnover.

Table IV.2   *The Sample of 160 Towns by Value of Retail Sales, 1961*

Retail Sales, 1961 (£ millions)	Number of Towns	Average Total Population, 1961 ('000)
10 < 12·25	31	61
12·25 < 15	31	72
15 < 19	30	83
19 < 30	34	112
30 and over	34	319

Source: K.D. George, *Productivity in Distribution*, p. 16 and pp. 86–90.

may have produced a possible over- or under-estimate of the importance of such retailers; more especially, however, the sample area may have contained unrepresentative proportions of the various kinds of business. This applies principally to 'Confectioners, tobacconists and newsagents' (C.T.N.'s), a comparatively large number of which are small shops; certainly in the case of a few towns, the figures for this kind of business show substantial changes between 1961 and 1966.[1] We should say that possible estimation errors tend to cancel out over the towns as a whole — so that the national totals are unlikely to be significantly biassed — and indeed to become less important the larger the size of town. Moreover the figures for the individual kinds of business are more likely to be subject to errors of any size than the overall totals for each town.

Fortunately, there were no changes in the 'definition' of the towns between the two Censuses, as both used the boundaries as defined by the 1961 Census of Population. However there are small differences in the coverage of the Censuses and two minor changes in the classification of certain types of shop for which it is not possible to make any allowance. Thus the 1966 Census did not cover 'street traders and market traders trading other than from lockable premises', which were included in 1961. The figures we derive for changes in turnover, establishments and persons engaged will therefore tend to be slight under-estimates of the actual changes, while the reverse is true for changes in sales per person engaged and sales per establishment. This represents a minor qualification to the findings, only insofar as market traders vary in importance between towns, but overall they accounted for a very small part of total retailing in 1961.[2]

The changes in classification involve 'other food retailers' which were transferred from the 'Other Food' category to 'Grocers and provision dealers' and 'soft furnishing shops' which were reclassified from 'Household goods' to 'Clothing and footwear', between the two Censuses. In the first case, this represents a change of less than one per cent to the turnover of each, in the second, one of about four per cent. It is reasonable to suppose therefore that both changes are of little consequence as far as our findings are concerned.

1 These may not necessarily be due to errors of estimation; for example, the development of vending machine sales of cigarettes might have had a significant effect on sales.

2 1 per cent of turnover, 6 per cent of establishments and 1·5 per cent of persons engaged (on a full-time basis); their importance was greatest in respect of the 'Other Food' kind of business, in which 47 per cent of their sales took place, but even here they were responsible for only 2·5 per cent of turnover, 10 per cent of establishments and 3·5 per cent of employment.

4. Inter-town Comparisons of Productivity

(i) Differences in Business Composition

As we made clear at the outset, we adopt the convention of identifying productivity with sales per person engaged. Quite apart from the possible qualifications to the interpretation of the results that stem from the use of this measure, which we outlined at the beginning of the study, there are difficulties involved in comparing the performance of different towns. These arise from the fact that there are significant variations between our sample of towns both in the business composition of their retail sectors and in the change in composition over the period under investigation. Thus in 1961, retailers included in the 'Grocery and provision dealers' category, for example, accounted, on average, for about 22 per cent of the total sales of individual towns. In respect of one town (Wolverhampton), however, their share was only 15 per cent while in another (Salford), it was over 32 per cent. Similarly, 'Clothing and footwear' retailers were responsible for an average of 18 per cent of town sales, but the proportion ranged from 13 per cent (in South Shields) to over 29 per cent (in Swindon). Moreover, while the average percentage of sales made by grocery stores was virtually the same in 1966 as in 1961 for the sample, one town (Bradford), for instance, showed a rise of almost five percentage points, whereas another (York) showed a decline of the same magnitude. A similar variation is evident for the other kinds of business.

If we assume that the difference in business composition between towns reflects a similar difference in the composition of the demand for goods, difficulties of comparing productivity arise, firstly, because the labour needed (or rather commonly used) to retail a given value of goods varies according to the commodity in question. This means that the level of sales per person engaged at any one point in time differs markedly between kinds of business. For example, in 1966, sales per person engaged in 'Grocery and provision dealers' were on average about £6·7 thousand over the country as a whole as opposed to about £4·7 thousand in 'Boot and shoe shops'. In part this may reflect differences in the amount of service included with sales. This not only affects comparisons of sales per person engaged between towns in any one year but also comparisons of changes over time. Thus any change in the composition of demand is liable to alter the total labour requirements of retailing for any given level of sales. In other words, overall sales per person engaged in a town may change over the period under investigation even if productivity as measured were to remain constant in each kind of business.

As far as inter-town comparisons of levels of productivity are concerned, we explicitly allow for differences in business composition by weighting the inverse of sales per person engaged in each kind of business by the average percentage of sales for which each is responsible over the towns as a whole. As far as comparisons of changes are concerned, a second factor needs to be taken into account.

Just as the level of productivity varies markedly between business categories, so too does the change over the period 1961 to 1966. Thus the change in productivity at the national level ranged from an increase of almost 19 per cent in respect of 'Grocery and provision dealers' to a decline of seven per cent in respect of 'C.T.N.'s' It seems reasonable to suppose that this disparity results in part from the different opportunities available for introducing labour-saving methods of operation as between trades. As we have shown elsewhere, it is possible to explain most of the productivity growth of grocery stores over this period in terms of the development of self-service, which may not really be viable for the sale of some goods (tobacco, for instance — except through vending machines). It therefore follows that the change in overall sales per person engaged with respect to any town is in some degree likely to be related to the initial composition of its retail sector, in the sense that a town which happens to include a relatively high proportion of grocery stores, for example, may be expected to show a larger gain in productivity than one which has a low proportion. Assuming that the scope for improving labour 'efficiency' over the period varied between kinds of business generally (and was not limited to grocery stores as against non-grocery stores), it is more convenient to adjust the measure of productivity movement for individual towns and to allow for this factor explicitly, rather than to introduce it in the form of explanatory variables.

Consequently, to take account of both initial differences and changes in business composition between towns, we have adopted the procedure of basing the analysis on weighted average movements in productivity for each town. These are calculated by weighting the change in the volume of sales per person engaged in each kind of business, by the average percentage of the labour force engaged in each kind of business for the 50 towns in 1961. In other words, the measure of productivity change used embodies the assumption that the distribution of employment between trades was initially the same in each town and remained the same over the period under investigation.[1]

This measure seems to represent the most satisfactory one for our purpose, which at the same time is readily calculable. We recognise that it is not ideal, insofar as the assumptions embodied in its use may not be valid in certain cases. Thus while we have assumed that the business composition of retail sectors reflects the pattern of demand for goods, this is not necessarily so, as not all sales of a given commodity are made in shops classified to the kind of business defined by the Census as specialising in its distribution. In particular, a significant part of the sales of goods sold by 'Clothing and footwear' and 'Household goods' shops takes place in 'General stores'. This gives rise to the possibility that a shift in employment between kinds of business within a town may occur in response to a switch in consumers' preference for buying a given commodity from one type of shop rather than another, and not necessarily in response to a shift in demand between commodities. Retailers included in one kind of business may therefore have increased their sales over the period relative to those included in other categories because, for instance, they offered a better deal to customers in terms of price and service, and not necessarily because they happened to sell the types of goods whose sales were expanding at a rapid rate. To the extent that such a switch in the source of supply changes a town's overall labour requirements in retailing a given group of commodities, then it can be argued that this ought to be reflected in any measure of productivity change, but it is not reflected in our measure.

The legitimacy of excluding this source of productivity change from the analysis clearly depends on how important it is considered to be. Our belief is that changes

1 While we can take account of differences between business categories, we have not sufficient data available to adjust for variations *within* business categories, and this may be a factor of some importance.

in the business composition of retail sectors are less likely to reflect shifts in consumer preference between types of shop than changes in the pattern of demand for goods. Moreover there is the 'service' aspect to be considered, in the sense that differences in the level of sales per person engaged between kinds of business may be a poor indicator of differences in the amount or quality of the service included with the goods sold. We cannot therefore necessarily treat sales of a given commodity taking place in one kind of business as equivalent to sales taking place in another.

(ii) Prices

A further point of qualification which is clearly related to the above discussion concerns the price indices used to express sales in 1966 in terms of 1961 prices. This, of course, is directly relevant to our estimates of changes in the volume of goods sold by retailers which we use below as a variable in its own right and not only as an interim step in the calculation of productivity movements. For each town we have deflated the sales of each of the seven principal kinds of business by a price index representing some weighted average for the goods sold by the various retailers included in that particular business category.[1] This procedure not only assumes that the movements in the price of individual commodities were uniform across towns over the period, but further that both the relative importance of the different types of shop constituting a business category and the composition of turnover of the shops did not vary significantly between towns, in both 1961 and 1966. As little information is available on any of these points, we can only trust that these assumptions are fulfilled.[2]

Certainly it is likely that variations between towns in the composition of retail sales are a far more serious possibility than variations in the price level or price movement for a given product.[3] Differences in the level of income per head in particular may be a factor of some importance in this regard, being associated with differences in the average unit value of purchases. The consequences of this for productivity were outlined in our introductory chapter and are considered in the subsequent analysis.

---

1 Specifically we have largely relied upon price indices calculated by the D.T.I. from details supplied by the contributors to the Monthly Retail Sales Index.

2 The problem would be less acute if the prices of the different commodity groups sold by the shops included in any kind of business changed at similar rates over the period. This is palpably not so in the case of 'Household goods' shops, for which the Department of Employment figures indicate that, between 1961 and 1966, prices for furniture, floor-coverings and soft furnishings increased by 15 per cent, for pottery, glassware and hardware by about ten per cent, while for radio, television and other household appliances, prices decreased by about one per cent, and for television hire it is estimated that prices fell by between ten and 15 per cent. On the other hand, the prices of the goods principally sold by 'Clothing and footwear' shops show very similar movements.

3 Differences in the intensity of retail competition between towns, however, may cause some small variations in price. Thus, for instance, a survey undertaken in 1971 found that prices for branded grocery products tended to be higher in the north of the country than in the south, the average difference being three per cent between prices in Scotland and in the South of England. See *Which?* November, 1971.

5. Outline of Analysis

In the following chapters, we first examine the relationship between the productivity performance of towns and certain factors which might be expected on *a priori* grounds to have some bearing on performance. Secondly, we discuss the likely reasons underlying the relationships which are found to exist, with the object of identifying the main processes involved in the realisation of productivity gains in retailing.

To be more specific, Chapters V and VI deal with the differences between towns in sales per person engaged in respect of both 1961 and 1966. Such differences are related in turn to variations in the size of towns, the proportion of sales made by multiple organisations and cooperative societies, sales per shop, income per head, and labour market conditions. In part, these two chapters consist of a re-examination of the findings of the analysis conducted on the basis of 1961 data for 160 towns,[1] the aim being to see whether the relationships which held for 1961 are also valid for 1966 In addition, the availability of details for 1966 which were not collected in 1961 enables us to extend the analysis in a number of directions. This is particularly so in Chapter VI which looks at average wages in retailing, the composition of the labour force and their relation to the state of the labour market.

Chapters VII and VIII are concerned with changes over the period 1961 to 1966 in respect of our sample of fifty towns. The inter-town variation in productivity growth is assessed and related to differences in the rate of change in the factors listed above. Again the influence of each variable is, for the most part, examined individually the aim being to find out whether the implications with respect to changes over time which might be drawn from the analysis of Chapters V and VI are supported by the evidence on the pattern of change over this five-year period.

Finally in Chapter IX, we bring together the findings of the previous four chapters and discuss the light which they throw upon the process underlying improvements in the efficiency with which labour is used in the retail trades. In particular, we consider whether the evidence is consistent with any of the hypotheses as to the major source of productivity growth in this sector, which we outlined in the introductory chapter. The inter-relation between the explanatory variables is examined and multiple regression techniques are adopted to see how much of the inter-town difference in labour productivity in 1961 and 1966 and in the change which occurred between the two years can be 'explained' by the factors which we have identified. In addition, an attempt is made to assess the relative importance of each factor.

Before commencing the analysis, however, it is as well to emphasize that the factors identified as having some bearing on labour productivity in retailing are by no means comprehensive. In particular they exclude the effect of, for example, town planning regulations, the level of local authority rates, and the general attitude to new and re-development, all of which can clearly have a crucial influence on the efficiency with which labour is used in retailing and the service which the sector is able to provide for shoppers. Differences in such factors cannot be taken into account by their very nature, but it is important to recognize that they might, for instance, cause the observed level or change in productivity with respect to certain towns to differ from what we would expect to find on the basis of the variables which we can

1 See K.D. George, *op. cit.*

identify. This point should be borne in mind throughout the subsequent analysis and we shall inevitably return to it on a number of occasions.

This, of course, is not to attribute all deviations from what we would expect to find to varying degrees of restriction at the local authority level. Clearly the value which we observe for any variable at any one point in time may lie some way from the 'equilibrium' value given the underlying conditions and the values of other relevant variables. This applies equally to movements over time, especially over the relatively short period which we shall be considering, the basic reason being that the full adjustment of one factor to change in another takes time to accomplish. Local authority regulations, however, are likely to play a central role in a number of instances in determining just how long the adjustment period is and the extent of the 'disequilibrium' which is allowed to prevail.

V
Labour Productivity, 1961 and 1966 – the Effect of Size, Structure and Income

1. Overview

A principle object of this chapter and much of the next is to test the general validity of the relationships formulated on the basis of the 1961 figures for retailing in towns, or in other words to see whether those factors which were found to influence the level of sales per person engaged in 1961 continued to exert a similar effect in 1966. We therefore begin by re-stating briefly the main findings of the 1961 study.[1]

1. There were significant differences in the level of productivity between towns, but these were not related in any systematic way to the size of towns. This applied both to retailing as a whole and to independents and multiples and coops taken separately,[2] the productivity ranking of towns by form of organisation being similar to the ranking for all retailing.
2. There was a positive association between the level of productivity in a town and the market share of multiples and coops but variations in the latter between towns represented only a minor source of overall productivity differences.
3. There was also a positive association between sales per person engaged and both the average sales-size of shop and the level of income per head.
4. A strong positive correlation was found between labour productivity and the degree of tightness in a town's labour market. The level of productivity was also related to the use of part-time labour, which reflected the association between the latter and labour scarcity. The greater part of part-time employment, however, occurred independently of labour market conditions.
5. The degree of labour market tightness together with the market share of multiples and coops, sales per shop and income per head provided a high degree of explanation of inter-town variations in labour productivity, the labour market variable appearing to be the most important factor.

An additional result which might be added to the above list was that productivity tended to be higher in central shopping areas than in other parts of the towns. However, the necessary data were not collected in 1966 to test whether this was also a feature of that year. Certainly it was an unsurprising result of the 1961 analysis,

---

1 See K.D. George, *op. cit.*

2 The data available do not allow multiples and coops to be separately distinguished.

because, for instance, of the generally larger size of shop and greater importance of multiples in town centres than elsewhere.

With the exception of this point, our intention is to look at each of the above findings and to compare their relevance in 1966 with that in 1961. In this chapter we consider the first three findings in turn, examining the influence on labour productivity of the size of town, the structure of the retail sector and income per head. The following chapter is concerned partly with the fourth finding listed above and looks at the influence of labour market conditions on productivity and the importance of part-time working. In addition, the availability of data for 1966 which were not collected in 1961 enables us to extend the analysis to consider the composition of the labour force in greater detail and to assess the association between average wages per employee in retailing and both the degree of labour scarcity and the level of productivity. It should be said that in both this chapter and the next, our main concern is to summarize the relationships which exist between variables and not to delve too deeply into their implications for the process involved in the realisation of productivity gains in retailing. These aspects are considered after we have examined the evidence on changes over the period 1961 to 1966, when we also deal with the fifth finding of the 1961 study listed above and assess the combined impact on productivity of all the four explanatory variables identified.

2. Productivity Differences and Market Size

(i) Inter-town Differences in Productivity

For purposes of analysis, the 1961 study divided the 160 towns into five fairly equal size-classes; the towns in each class were then arranged in descending order of sales per person engaged and split into five groups of six or seven towns. The average difference in the level of productivity between those towns included in the 'top' group of each size-class and those included in the 'bottom' group was found to be about 27 per cent, with comparatively little variation between classes. Adopting a similar procedure with respect to our sample of fifty towns — except for omitting the first step of dividing them into size-classes — produces the picture shown in Table V.I. In this case, the towns are arranged into two sets of five groups of ten, according to, firstly, the value of sales per person engaged in 1961, and, secondly, the value in 1966. The figures in brackets show the average levels of productivity in 1966 for the 1961 groups.

A comparison of average sales per person engaged for Groups A_0 to E_0 and Groups A_1 to E_1 reveals that the disparity between towns was much the same in 1966 as it had been in 1961. In particular, the difference between the two extreme groups is 20 per cent for 1961 and 19 per cent for 1966. Moreover if we take the average level of productivity of the 'top' six towns and of the 'bottom' six towns in 1966 we find a difference of 24 per cent,[1] which compares with the average variation of 27 per cent with respect to the 160 towns, as we noted above.[2]

1   23 per cent for 1961.

2   The slightly greater variation with respect to the 160 towns arises from the inclusion of towns in the close vicinity of London, which generally had the highest sales per person engaged in 1961.

Table V.1   *Sales per Person Engaged by Town Group, 1961 and 1966*

Town Group (ten in each)	Sales per person engaged, 1961[a]	Town Group (ten in each)	Sales per person engaged, 1966[a]	
A_0	4435	A_1	5594	(5564)
B_0	4142	B_1	5261	(5206)
C_0	3941	C_1	5094	(5066)
D_0	3843	D_1	4934	(5010)
E_0	3685	E_1	4697	(4736)

Note: The towns are divided into the groups A_0 to E_0 according to sales per person engaged in 1961 and into groups A_1 to E_1 according to sales per person engaged in 1966. The figures in brackets correspond to groups A_0 to E_0.
a Standardised as explained in the previous chapter.

It is also apparent, if we turn our attention to the figures in brackets in Table V.1, that the towns with a relatively high level of productivity in 1961 tended to have a similarly high level in 1966, the converse being true for towns with low productivity. Indeed if the fifty towns are ranked according to sales per person engaged in 1961 and according to sales per person engaged in 1966, the (Spearman's) coefficient of rank correlation between the two rankings is found to be 0·81. In other words, there is evidence of a considerable degree of stability in the relative sales per person engaged of the individual towns within our sample over this five-year period. This suggests, for instance, that the differences observed at one point in time tend not to be of a transitory nature.

(ii) The Size of Town

In retailing as in other activities, the realisation of any economies of scale depend, upto a certain point, upon the size of the market. As we have identified the 'town' with the retail market, it might be thought that the size of the former would influence the level of productivity in retailing, through its bearing on the size of shop which the town is able to support. However there are three considerations that need to be taken into account in this respect. Firstly, while a market above a certain size might be a necessary condition for the attainment of scale economies, it is not a sufficient condition, in the sense that a town may have a large number of small shops rather than fewer large ones. Secondly, the towns included in our sample are all almost certainly large enough to support shops of sufficient size to enjoy most of the major economies that are to be gained in respect of most kinds of business. Thirdly, the simple view expressed above neglects the likelihood that equally (if not more) important economies of scale in retailing are of the 'multi-plant' variety. While the size of retail establishments might be a function of the size of the total market, the same is not obviously true of retail organisations. The level of labour productivity in any town is therefore likely to be related not only to the average size of shop but also to the average size of organisation to which the shops belong. In any particular instance, the latter consideration may offset the former.

The absence of any systematic association between town size and productivity with respect to the 1961 data can clearly be rationalised in terms of these three observations. The evidence for 1966, which is set out in Table V.2, confirms the findings of the 1961 study. Thus it is very apparent that there is no tendency for

Table V.2   *Productivity and Sales per Shop by Size of Town, 1966*

Town Groups (ten towns in each)	Average Value of Total Retail Sales (£000)	Average Sales per Person Engaged (£)	Average Sales per Establishment (£000)
A	151,840	5,140	24·66
B	64,586	5,060	23·80
C	47,335	5,114	25·95
D	36,026	5,289	27·80
E	26,352	4,976	22·92

Notes: The towns are grouped according to the value of retail sales in 1966. Both sales per person engaged and sales per establishment are standardised, as explained earlier, to adjust for the differing importance of the various kinds of business between towns.

either sales per person engaged or sales per shop to vary in any discernible way with the size of town.[1]

This conclusion remains unaltered when the data are broken down by form of organisation, as is evident from Table V.3, in which the towns are divided into the same groups as in Table V.2 and the corresponding average levels of productivity in multiples and coops and in independents are shown.

One point to make clear is that the use of retail sales as a measure of town size, rather than population which would appear the most obvious measure, is dictated by the fact that the latter does not include those people living outside a town who shop in the town, and makes no allowance for those living inside who shop outside. The importance of these two considerations varies markedly between towns, as is indicated by the variation in sales per inhabitant. Thus there was a difference of 168 per cent between the two extreme values of the latter in 1966, and the average value for the ten towns where sales per inhabitant was highest exceeded the average value for the ten where it was lowest, by 73 per cent. Of course, such differences may in part reflect variations in expenditure per head of population between towns. This in turn may show itself in the different levels of income per head. As far as the latter can be estimated, the difference in income per head between the two towns with extreme values of sales per inhabitant was four per cent, while that between the two extreme groups of ten towns, in terms of sales per inhabitant, was less than one per cent.[2] Consequently, even if we assume vastly different average propensities to consume, the relative importance of migrant custom would appear to be the major determinant of variations in sales per inhabitant — assuming that our income per head estimates are not too far out.[3]

Moreover the towns with high sales per inhabitant tend to be important regional shopping centres, such as Cambridge, Oxford and Norwich, while those with the low values are often part of a conurbation and are situated on the outskirts of a major

1   It should be noted that some association between sales per person engaged and sales per shop is evident. This is considered explicitly later in the chapter.

2   The income per head estimates are explained later.

3   This is rather an heroic assumption as we explain below, but clearly substantial errors are necessary to account for the marked differences in sales per inhabitant, if migrant custom is to be ascribed a minor role.

Table V.3 *Productivity in Multiples and Coops and in Independents by Size of Town, 1966*

Town Group (ten in each)	Average Value of Total Retail Sales (£000)	Sales per Person Engaged	
		Multiples and Coops (£)	Independents (£)
A	151,840	5,973	4,559
B	64,586	5,999	4,452
C	47,335	5,858	4,544
D	36,026	6,353	4,552
E	26,352	6,064	4,459

Notes: The towns are grouped according to the value of retail sales in 1966. Sales per person engaged in this case are *not* standardised owing to the lack of the necessary details by form of organisation. Multiples are defined as those organisations owning ten or more branches.

city. Examples of the latter in our sample are Salford, South Shields and Birkenhead. Indeed the boundaries of such towns may be so drawn that many of its inhabitants live closer to the neighbouring city centre than do many of those of the latter.

The importance of migrant custom (whether in or out) is likely to have a significant bearing on the structure of retailing within towns. In general terms, we might expect those towns with a high 'immigrant' custom to specialise more in the retailing of 'shopping goods' than towns with a high 'emigrant' custom. This is confirmed if we look at the relationship between sales per inhabitant and the proportion of total town sales accounted for by grocery shops. For our sample of 50 towns, a clear negative association emerges, which is summarized by the equation:

$$G = 35 \cdot 1 - 0 \cdot 063V \qquad r^2 = 0 \cdot 50$$
$$(0 \cdot 009)$$

where G is the percentage share of 'grocery and provision dealers' and V is the value of sales per inhabitant, both for 1961.[1] Thus in a town where sales per inhabitant were £100 above average, the share of grocers tended to be over six points below average. For the specific towns mentioned above, grocery stores were responsible for about 20 per cent of total retail sales in Cambridge and Oxford, but for about 30 per cent in Salford and South Shields.

This type of variation in the pattern of consumer demand between towns provides the rationale underlying our standardisation of sales per person engaged figures, our essential purpose being, as we have explained before, to compare the amount of labour used to retail a *given* parcel of goods between towns.

(iii) Productivity by Form of Organisation

The final part of the first of the main findings formulated on the basis of the 1961 data was that towns with a high level of overall productivity in retailing also tended to have a high level of productivity with respect to both independents and multiples and coops. This was not an unexpected result in view of the plausibility of supposing

---

1 The equation is calculated for 1961 as there are greater errors involved in estimating sales per inhabitant for 1966, because of the boundary changes adopted by the Census of Population. A similar relationship is evident for 1966.

that the factors which influence productivity are unlikely to 'discriminate' between types of retailer. However the evidence for 1966 does not altogether support this supposition.

If the towns are ranked according to the value of sales per person engaged in retailing as a whole in 1966 and according to the value for independents, we find a rank correlation coefficient of 0·76 between the two rankings. Comparing the order of towns ranked by overall productivity of multiples and coops, yields a rank correlation coefficient of 0·55. Performing the same exercise on the basis of the 1961 data for fifty towns, produces coefficients of 0·76 − exactly the same as for 1966 − and 0·71, respectively.[1]

However if the towns are ranked according to the sales per person engaged of independents and according to the sales per person engaged of multiples and coops, the coefficient of rank correlation is as low as 0·10 for 1966, whereas for the same towns in 1961, it is 0·42. Thus while some association is evident for 1961, the coefficient being highly significant, as far as 1966 is concerned, we can safely say that there was little relationship at all between the two variables. Towns with a relatively high level of productivity in independents in 1966 did *not* tend to have a similarly high level in their multiple and coop outlets.

There are a number of possible explanations for the difference between the two years. In particular, there was a change in the Census definition of multiples − and hence of independents − at the town level. Thus in 1961, multiples were defined as those organisations owning five or more retail establishments, whereas in 1966 the minimum requirement was increased to ten establishments. It may therefore be that a comparison on the basis of the 1961 definition would have yielded similar results in both years. At the same time, the observed difference might be held to reflect the possibility that the productivity performance of shops belonging to large retail organisations is less closely influenced by the features of any particular town in which they happen to be located than is the case for smaller concerns. In other words, operations might be centrally directed in the case of the former, whereas the outlets of smaller traders tend to be concentrated within a particular locality. This point is pursued more fully in the next chapter, when we come to discuss the influence of labour market conditions.

Alternatively it may be argued that at least part of the difference between the two years is attributable to the nature of the 1966 data, insofar as the Census information for independents is subject to sampling errors of unknown importance.

3. The Market Share of Multiples and Coops

In Chapter III above, we noted the significant difference in the level of sales per person engaged between multiple stores and independent shops. This disparity is also evident at the town level. For this reason alone it is to be expected that the overall sales per person engaged in any town would be related in some way to the

1 As there are no details available to 'standardise' productivity by form of organisation, the comparisons are carried out in terms of the ratio of total retail sales to total persons engaged in each town as a whole and in each form of organisation within the town. In fact, there is little difference between towns ranked according to this 'crude' measure and ranked according to 'standardised' productivity, the rank correlation coefficient being 0·96 in both 1961 and 1966.

Table V.4.   *Regressions of Productivity on the Market Share of Multiples and Coops, 1961 to 1966*

Equation	Year	No. of Towns	Constant	Regression Coefficient	r^2
1.	1966	50	3,829	26·81 (6·15)	0·28
2.	1961	50	3,023	19·31 (5·19)	0·22
3.	1961	160	2,690	27·33 (3·36)	0·30

Note: For 1966, multiples are defined as those organisations owning ten or more retail establishments; for 1961, as those owning five or more establishments.

proportion of trade made by multiple and coop outlets.[1] This indeed was found to be the case in 1961, and the evidence for 1966 shows a similar pattern, as can be seen from the regression equations described in Table V.4.

Equation 1 indicates that, in 1966, a rise of one percentage point above average in the percentage of sales made by multiples and coops tended to be associated with an increase of £27 above average in the overall level of sales per person engaged in retailing, which is almost identical to the overall relationship which existed for the 160 towns in 1961. The difference in the definition of multiples as between the two years should, however, be borne in mind.

At the same time, this does not mean that the variation in sales per person engaged between towns can be ascribed primarily to the fact that multiples and coops have a higher level of productivity than independents and that these differ in importance between towns. Thus if we take explicit account of such differences, by calculating overall sales per person engaged on the assumption that the distribution of retail turnover between the two forms of organisation was the same in each town, there still remain substantial variations within our sample. For 1966, this adjustment only serves to reduce the difference in sales per person engaged (necessarily unstandardised) between the ten towns where this was highest and the ten where it was lowest, from 17·3 per cent to 15·6 per cent. The equivalent exercise with respect to the 1961 sample of towns produced a similar result, the average difference between the 'top' (six or seven) towns and the 'bottom' (six or seven) towns, in terms of productivity, being reduced from 29 per cent to 25 per cent. In consequence, the conclusion which emerges is the same for both years: inter-town variations in productivity within each type of organisation are considerably more important than those arising from any differences in the market share of multiples and coops.

However perhaps a more interesting question is whether the relative importance of multiples and coops has any bearing on the overall labour productivity of towns, *other than* through the mere fact of their superior level of sales per person engaged. In other words, the question is whether a high proportion of multiples and coops

1   As at the national level, multiples are considerably more important than coops in respect of our sample of towns. In 1961, for example, in the towns for which separate information on coops was given, these organisations accounted for 12 per cent of turnover on average, whereas multiples accounted for 40 per cent. The differential is, of course, likely to have widened since then.

Table V.5　　*The Market Share of Multiples and Coops, Overall Productivity and Productivity in Independents, 1966*

Town Group (ten in each)	% Multiples and Coops	Sales per Person engaged:[a]		
		Overall (£)	Adjusted (£)	in Independents (£)
A	56·9	5,346	5,202	4,645
B	51·5	5,204	5,186	4,498
C	47·9	5,066	5,043	4,439
D	44·8	5,116	5,152	4,570
E	38·7	4,847	5,066	4,415

Notes: The towns are grouped according to the percentage of sales made by multiples and coops.

a The figures in the 'overall' column are the standardised values of sales per person engaged in all retailing; the figures in the 'adjusted' column allow explicitly for the differing proportion of multiples and coops between towns. The latter are derived by weighting persons engaged per £100,000 turnover in independents and in multiples and coops by their average percentage of sales for all towns.

stimulates greater efficiency in other types of shop through creating a more competitive market environment. In Table V.5, the towns are arranged in descending order of the market share taken by multiples and coops and again divided into five groups of ten. The corresponding average values of sales per person engaged for retailing as a whole — both unadjusted and adjusted to allow for the varying proportions of multiples and coops between towns — and for independents, are shown along with the average share of multiples and coops. A clear tendency emerges for overall productivity to vary with the relative importance of the latter two forms of organisation, as would be expected from Equation 1 of Table V.4. But when productivity is adjusted to take explicit account of inter-town differences in the proportion of multiples and coops, such a tendency becomes much less apparent, the 'excess' of the average productivity for Groups A and B over that of Groups D and E being reduced from six per cent to less than two per cent.[1] Similarly the sales per person engaged in independent shops is only slightly higher, on average, in those towns where multiples and coops are of greatest importance than in those where they are of least importance.

The evidence therefore suggests that the market share of multiples and coops has only a small effect on the efficiency of other types of retailer. At the same time, the form which the above 'test' has taken is open to criticism, insofar as the overall percentage of sales made by multiples and coops combined conceals both the respective shares of these two forms of organisation and the distribution of multiples between kinds of business. Thus it might be expected that such organisations would have a greater influence on independents in respect of, say, the grocery trade than in respect of, say, the C.T.N. trade. However if we examine the figures for the grocery trade, the evidence does not suggest that the relationship between the two variables under consideration is any closer than at the aggregate level. The difference in the productivity of independent grocers as between the ten towns where multiples and coops are of greatest importance in respect of this

---

1 Recalculating the regression of productivity on the market share of multiples and coops using the adjusted measure of productivity, yields an r^2 of only 0·03.

trade and the ten where they are least important, is only two per cent. On the other hand, the difference in the average productivity of multiples and coops as between the same two groups of towns is nine per cent, which suggests perhaps that the degree of competition is increased by more among multiples and coops themselves than across the market as a whole. Thus it might be, for example, that independents are, to some extent, protected from competition by the nature of their trade, which may well be different from that of multiples in particular, the latter tending to be concentrated in central shopping areas while the former cater for a much more local demand. But this result is not repeated at the aggregate level, the average productivity of multiples and coops in the towns included in Group A of Table V.5 being actually *less* than that in the towns in Group E (by about one per cent).

In the above analysis we have not considered the basic question of why multiples and coops should have a higher level of sales per person engaged than independents. There are any number of explanations for the difference. It might be argued, for example, that multiples — and to a much less extent coops — tend to adopt more up-to-date methods of selling than do independents, or alternatively, that they tend to organise their labour force more efficiently. In addition, part of the explanation would seem to lie in the centralisation of certain activities which independents perform at the shop level, and also in the greater degree of specialisation permitted by the larger scale of operation. At the same time, however, it might be claimed that the observed disparity in sales per person engaged as between the two forms of organisation is not a reliable indicator of the actual difference in output per head, if output is defined to include the services provided with the goods sold. In other words, the sales of independents might be considered to include a greater element of service than those of multiples. This is clearly a factor to be taken into account, but it is open to debate whether it operates in this direction rather than the other. This debate, however, as we have noted before, is not one which can be resolved in any objective way and is not one with which we want to become too closely embroiled.

4. Inter-Correlation between Explanatory Variables

One point which needs to be considered at this stage is the possibility that the observed relationship between productivity and the importance of multiples and coops arises in some measure from the fact that both are related to a third variable. Indeed it is conceivable, in the extreme, that the market share of these two forms of organisation has no systematic influence on sales per person engaged at all, but merely serves as a proxy for another factor. As we pointed out at the beginning of the chapter, the 1961 study identified four principal explanatory variables of inter-town differences in productivity; each of these was correlated to a certain extent with each of the other three, but none so closely as to lose any 'identity' of its own and to give rise to the extreme possibility just mentioned. Nevertheless it is necessary to bear in mind the degree of inter-correlation between factors when considering the interpretation to be placed on the association discussed in the previous section and on those to be examined in the remainder of the chapter.

Table V.6 shows the squares of the coefficients of correlation between the four explanatory variables, with respect to both 1961 and 1966. With the exception of the correlation between the market share of multiples and coops and sales per

Table V.6   *Inter-Correlation between Explanatory Variables, 1961 and 1966*

Variables correlated	r^{2} [a]		
	1966: 50 towns	1961: 50 towns	1961: 160 towns
% M.C. and Sales per Shop	0·32	0·33	0·37
% M.C. and Income per head	0·12	0·03	0·05
% M.C. and Labour Market	0·05	0·00	0·06
Sales per shop and Income per head	0·10	0·00	0·12
Sales per shop and Labour Market	0·08	0·04	0·20
Income per head and Labour Market	0·37	0·33	0·42

Notes: % M.C. is the percentage market of multiples and coops. 'Labour market' refers to percentage vacancies less unemployed, averaged over the period 1962 to 1966 in respect of 1966 and averaged over the period 1957 to 1961 in respect of 1961. More details on this and the other two variables are given below in the appropriate sections.
a All values of r are positive.

shop and that between income per head and labour market conditions, the values of r^2 are generally very low. Moreover, in respect of each pair of variables, the latter is of a similar order of magnitude for both years and for both samples.

5. Productivity and the Effect of Sales per Shop and Income per Head

(i) Sales per Shop

The higher level of sales per person engaged in multiples than in independents is associated with a substantial difference in the average size of shop,[1] which may well be a contributory factor and which largely accounts for the comparatively high degree of correlation between the relevant two variables in Table V.6 above (r^2 equalled 0·32 in 1966). As we have observed, there is evidence of economies of scale in retailing at the establishment level. These can be explained in terms of the imperfect divisibility of capital and labour. For example, large scale is often a *sine qua non* for the successful introduction of self-service or self-selection methods of selling, while the attainment of the advantages of specialisation is related to the size of the labour-force. In consequence, it is to be expected that towns which have relatively large shops would show relatively high levels of sales per person engaged. This indeed was a finding of the 1961 study and it is supported by the evidence for the 1966 sample of towns.

The relationship between sales per shop and productivity, for both 1961 and 1966 is summarized in the regression equations contained in Table V.7. Equations 1 and 2 indicate that, for the sample of fifty towns in both years, there was a tendency for towns which possessed shops with an average annual turnover of £1,000 above average to have a level of sales per person engaged of about £40 above average. The higher regression coefficient shown by Equation 3, which summarizes the relationship for the 160 towns in 1961, seems to be a consequence

1 Over the country as a whole, multiples employed on average about eight 'full-time equivalent' persons in each branch, which compares with an average of three 'full-time equivalent' persons engaged in each independent outlet.

Table V.7   *Regressions of Productivity on Sales per Shop, 1961 and 1966*

Equation	Year	No. of Towns	Constant	Regression Coefficient	r^2
1.	1966	50	4,127	0·040 (0·007)	0·40
2.	1961	50	3,272	0·039 (0·009)	0·28
3.	1961	160	3,008	0·059 (0·005)	0·45

Notes: The equations are based on standardised measures of sales per shop, which, as for sales per person engaged, take explicit account of inter-town differences in the distribution of retail sales between kinds of business.

of including in the sample the high productivity towns situated close to London, rather than of reducing the average size of town covered. Thus with respect to these towns, a given rise in sales per shop appears to have a comparatively large impact on sales per person engaged, although, in these particular cases, this may conceal the effect of other factors, such as income per head and labour market conditions, which we consider below.

(ii) Income per Head

The principal influence of the level of income per head on the value of sales per person engaged is through its effect on expenditure per customer, and hence on the value of individual transactions. As was argued in the introductory chapter, a rise in the latter is likely to be associated with a less than proportionate increase in selling effort or staff requirements. This applies whether such a rise takes the form of an increase in the number of units purchased at any one time or of an increase in the unit value of purchases, although clearly we would not necessarily expect the actual additional labour required to be the same in both cases. Moreover as well as raising average transaction size directly, higher levels of income per head are also likely to be associated with greater consumer mobility and better home storage facilities, both of which are conducive to customers purchasing more per shop visit. In addition it should be noted that as consumers become more mobile, there may well be a tendency for the retail market to become less imperfect insofar as the protection enjoyed by certain traders by virtue of their favourable location is reduced.

At the same time, however, the level of retail sales demanded by customers — including a wider variety of goods or shops, or more luxurious shopping facilities — may also be positively related to their income, with the result that any rise in the latter has a dampening effect on productivity as measured. In other words, an increase in the amount of retail services provided is likely to imply a rise in employment per unit of sales.

The conclusion to emerge from the 1961 study was that the positive effect of income per head on productivity outweighed any negative effect, and the evidence for 1966 supports this finding. This evidence is summarized in Equation 1 of Table V.8, which also contains the results of regressing productivity on income per head for both samples in 1961. Again the regression coefficients are all highly significant, and are similar for both years with respect to the sample of fifty towns. In 1966,

Table V.8 *Regressions of Productivity on Income per Head, 1961 and 1966*

Equation	Year	No. of Towns	Constant	Regression Coefficient	r^2
1.	1966	50	330	4·55 (0·99)	0·31
2.	1961	50	299	5·21 (0·97)	0·38
3.	1961	160	−1,170	7·34 (0·56)	0·52

Notes: Income per head data are derived from the *Inland Revenue Reports* for 1962, 1963, and 1967 and from *Inland Revenue Statistics*, 1970, and refer to the 1959/60 financial year in respect of 1961 and to an average of the 1964/5 and 1967/8 financial years in respect of 1966. Fuller details are given in the text.

for example, a town with an income per head of £50 above average tended to have a level of sales per person engaged of about £228 above average. For the larger sample of towns, it is once more the case that a given difference in income per head has a seemingly greater impact on productivity. This as before seems directly attributable to the inclusion of the high productivity towns in the London area.

However it should be emphasized that the above analysis is based on data for income per head which are less than satisfactory. Specifically, as there are no statistics published on a town basis, we have been forced to use Inland Revenue figures for counties and conurbations, attributing to each town, the average level of income per head for the county or conurbation in which it is located.[1] Clearly this involves an assumption which is unlikely to be valid in certain instances, inasmuch as the actual average income per head for a particular town may well diverge significantly from that of the county of which it forms only a part. We have no way of knowing how important such divergences are within our sample.

For this reason, the above findings should be regarded with a good deal of circumspection, and we would emphasize the fact that a positive relationship between income per head and productivity is apparent, rather than attach any great significance to the precise association between the two.

6. Summary of Main Findings

To sum up, therefore, the first four findings of the 1961 study which were listed at the beginning of the chapter are generally supported by the 1966 data for fifty towns. No clear association was found between town-size and productivity, while the market share of multiples and coops, the size of shop and income per head were all positively related to the level of sales per person engaged. With respect to sales per shop and income per head, a marked feature to emerge was that the values of the regression coefficients for the sample of fifty towns were much the same in 1966 as in 1961, suggesting that a given difference in the value of either variable between towns had a similar effect on productivity in both years. The regression

---

1 These statistics used to be published periodically in *Inland Revenue Reports* and now appear in *Inland Revenue Statistics.* Where conurbation details are given, these are used instead of county data. For example, Liverpool and Birkenhead are both ascribed the average income per head of the Merseyside conurbation instead of that of Lancashire and Cheshire.

coefficients computed on the basis of the larger sample were higher, a possible reason being the inclusion of a number of towns situated in the London area, which had high levels of sales per person engaged.

The only real point of divergence between the results for 1966 and the 1961 study concerns the productivity in multiples and coops and in independents. Firstly, no correlation was apparent between the two with respect to 1966, while some relationship was evident on the basis of the 1961 data. Secondly, the suggestion of the 1961 study that a high market share of multiple and coops may stimulate a high overall level of productivity through its effect on the competitive environment, is not supported by the 1966 figures. Apart from these two relatively minor points, however, a significant degree of conformity emerges.

VI

Labour Productivity, 1961 and 1966 — the Effect of Labour Market Conditions and the Structure of Employment

In this chapter, our concern is, firstly, with the association between inter-town differences in labour market conditions and the variations in sales per person engaged in 1961 and 1966;[1] this is examined both for retailing as a whole and for multiples and coops and independents taken separately. Secondly, we attempt to discern the effect of labour market conditions on average wages paid by retailers and look at the relationship between the latter and the level of productivity. Thirdly, we examine the differences in the sex composition of the retail labour force and in the importance of part-time employment between towns with differing degrees of labour market tightness. The association between the use made of part-time workers and the level of sales per person engaged in 1966 is also considered to see whether the 1961 finding in this regard is repeated.

1. Labour Market Conditions and Productivity

(i) All Retailing

In 1961, as we have noted, there was a close association between the degree of tightness in a town's labour market and its level of sales per person engaged in retailing. There are a number of possible explanations for this result, each of which represents a reason for expecting a similar relationship to show itself with respect to 1966. These we referred to briefly when discussing the possible sources of productivity growth in our introductory chapter.

Thus tight labour market conditions are likely to be associated with relatively abundant job opportunities in sectors other than retailing, and particularly in manufacturing which tends to pay higher wages than retailing for comparable workers. Retailers are therefore likely to find greater difficulty at such times in retaining employees or recruiting suitable staff, either to replace those that have left or to meet any expansion in sales. This may mean that traders are obliged to operate with fewer assistants than they would ideally require; alternatively, (or additionally), it may mean that they are forced to pay higher wages to prospective and, probably, existing employees. Both consequences may have similar effects on productivity.

Firstly, in the short-run, as we have argued above, the most likely result is that customers have to wait longer before being served. However it is possible that, in

---

1 We postpone until Chapter VIII below an examination of the relationship between
   labour market conditions and productivity growth over the period 1961 to 1966.

some instances, changes in internal organisation can be implemented to increase the efficiency with which existing staff is used, and these may prevent any reduction in service taking place, or lessen the deterioration which is necessary. This, of course, implies that the retailer was operating at less than optimal efficiency before the increase in labour scarcity occurred, which gives rise to the question of why such changes had not already been introduced. A plausible answer is that business enterprises tend not to assess their current working methods too closely until they are forced to do so by some change in circumstances.[1]

Secondly, if the tight labour market conditions persist, they may lead to more fundamental changes in working methods, and most notably to the introduction, or greater dependence on, self-service or self-selection techniques of selling. These not only shift some of the retail function onto shoppers, but also enable greater continuity to be achieved in the work of employees, by reducing the proportion of staff whose work is dependent on the physical presence of customers. Insofar as such techniques involve greater capital intensity, their adoption is encouraged not only by the absence of suitable staff but also perhaps by the associated increase in the costs of employing labour relative to capital.

Thirdly, persistently tight labour market conditions may be associated with a reduction in the number of retail outlets, through their effect on real wages and because of the job opportunities available in other sectors. Thus under the monopolistic competition hypothesis, an increase in labour costs implies a decrease in net profits and, consequently, the elimination of those outlets which were just able to cover the costs of remaining in business at the previously prevailing wage rate. At the same time, the lower net profits are likely to discourage new entrants from setting up business, while the greater number of vacancies in other sectors may tend to increase the opportunity costs of being self-employed in retailing. The likely result is therefore that sales are concentrated on fewer retail outlets of relatively high efficiency, which are able to spread the higher overhead costs (stemming from higher real wages) over a greater volume of output.

Each of these potential consequences leads us to expect a positive relationship between the degree of labour market tightness and productivity. On the other hand, there are other forces pulling in the opposite direction. In particular, the difficulty of recruiting suitable staff may give rise to the employment of less qualified workers or to the adoption of a 'second-best' employment policy, such as taking on part-time employees instead of full-timers. Both may have a dampening effect on the level of output per person engaged, the former through reducing the average 'quality' of staff, the latter through increasing the problems of organising labour efficiently. This is not to deny the potentially substantial gains from employing part-timers, which are associated with countering the 'peakiness' of demand, but to recognize that there are costs involved in increasing the employment of part-timers at the expense of full time staff.

1 This is not necessarily an inefficient way of operating, if we recognize the fact that there are costs of making assessments and introducing alternative working methods and these need to be more than offset by the potential returns. The potential returns are likely to be considered greater if the costs of operating under existing working methods have increased.

Table VI.1   *Regressions of Productivity on the Degree of Labour Market Tightness, 1961 and 1966*

Equation	Year	No. of Towns	Constant	Regression Coefficient	r^2
1.	1966	50	5,150	126·59 (32·75)	0·24
2.	1961	50	4,078	127·90 (21·54)	0·42
3.	1961	160	4,108	164·25 (13·38)	0·49

Notes: The degree of labour market tightness is measured by percentage vacancies minus unemployed, averaged over the period 1962 to 1966 in respect of 1966, and averaged over the period 1957 to 1961 in respect of 1961.

As a further qualification, it should be noted that we measure the degree of labour market tightness in any town only by reference to the number of unfilled vacancies less the number unemployed as a percentage of the total labour force. This leaves out of consideration inter-town differences in, for example, the occupational, age and sex structure of the labour force, which also have a bearing on the recruitment problems of retailers and on the level of labour costs.

To turn to the evidence, the data for the 1966 sample of towns support the 1961 findings. Thus if we follow the procedure of the latter study and measure the degree of labour market tightness in 1966 in terms of the average percentage vacancies minus percentage unemployed over the period 1962 to 1966,[1] a positive association emerges between this and inter-town variations in productivity. This is illustrated in Table VI.1 which also shows the relationship between the relevant two variables in 1961 for both sizes of sample. Again it should be noted that the regression coefficients are almost identical with respect to the fifty towns for both years – a town in which the degree of labour scarcity was one point above average tending to show a level of sales per person engaged of almost £130 above average. The point made in the previous two sections on the effect of excluding the towns close to London from the sample seems to be equally valid here. However it does appear that there was a much weaker association between the two variables in 1966 than in 1961 – r^2 being only 0·24 instead of 0·42 and 0·49.

A somewhat better 'fit' is obtained if we extend the 1961 analysis and postulate a non-linear relationship between the two variables, of the form $P = a + b_1 L + b_2 L^2$, where P equals productivity and L is the degree of labour market tightness as defined

---

1   An average is taken over a five-year period to enable longer-term adjustments to a labour shortage to take place and to smooth any short-term fluctuations in vacancies less unemployed. This procedure also helps to reduce the importance of the (generally small) differences in the timing of cycles between the towns and in their amplitude, five years being the period covered by a complete cycle in almost all cases. The figures are for June in each year and refer to the number of unfilled vacancies notified to, and the number of unemployed reporting to, employment exchanges classified to each town. Statistics on unemployment on a town-basis are published monthly in the *Department of Employment Gazette* (previously *Ministry of Labour Gazette*); data on vacancies are not published in this form, and I am grateful to the Department of Employment for allowing me to extract the relevant details from their records. The tentative nature of the vacancy statistics should be emphasized.

Table VI.2   *Non-linear Regressions of Productivity on the Degree of Labour Market Tightness 1961 and 1966*

Equation	Year	No. of Towns	Constant	Regression Coefficients		r^2
				L	L^2	
1.	1966	50	5,078	210·4	57·1	0·36
				(41·0)	(18·9)	
2.	1961	50	4,063	172·2	18·1	0·45
				(35·7)	(11·7)	
3	1961	160	4,046	201·3	23·3	0·57
				(14·4)	(4·6)	

Notes: L equals percentage vacancies minus percentage unemployed for the period 1962 to 1966 with respect to 1966 and for the period 1957 to 1961 with respect to 1961.

above.[1] Such an equation embodies the *a priori* expectation that, after a certain degree of labour scarcity has been reached, a further tightening of the labour market would tend to have a more than proportionate effect on the level of sales per person engaged, while, at the other end of the scale, once a given degree of 'slack' has appeared in the labour market, further slackening would tend to have little effect. The results of fitting this type of equation to the data for 1961 and 1966 are contained in Table VI.2.

For both years, it is apparent that a quadratic equation gives a higher degree of explanation of the observed variations in sales per person engaged between towns than does a linear equation – r^2 being increased from 0·24 to 0·36 with respect to 1966 and from 0·49 to 0·57 with respect to the 160 towns in 1961. There are, however, greater differences between the regression coefficients, particularly with regard to the squared term, than emerged from Table VI.1. Thus a rise in percentage vacancies less unemployed from +1·0 per cent to +2·0 per cent has a greater impact on the level of productivity in 1966 than in 1961, whereas a change from −2·0 per cent to +1·0 per cent is associated with a greater difference in productivity in 1961 than in 1966. It is not immediately apparent why this should be.

To compare Equation 1 in Table VI.2 with Equation 1 in Table VI.1, the latter suggests that a change in the degree of labour market tightness from +1·0 per cent to +2·0 per cent, for example, tended to be associated in 1966 with a change in sales per person engaged from £5,276 to £5,403, while the former indicates that the same change is associated with a change in sales per person engaged from £5,346 to £5,727. A change from −2·0 per cent to −1·0 per cent would tend to change productivity from £4,897 to £5,024 according to Equation 1 of

---

1   Several different forms of non-linear equation were fitted to the data; the quadratic form gave the best fit.

Table VI.1, but from £4,886 to £4,925 according to Equation 1 of Table VI.2.[1]

The above analysis, as we noted, is based on a similar measure of labour market tightness as was used in the 1961 study. Specifically, the average percentage vacancies less unemployed over a five-year period was taken, the essential reason being to allow time for the possible long-term effects of a particular labour market situation on the operating policy of retailers to show themselves. However part of the explanation for the observed relationship between the degree of labour scarcity and productivity might, as we have argued, lie in a deterioration in the service offered to customers, taking the form especially of longer queues. This, we considered, was likely to be largely a temporary phenomenon. In an (admittedly rather crude) attempt to assess the importance of such short-term consequences, *vis à vis* more 'fundamental' changes in productivity, we have extended the 1961 analysis, by relating sales per person engaged in 1961 and 1966 to the degree of labour market tightness in those particular years. Thus if the short-term effect, or what might be termed the 'lagged adjustment' effect, predominates, we might expect to find a closer association between inter-town variations in sales per person engaged in 1961 or 1966 and differences in percentage vacancies less unemployed for the year in question, than between the former and differences in percentage vacancies less unemployed *averaged* over a five-year period. In other words, *other things being equal*, if the short-term explanation of the relationship between labour market tightness and sales per person engaged is the main one, any extension of the period over which labour market tightness is assessed is likely to weaken the observed association between the two variables.

The results of regressing productivity in 1961 and 1966 on percentage vacancies less unemployed in each year are shown in Table VI.3. Again we have adopted the quadratic form of equation, as we would expect the difficulty of recruiting staff to intensify more than in proportion to the increase in labour scarcity, once a certain degree of tightness has been reached. For 1966, in fact, this form of equation gives a slightly better fit than the linear equation, while for 1961, there is little difference between the two forms in terms of r^2. In both cases, however, the association between the two variables is less close than in Table VI.2 above, in which a five-year average measure of labour market tightness is used. Thus a comparison of Table VI.3 with Table VI.2 suggests the existence of a long-term influence of a period of labour market tightness on sales per person engaged.

At the same time, the relationships described in Table VI.3 cannot be taken as indicating the strength of short-term factors. There is a close association between differences in the degree of labour shortage between towns in 1961 and 1966 and

---

1 A qualification to the use of quadratic equations which should be recognized arises from the fact that they describe a parabola, and therefore have an economic meaning only within a particular zone. Thus the equations in Table VI.2 predict that, after a certain degree of slackness in the labour market has been reached, further slackening will result in a *rise* in sales per person engaged — whereas we would expect little change. The critical point is reached for 1966 when percentage vacancies less unemployed equals between −1·8 and −1·9 per cent, and for the 160 towns in 1961, when the measure equals −4·3 per cent. Six of the fifty towns in 1966 had a greater degree of labour market slackness than −1·9 per cent and three of the 160 towns in 1961 had a greater degree of slackness than −4·3 per cent.

Table VI.3   *Non-linear Regressions of Productivity on the Degree of Labour Market Tightness, 50 Towns, 1961 and 1966*

Equation	Year	Constant	Regression Coefficients		r^2
			L	L^2	
1.	1966	4,986	71·2	53·4	0·32
			(50·6)	(23·3)	
2.	1961	4,005	82·3	−4·9	0·24
			(28·7)	(12·0)	

> *Notes:* L refers to percentage vacancies minus percentage unemployed in 1966 with respect to 1966 and in 1961 with respect to 1961. Unfortunately the data necessary to carry out the same exercise for the 160 towns in 1961 are not to hand.

the differences which prevailed over the previous four-year period in each case.[1] Thus the measure used in Table VI.3 tends to reflect labour market conditions over a much longer period, which implies that it is not possible to isolate what we have termed the lagged adjustment effects of labour shortage from the more 'permanent' effects. All we can conclude is that the evidence is consistent with the existence of the latter type of influence.[2]

(ii) Productivity by Form of Organisation

We referred in a previous section to the absence of any association in 1966 between the relative level of sales per person engaged of a town's multiple and cooperative outlets and that of its independent shops. This seemed to suggest that factors affecting productivity in a town's retail sector might have a differential impact as between these two forms of organisation. To pursue this point, we have examined the relationship between the state of the labour market and sales per person engaged by form of organisation.

There are a number of conflicting *a priori* arguments as to what we would expect to find. Superficially, it might be thought that as independent retailers are likely to be more 'specific' to a particular town than multiples or coops, they would tend to be more affected by the individual environmental characteristics of that town than would be the latter, the operating policy of which may be centrally determined. On closer consideration, however, there are a number of reasons why the reverse might be more valid. Firstly, the majority of independent shops are one-man or family concerns, which actually have no or very few employees in the strict sense of the term. This being the case, it clearly limits the possible influence of labour market conditions on employment policy, although it might be that the number of

---

1   The coefficient of correlation between our measure of labour market tightness in 1961 and the average for the years 1957 to 1960 is +0·87, while that between our measure in 1966 and the average for the years 1962 to 1965 is +0·84.

2   We also examined the relationship between productivity and percentage vacancies less unemployed averaged over a two-year period – 1960 and 1961 with respect to 1961, and 1965 and 1966 with respect to 1966. Fitting a quadratic equation to the data yielded values for r^2 of 0·33 for 1966 and 0·31 for 1961, which are slightly higher than those reported in Table VI.3 but again less than those derived when basing the analysis on five-year averages.

unpaid family helpers would be greater where there are relatively few job opportunities in other sectors.[1] There is consequently more scope for labour market conditions to affect the operating policy of multiples and coops than that of independents. Secondly, although multiples and coops may not be specific to any town, their shops are, in many instances, concentrated in a particular region, over which the state of the labour market may be very similar to that in the town in question. Thirdly, while the operating policy of multiples may well be centrally determined, nevertheless a number of major concerns are known to use payroll-sales ratios as indicators of the relative performance of individual branches, which is likely to act as an inducement to branch managers to adjust their methods of operation to local labour market conditions.

The evidence on this question is summarized for the sample of fifty towns in 1961 and 1966, in Table VI.4.[2] The regressions described in the table show very clearly that there is a far closer association between sales per person engaged and the degree of labour market tightness with respect to multiples and coops than is the case with respect to independents, the value of r^2 being considerably greater in both years for the former than for the latter. Moreover a given difference in labour market conditions between towns is associated with a much greater variation in the productivity of multiples and coops than in that of independents, as is indicated by the relative values of the regression coefficients.

The conclusion to emerge is therefore that there are marked differences between forms of organisation in the relationship between sales per person engaged and the degree of labour shortage. Furthermore it seems to be that multiples and coops adapt their methods of working to the prevailing labour market conditions to a greater extent than do independents. We have argued that this result arises in part from the limited scope which independents have to adjust their labour force.

As a final remark, however, we should note the possibility that the turnover of independents in tight labour market towns embodies a greater service element than does that of similar shops in 'slack' towns, because of the correspondingly higher level of income per head in the former than in the latter. Thus it is to be expected that any such differences in the amount of service provided would be most apparent with respect to independent retailers than with respect to multiples and coops. While it is very difficult to test this hypothesis in any satisfactory way, the evidence which we have on independent gross margins does not suggest that these differ significantly between towns with widely different labour market conditions. This is illustrated by Table VI.5, which shows the average level of gross margin in 1966 for 'Grocery and provision dealers' and for 'Clothing shops' in the ten towns which had the tightest labour market conditions over the period 1962 to 1966 and in the ten which had the slackest. Clearly any difference in gross margin within the sample should show itself most markedly in respect of these two extreme groups. It is apparent however that the average gross margin earned by retailers in the Group A towns is only very slightly higher than that earned by those in the Group B towns.

---

1   In addition, we might expect to find a greater proportion of self-employed in 'slack' than in 'tight' towns, as we have mentioned.

2   Again we have not conducted a similar exercise for the 160 towns.

Table VI.4   *Regressions of Productivity by Form of Organisation on the Degree of Labour Market Tightness, 50 Towns, 1961 and 1966*

	Equation	Year	Constant	Regression Coefficient	r^2
Multiples and Coops:	1.	1966	6,106	214·21 (36·75)	0·41
	2.	1961	4,675	181·69 (26·34)	0·50
Independents:	3.	1966	4,526	48·54 (34·81)	0·04
	4.	1961	3,610	79·46 (21·92)	0·21

Notes: The figures for productivity are not standardised. Multiples are defined as organisations with five or more branches in 1961, and as organisations with ten or more branches in 1966. The degree of labour market tightness in 1966 is measured by average percentage vacancies less unemployed over the period 1962 to 1966 and in 1961 by the average over the period 1957 to 1961.

Table VI.5   *Gross Margins in Independent Grocery Stores and Clothing Shops, by the State of the Labour Market, 1966*

Town Group (ten in each)	Percentage Vacancies less Unemployed, 1962–66	Gross Margin: Grocery	Clothing
A	1·1	15·1	30·7
B	−2·4	14·9	30·3

Notes: Group A consists of the ten towns in which the degree of labour market tightness was greatest over the period 1962 to 1966, Group B of the ten in which the labour market was slackest.

This of course cannot be regarded as conclusive evidence that there is little difference in the amounts of service provided as between the two groups. There are a large number of possible explanations for any given level of gross margin, of which the service element is but one. Thus it is quite conceivable, for example, that variations in efficiency or the degree of monopoly within our sample tend to conceal differences in the amount of service provided.

2. Wage Differences

(i) The Effect of Labour Market Conditions on Average Wages in Retailing
We argued earlier in the chapter that the relationship between conditions in a town's labour market and the level of sales per person engaged in retailing may arise from two essential sources. Firstly, differences in the former are likely to reflect differences in the difficulty of recruiting suitable staff, and secondly, they may reflect differences in the cost of employing labour. In reality, it is difficult to distinguish precisely between these two elements, if it is allowed that labour is always available 'at a price'. We have attempted to examine the association between the degree of labour market tightness and average earnings per employee for our sample of fifty towns in 1966, on the basis of wages and salary figures for independent retailers.

The specific question to which we have addressed ourselves is whether a given worker was, on average, paid more in towns where labour was relatively scarce than in towns where labour was relatively abundant. To answer this, we have estimated the wages per full-time male equivalent employee in independent shops with respect to individual towns. This measure is based on the assumption that, in each town, the *relative* earnings of each of the four categories of worker for which we have information — namely, full-time male, full-time female, part-time male and part-time female employees — conformed to their relative earnings at the national level. Specifically, we assume that the information collected in the Retail Earnings Survey for 1966[1] gives a satisfactory indication of the average wages paid, for example, to full-time male employees in relation to full-time female employees, or to full-time female employees in relation to part-time female employees, in independent shops in each of the fifty towns. Clearly this is rather an heroic assumption to make, but it represents the least unsatisfactory method of approach. For this reason, the results of the exercise are of an extremely tentative nature.

Average wages per full-time male equivalent employee in independent shops, derived on the basis of the above procedure, are shown in Table VI.6 for groups of towns arranged according to the degree of labour market tightness. It is apparent that there is some tendency for wages to be higher in those towns in which labour was comparatively scarce over the period 1962 to 1966, than in those where it was comparatively abundant. Thus a full-time male worker in retailing received, on average £887 in the Group A towns whereas he tended to receive almost £40 a year less in the Group E towns. On the other hand, it has to be admitted that the differences in average wages between Groups A, B and D are very small.

Although there appears to be some association between the two variables, there is not a particularly close linear relationship, as is indicated by the regression equation:

$$W = 874 + 11 \cdot 72L \qquad r^2 = 0 \cdot 06$$
$$(6 \cdot 79)$$

where W equals wages per full-time male equivalent employee in independent shops for the sample of fifty towns in 1966, and L is percentage vacancies minus percentage unemployed, averaged over the period 1962 to 1966. Thus the value of r^2 is very low, while the regression coefficient is not significant at the five per cent level of confidence.

One point which should be noted with regard to the picture shown by Table VI.6 is that, as average wages differ between kinds of retail business, it is possible that at least part of the variation in wages per employee arises from differences in the composition of businesses as between groups. However inspection of the data reveals that this is likely to be only a minor factor in the explanation, as no marked differences in composition are discernible. Moreover if we examine, for example, 'Grocery and provision dealers' and 'Clothing shops' separately, a similar pattern emerges as for all independent retailers. Thus, for the former trade, the towns in Group A, as defined in Table VI.6, showed average wages per full-time male equivalent employee of £827, as opposed to £796 with respect to the Group

1 Published in *Ministry of Labour Gazette*, December 1966.

Table VI.6 *Wages per Full-time Male Equivalent Employee in Independent Shops by State of the Labour Market, 1966*

Town Group	Percentage Vacancies less Unemployed, 1962–66	Wages and Salaries per Full-time Male Equivalent Employee, 1966 (£)
A (10)	1·1	887
B (9)	0·4	881
C (10)	0·2	866
D (10)	−0·5	878
E (11)	−2·3	848

Notes: The towns are grouped according to the degree of tightness in the labour market over the period 1962 to 1966; the figures in brackets show the number of towns in each group, the differences arising from a concern to put towns with similar percentage vacancies less unemployed in the same group.

Full-time male equivalent employees are estimated by applying weights of 1·0, 0·5, 0·25 and 0·125 to full-time male, full-time female, part-time female and part-time male employees respectively. These weights are derived from information on earnings in a sample of retail establishments with 11 to 24 employees, in the Retail Earnings Survey for 1966, *Ministry of Labour Gazette*, December, 1966.

E towns, while for 'Clothing shops', Group A towns showed an average of £981 and Group E an average of £909.

A further point to emphasize is that we would not, of course, expect the degree of labour market tightness to be the sole determinant of relative earnings in retailing as between towns. The wages paid to a given worker will depend in large measure on the prevailing level of wage rates in other sectors — given the low degree of unionisation in the retail trades — which in turn will be influenced, for example, by the precise industrial composition of these sectors. By virtue of this consideration alone, we might not expect to find a completely systematic association between labour scarcity and average wages. In consequence, the fact that any relationship emerges at all might be regarded as more note-worthy than the fact that the relationship is weak — especially if the crude nature of the average wage indicator is also taken into account.

Finally we should note that we have only been able to estimate average wages per employee in independent shops, and that the pattern might well be different with respect to multiples and coops. Thus within a nationwide retail organisation it is unlikely that wage-rates for a particular job vary substantially between branches — apart from the usual 'London-allowance' — although at the same time this might not apply with equal force to actual earnings. This being so, branch managers in tight labour market towns, for instance, might have an incentive to adjust the composition of their labour force, with regard to the male/female, part-time/full-time breakdown, insofar as they have difficulty, for example, in recruiting male or full-time staff at the going wage-rate.

A more general point is that, given the large disparity between male and female wage-rates, retailers have the potential ability to adjust their total labour costs by changing the sex composition of their labour force. The actual variation in composition between towns is examined after we have considered the association between our estimates of average wages per employee and the level of productivity.

(ii) Average Wages and Productivity

The question now arises as to whether the evidence for the sample of towns in 1966 is consistent with the hypothesis that the level of wages in retailing is likely to have a positive influence on sales per person engaged. This hypothesis is based on the view that labour costs do not directly enter into the determination of retail price — or the retail gross margin — with the implication that differences in wages between towns constitute differing incentives to raise output per worker. In other words, if retailers have difficulty in passing on any increase in labour costs — either because these are regarded as fixed costs or because price is determined by the application of a conventional mark-up[1] — their net profits may be reduced, and the attempt to restore these is likely to result in some increase in sales per person engaged.

We have examined both aspects of this hypothesis. Firstly, there is no discernible tendency within our sample of towns for the average gross margin of independent retailers to vary with the average level of wages per full-time male equivalent employee. This is illustrated by the finding that the ten towns which show the highest value for the latter have an average gross margin of 24·2 per cent with respect to their independent retailers, while the ten towns which show the lowest value have an average gross margin of 24·4 per cent. We can therefore conclude that there is no significant difference between these two 'extreme' groups with regard to the level of gross margin — assuming of course that the business composition of their retail sectors is similar — which is consistent with the above hypothesis.

Secondly a positive association between average wages and sales per person engaged emerges from the data and this is summarized by the regression equation:

$$P = 3101 + 2\cdot31W \qquad r^2 = 0\cdot19$$
$$(0\cdot70)$$

where P is the overall level of productivity and W is the average wages per full-time male equivalent employee in independent shops, for the fifty towns in 1966. The equation suggests, therefore, that a difference of £100 in the average earnings per employee tended to be associated with a difference of £231 in the level of sales per person engaged.[2]

The conclusion which again must remain rather tentative, is therefore that the evidence supports the view that the level of average wages exerts a positive influence on the level of sales per person engaged. It should be recognized, however, that this relationship is equally explicable in terms of the income effect of higher wages, as well as in terms of the hypothesis outlined at the beginning of the section.

---

1 This was explained more fully in Chapters I and II above.

2 If we take the productivity of independents instead of that of all retailers, the equation is

$$P_I = 2837 + 1\cdot92W \qquad r^2 = 0\cdot14$$
$$(0\cdot68)$$

where P_I is the sales per person engaged in independents and W is as in the text. It should be noted that there is a closer association between these two variables than between the productivity of independents and the degree of labour market tightness, with respect to 1966. See Equation 3, Table VI.4.

In other words, higher wages are likely to lead directly to an increase in the average transaction size, with corresponding implications for sales per person engaged.[1]

3. Structural Differences in Employment

(i) The Composition of the Labour Force and Labour Market Conditions
The 1961 study found a tendency for part-time working to be more important in relatively tight labour market towns than was the case in relatively slack towns, the possible underlying rationale being that retailers use more part-time labour where full-time workers are not readily obtainable. Our concern here is both to re-examine this finding in the light of the 1966 data and to extend the analysis to consider the male/female composition of the retail labour force in relation to labour market conditions. Thus we have seen that a given worker may receive a higher wage in towns where labour is scarce, the question now arises, for example, of whether retailers in such towns tend to employ a higher proportion of female staff than elsewhere, in an attempt to keep down payroll costs or because male employees are not available. This assumes, of course, that male and female staff are to some extent interchangeable, which for certain functions is not so; for example, shop assistants in 'Womenswear' shops clearly need to be female, the reverse being true of 'Menswear' shops. We return to this point below.

The evidence on the relationship between labour market conditions and the composition of employment is summarized in Table VI.7. The pattern that emerges is quite remarkable. There is a completely systematic tendency for the proportion of female employees, whether full-time or part-time, to vary inversely with the degree of labour scarcity. In those towns where labour is in comparatively short supply, retailers tend to employ a relatively high proportion of men; in towns where there is a comparative abundance of labour, retailers tend to employ a relatively high proportion of women.

Retailers in tight labour market towns do not appear therefore to keep down labour costs by employing more female staff. Indeed variations in the sex composition of employment between towns seems to be a factor in increasing the difference in average earnings per worker rather than a factor in reducing the difference. We must temper this observation, however, by noting that the average age of staff as between towns remains unknown; it is possible therefore that retailers in tight towns employ more juveniles than is the case elsewhere.[2]

---

1 In a further attempt to test the hypothesis, we examined the relationship between the level of sales per person engaged and the figures for average earnings of full-time manual female employees by sub-region, published in the D.E.P., *New Earnings Survey* for 1968. These represent the closest approximation to earnings by town and their use is based on the rather heroic assumption that they may reflect inter-town differences in retail labour costs. Although a positive association between the two variables emerged, it was nevertheless very weak ($r^2 = 0.06$). We can record, however, that the average level of productivity was £5,484 in the ten towns where average earnings were highest as against £5101 in the ten where they were lowest.

2 It might also be that there is less of a disparity between male and female earnings in 'tight' towns than in 'slack' towns, which would reduce the differential cost of employing male assistants. If this is so, it would mean that average wages per full-time male equivalent employee have been overestimated for 'tight' towns in the preceding exercise.

Table VI.7   *The Composition of Employees in Retailing and the Degree of Labour Market Tightness, 50 Towns, 1966*

| Town Group | Percentage Vacancies less Unemployed, 1962–66 | Average Percentages of Total Employees: | | | | | | |
| | | Full-time | | | Part-time | | | |
		Male	Female	Ratio	Male	Female	(Total)	Ratio
A (10)	1·1	30·6	32·7	1·07	10·1	26·7	(36·8)	2·64
B (9)	0·4	29·6	34·8	1·18	9·0	26·7	(35·7)	2·97
C (10)	0·2	29·0	36·4	1·26	8·4	26·2	(34·6)	3·12
D (10)	−0·5	27·4	40·5	1·48	6·3	25·7	(32·0)	4·08
E (11)	−2·3	24·8	43·2	1·74	5·3	26·8	(32·1)	5·06

Notes: The towns are grouped according to the average degree of labour market tightness over the period 1962 to 1966, the figures in brackets showing the number of towns in each group.

The percentages cover the paid employees in the total retail sector of towns. The figures in the 'ratio' columns show the ratio of females to males.

On the other hand, the proportion of part-time workers employed (the figures in brackets in the table) is positively related to the degree of labour scarcity, which supports the 1961 finding.[1] However the relationship with respect to the 1966 sample is not a continuous one, in the sense that the linear regression equation yields an r^2 of only 0·05, as opposed to 0·26 for the 160 towns in 1961.

But the important question still remains as to the underlying rationale for the quite distinct pattern shown by Table VI.7. Unfortunately there appears to be no definitive answer, and we can only suggest one or two tentative explanations, while noting that this is a matter which seems worthy of much closer consideration than we can devote to it in the course of this study. Thus two possible contributory factors seem to us to be firstly, that in tight labour market towns, there are likely to be relatively many job opportunities open to women in sectors other than retailing which tend to pay much higher wages. Retailers therefore are obliged to employ male workers where women would be employed in towns where vacancies in other sectors were much fewer. Secondly, the towns where labour market conditions are relatively slack tend to be towns which are important centres of declining heavy industry, such as ship-building, for example, and in which, correspondingly, there are comparatively few job opportunities for women in industry. In such areas it may well be that there is a general lack of acceptance of male employees in retailing, on the part of both management and worker, coupled with a greater availability of female labour than in 'tight' towns – the tendency being perhaps for the wife to work in a shop if the husband becomes unemployed. In general, therefore, if retailers are able to recruit 'cheap' female labour there is clearly little incentive to start recruiting males.

At the same time, we have to take account of the possibility that the pattern shown by Table VI.7 owes something to inter-town differences in business composition. All we can say on this point is that there is no sign of any significant variation in the proportion of total sales made by the seven major business categories as between the town groups. Clearly variations within business categories

1 It should be noted that the 1961 finding was based on total persons engaged as the Census did not give details on the number of working proprietors and unpaid helpers.

may be important — such as between 'Womenswear' and 'Menswear' shops — but these cannot be assessed from the information available.

(ii) Part-time Working and Productivity

Finally, the 1961 study revealed a fairly marked tendency for those towns with relatively high sales per person engaged to have relatively more persons engaged on a part-time basis than other towns. The possible rationale for this was firstly that the importance of part-time working reflected the degree of labour market tightness and secondly that it might also reflect the degree of attention devoted by retail management to the problem of peak demand. The 1966 data however do not show any systematic relationship between productivity and the percentage of part-time workers employed in retailing. Thus, for example, the linear regression equation yields an r^2 of 0·004, whereas that derived for the 160 towns in 1961 was 0·32. At the same time, there is only a weak correlation between the two variables in 1961 with respect to the sample of fifty towns. Close inspection of the data again suggests that the explanation for the difference lies in the exclusion of the towns in the London area, which in 1961 tended to have both a high level of productivity and a high proportion of part-time persons engaged in retailing.

4. Summary of Main Findings

As in the previous chapter, the conclusions formulated on the basis of the 1961 data tend to be supported by the evidence for 1966. In particular, a positive relationship was found between the degree of labour market tightness and sales per person engaged — the regression coefficient for the former being much the same in 1961 and 1966 with respect to the sample of fifty towns — and between the degree of labour market tightness and the importance of part-time working — although in 1966 the relationship did not appear to be continuous. On the other hand, no association was found between the use made of part-timers and productivity in 1966.

The 1961 analysis was extended in a number of directions. Firstly, sales per person engaged in 1961 and 1966 were related to the degree of labour shortage in 1961 and 1966, respectively, instead of to a five-year average. A positive association was found, but this was weaker than when a longer period measure of labour shortage was used, whereas if 'short-term' influences predominated, a stronger association might have been expected.

Secondly, the degree of labour market tightness was found to exert a greater influence on the productivity of multiples and coops than of independents. An important part of the explanation for this was argued to be the difference in the scope for adjusting the labour force and working methods.

Thirdly, some tendency emerged for average wages per full-time male equivalent employee in independent shops to vary with the degree of labour scarcity. In addition there was a positive relationship between the former and sales per person engaged, which might suggest that higher labour costs represent an incentive to raise productivity, particularly as little variation in gross margin between towns is apparent. At the same time, however, the income effect of higher earnings needs to be taken into account.

Fourthly, a remarkably consistent pattern emerged when the composition of the retail labour force was related to labour market conditions. Towns with tight labour markets tended to have a higher proportion of male employees than towns where labour was relatively abundant. This applied with equal force to both full-time and part-time staff. It was considered that part of the explanation for this might lie in the number of job opportunities available for women in other sectors. Its effect would seem to be to raise the labour costs of retailers in towns where average wages for any given worker already tended to be relatively high.

VII

Changes in Labour Productivity, 1961 to 1966 – the Growth of Sales, Sales per Shop and Income

1. Overview

We come now to consider the changes which occurred over the period 1961 to 1966 with respect to our sample of fifty towns. Basically our concern is to examine the influence on productivity growth of movements in the variables identified in the previous two chapters, which appeared to be positively related to sales per person engaged in both 1961 and 1966. In this chapter, we assess the effect of changes in the volume of trade, the number and size of shops, population, income per head and the change in the market share of multiples and coops. In the next, we look at the relationship between productivity change and labour market conditions. As before, our intention is to consider the association between each variable and productivity change individually, outlining briefly what we would expect to find on an *a priori* basis. Having done this, we go on, in a later chapter, to assess the combined impact of the explanatory variables on productivity growth and discuss more fully the light which our findings throw on the process underlying improvements in labour utilisation in retailing.

A further point to note is that the subsequent analysis concentrates upon the changes for retailing as a whole. Unlike the previous two chapters, insufficient information is available to separate the experience of independents from that of multiples and coops. Some consideration is however given to differences between kinds of business, although it is not our intention to report the findings for each individual category in full as this would merely complicate the exposition without adding greatly to the analysis, as will become clear later in the chapter.

2. Inter-town Differences in Productivity Change

In the introduction to the town analysis we discussed the problems involved in comparing productivity between towns and outlined the reasons for basing the analysis on standardised measures which explicitly allow for differences and changes in the business composition of retail sectors. Before examining the influence of various characteristics of the towns on the change in productivity over the period 1961 to 1966, it is as well to give an indication of the variation in the latter in respect of our sample. The increase in productivity between these two years, on the basis of our weighted average measure, varied from a high of 22 per cent to a low of 4·5 per cent, six towns experiencing a gain of over 16 per cent and four towns a gain of less than six per cent. Fuller details are shown in Table VII.1.

An alternative way of illustrating the variation in performance between towns

Table VII.1 *Frequency Distribution of Productivity Growth by Town, 1961 to 1966*

Percentage Rise in Productivity 1961 to 1966[a]	Number of Towns
16·0 and over	6
14·0 to 15·9	9
12·0 to 13·9	6
10·0 to 11·9	10
8·0 to 9·9	9
6·0 to 7·9	6
Less than 6·0	4

a Weighted average movement.

Table VII.2 *Productivity Growth and the Ratio of the Change in Sales to the Change in Persons Engaged by Town Group, 1961 to 1966*

Town Group (ten in each)[a]	Percentage Rise in Productivity (weighted average movement)	Ratio of Change in Sales to Change in Employment as a Percentage
A	16·7	16·1
B	13·9	13·3
C	11·6	11·2
D	9·0	8·2
E	6·1	6·2

a Towns grouped according to the weighted average increase in productivity.
b As throughout the study, the change in sales is expressed in real terms and the change in employment is calculated on the basis of full-time equivalent persons engaged.

is shown in Table VII.2, in which towns are ranked in descending order of produc-·
tivity increase and divided into five groups of ten. This indicates, for instance, that
the average rise in productivity in the ten towns which experienced the greatest
increase over the period was almost three times as great as for the ten towns which
experienced the smallest gain (16·7 per cent as against 6·1 per cent).

Table VII.2 also shows the average rise in the overall volume of sales per person
engaged — unadjusted that is for inter-town variations in business composition — for
the towns in each group, and demonstrates that although this is generally slightly
lower than the weighted average increase there is little difference between the two
measures of productivity change. This is further indicated by the fact that the productivity ranking of towns does not vary significantly according to which measure
of change is used, the rank correlation coefficient between the two indicators
being 0·93. It follows therefore that the subsequent findings would not be much
altered by the use of an unadjusted measure of productivity change. This is reassuring
in view of the qualifications surrounding the standardising procedure.

3. Inter-correlation between Explanatory Variables
Our intention, as we have said, is to look at the relationship between productivity
growth and movements in each variable individually, leaving to a later stage examination of the combined effect on productivity change of all the factors identified.
Nevertheless it is as well to consider at the outset the relationship which exists
between the individual explanatory variables, in order to obtain some indication
of the extent to which an observed correlation between productivity change and

another factor is likely to conceal the influence of a third factor. The values for the squares of the coefficients of correlation between the principal variables included in the subsequent analysis are contained in the matrix shown in Table VII.3. The table in fact is based on the evidence for 41 towns, because of the difficulty of comparing labour market conditions after 1961 with those prevailing before 1961 with respect to nine towns, the essential reason being that the official 'definition' of the towns changed between the two periods. For the other variables included in the table, however, there is little significant difference between the coefficients computed on the basis of 41 towns and those computed on the basis of 50 towns.

As might have been anticipated, the table shows a positive association between changes in income per head and changes in both the degree of labour market tightness and the volume of sales. In addition, the changes in the number of shops

Table VII.3   *Squares of the Coefficients of Correlation between the Variables used to explain Productivity Change over the period 1961 to 1966, 41 Towns*

Explanatory Variables	Squares of Correlation Coefficients:				
	Δ Sales	Δ Sales per Shop	Δ Shops	Δ Income	Initial Income
Δ Labour	0·09	0·002	0·05	0·20	0·20[a]
Δ Sales		0·001	0·42	0·23	0·05[a]
Δ Sales per Shop			0·49[a]	0·01[a]	0·03
Δ Shops				0·16	0·05[a]
Δ Income					0·21[a]

Notes: Δ Labour equals the average percentage vacancies less unemployed over the period 1962 to 1966 minus the average percentage over the period 1957 to 1961. Δ Sales and Δ Sales per shop are both expressed in real terms. Δ Income equals the change in income per head over the period 1959/60 to 1964/65 while Initial Income is the level of income per head in 1959/60.
a Signifies that the correlation coefficient is negative.

is related to sales growth and appears to have a strong influence on the changes in sales per shop. On the other hand, little correlation at all emerges between the latter and changes in the volume of trade, which is a rather unexpected feature in the light of the kind of business analysis of Chapter III above and is one which deserves to be carefully noted. In general we can conclude from the values of the coefficients shown in Table VII.3 that examination of the effect on productivity growth of each variable in isolation is unlikely to lead to any serious danger of misinterpretation.

4. The Growth of Towns
The evidence we examined in the earlier part of the study suggested that there is a positive relationship between productivity growth in retailing and the rate of sales increase over a period of time. Thus those kinds of business which experienced the largest expansion of trade between 1957 and 1966 also made, in general, the greatest gains in productivity. The object here is to examine the association between these two variables across our sample of towns for the period 1961 to 1966. Before looking at the evidence, however, we need to consider what we would expect to find.

Clearly the possible existence of a time-lag in the adjustment of the retail workforce to an increase in sales would be one reason for expecting a positive relationship between the two variables. More rapidly expanding towns, for example, may

92

be a little more behind in recruitment at the end of period than at the beginning than is the case for less rapidly expanding towns. Here the pattern of the movement in sales over the period is clearly relevant, there being a greater likelihood of the figures for productivity growth reflecting lags in adjustment if increases in sales happened to be concentrated in 1965 or 1966, for example. In this case much of the necessary rise in staff recruitment would only occur after the period under investigation.

Because of the shorter time period under consideration, such lag effects are of more potential importance than was the case for the kind of business analysis in Chapter III above, which was based on comparing changes over nine years. However the main arguments put forward to rationalise the results of that analysis may also apply to inter-town comparisons. Thus, as we mentioned, the introduction and spread of innovations in methods of retail operation are likely to be related to the rate of sales growth, the expansion of retail capacity being a major factor determining the speed with which such improvements are made. At the same time, a rise in the volume of sales may result in the fuller utilisation of staff in existing stores or may lead to a less than proportionate rise in work effort, to the extent that it takes the form of an increase in the average size of transaction.

However as between towns, over the length of time being considered, there are a number of reasons for expecting a given rise in sales to be associated with very different rates of productivity growth, in addition to the point made earlier concerning the timing of the sales increase. Firstly, it is possible that some towns provided exceptional scope for redevelopment in 1961 and that the construction of new stores, incorporating the latest methods of selling, took place in subsequent years independently of the rate of sales increase. Secondly, it is possible that local planning regulations may have restrained the growth of retail capacity (and indeed the extent of redevelopment) in certain towns over the period and hence induced an artificial lag effect. In general terms, the relevant point to be borne in mind is that the effect of an increase in sales on productivity will very much depend on the relationship between shopping capacity and sales at the beginning and at the end of the period under investigation. If, for example, there had been big increases in shopping capacity in earlier years, then the period under observation will tend to be one where any sales increase has an unusually large effect in terms of spreading overheads, including the important element of fixed labour costs, so that the productivity gains will be large. On the other hand, if the period begins with an exceptionally low ratio of shopping capacity to sales, then if there is a substantial addition to capacity during the period, the productivity gains may well tend to be damped, even though the new capacity may embody the most up-to-date working methods.

Thirdly, any systematic relationship between productivity growth and the change in sales may be concealed by the influence of other factors. For example, a rapid rise in the volume of trade may be accompanied in *some* towns by a significant slackening of labour market conditions, even though Table VII.3 reveals no general tendency for this to be the case. If recruitment in earlier years had been constrained by a lack of suitable applicants, then the period under investigation might witness a greater increase in retail staff than is needed to handle the rise in sales alone.

Fourthly, any change in the volume of sales is likely to incorporate two elements:

a change in the number of people making purchases and a change in the amount of purchases made by each person. These elements may not only vary in their relative importance between towns but, in addition, may both be associated with conflicting effects on productivity. Thus, as we have said, an increase in expenditure per customer is likely to mean an increase in purchases per shop visit or in the average unit value of goods bought, and hence it is likely to result in a less than proportionate rise in the work effort required of retail staff. But it also tends to be associated with higher levels of real income, which may lead to an increased demand for retail services, including a wider variety of shops and products, and may therefore have a depressing effect on productivity as measured. Similarly a given increase in shopping population may also have varying implications for productivity. Such an increase may result in a need for more retail capacity and more assistants, but it may also lead to a greater utilisation of existing shops and staff, depending in large measure on the timing of the additional purchases and to some extent on the location of the extra customers. Thus insofar as the capacity of the retail sector and the number of employees engaged is determined by demand at the peak, any increase in demand during off-peak periods may be accommodated with little or no rise in the resources devoted to retailing.

Unfortunately there are no reliable details available on the importance of changes in shopping population over the period as opposed to changes in expenditure per customer, which might help in forming an expectation as to the likely effect on productivity of the movement in sales experienced by each town. While information is available on the changes in population between 1961 and 1966, there is little reason why such movements should reflect changes in the number of people using a town's shopping facilities. For example the construction of a new shopping centre may have attracted more people into the town from outside, or alternatively the development of new shops in a neighbouring town may have led to an outflow of custom. In both cases the shopping population of the town in question may have changed significantly without there being any great change in the number of inhabitants living within its Census boundaries.

The evidence suggests that this type of change was of some importance for our sample even over the relatively short period of time being investigated. Thus there is no close association between the movement in sales experienced by individual towns and the change in population. The coefficient of rank correlation between the towns ranked according to sales growth and according to population increase is as low as 0·29 while the implied change in the volume of retail expenditure per inhabitant ranged from an increase of almost 29 per cent to a decline of over six per cent.[1] It is difficult to accept that a variation of this magnitude could obtain without there having been compensating movements in the importance of migrant custom.

---

1 The change in population for the towns is derived from the 1966 Sample Census of Great Britain. In the case of ten of the fifty towns, boundary changes were made between the 1961 and 1966 Censuses, but for these towns the 1961 figures are given on the 1966 definition so that movements between the two years can be calculated. As we have mentioned, both the 1961 and 1966 Censuses of Distribution were based on the 1961 Census boundaries, which means that for the above ten towns movements in retail sales and in population may not correspond exactly, but the difference should not be very great.

Table VII.4   *Changes in Sales and in Sales per Person Engaged for Town Groups, 1961 to 1966*

Town Groups (ten in each)	% Increase in the volume of sales	% Increase in productivity (weighted average movement)
A	24·4 (24·1)[a]	12·8 (14·4)[a]
B	17·1	14·6
C	12·0	10·6
D	8·9	8·8
E	2·1 (3·6)[b]	10·4 (9·0)[b]

Notes: The towns are grouped according to the increase in sales.

a Excluding two towns in which very big rises in sales were accompanied by very small gains in productivity.

b Excluding two towns in which declining or constant sales were accompanied by large gains in productivity.

An alternative would be to approach the problem from the opposite direction by directly estimating changes in sales per customer, and hence changes in shopping population, from income per head changes, but the necessary information, as we have remarked before, is not available in a sufficiently reliable form. We do, however, make some attempt later in the chapter to use the statistics that are published to give some indication of the relationship between income per head and productivity growth.

Considering all the points made in the above discussion, we might not expect to find a close association between productivity growth and changes in sales at the town level over the period in question. The expectation is borne out by the evidence presented in Table VII.4 in which the towns are arranged in descending order of sales increase and divided into five groups. The average rise in the volume of sales and in productivity for each group between 1961 and 1966 is shown in the table.[1]

Looking at the sales column first, it can be seen that even over this five-year period, the change in sales varied markedly between towns, the increase ranging from an average of over 24 per cent for those in Group A (the ten most rapidly expanding towns) to an average of two per cent for those in Group E (the ten experiencing the least growth). The corresponding movements in productivity show much less variation, although there is some tendency for the towns which experienced relatively high rates of sales growth to have made greater productivity gains than others.

The association between the two variables over fifty towns is further summarized by the regression equation:

$$P = 9\cdot8 + 0\cdot125T \qquad r^2 = 0\cdot07 \qquad\qquad (1)$$
$$(0\cdot065)$$

where P is the percentage change in labour productivity between 1961 and 1966

---

1   The rationale for adopting this method of presentation is to give a clearer indication of whether any relationship exists between the two variables in question than can be derived from a simple linear regression equation, which will only show an association if a continuous linear relationship obtains.

and T is the percentage change in the volume of retail turnover. The square of the correlation coefficient is only 0·07 and the standard error of the regression coefficient indicates that the latter is not significantly different from zero at the five per cent level of confidence.

The lack of a strong correlation between the two variables is, however, in large measure due to four towns, two of which experienced exceptional sales increases over the period but made very modest productivity gains and two of which experienced either a decline or no growth in sales but made relatively large gains in productivity.[1] Examination of the basic data for these towns suggest that their performance may have been affected by an abnormal relationship between shopping capacity and sales either at the beginning or at the end of the period under investigation, which was one of the reasons discussed above for expecting a less than systematic relationship between productivity and sales growth. Thus in respect of the two towns with high sales but low productivity growth, there is indirect evidence of a substantial addition to retail capacity over the period in the form of an increase in the number of shops – of 46 per cent in one case and 24 per cent in the other – which was far greater than for any other town included in our sample. With respect to the two towns showing the reverse pattern, there was *apparently* a large reduction in capacity with the number of shops declining by over 20 per cent in both cases, which again was more than for any other of the fifty towns. We should reiterate at this point that there is no necessary reason why changes in the number of individual retail outlets should reflect similar movements in the amount of floorspace devoted to retailing. This is particularly relevant with regard to the latter two towns mentioned, as the general tendency has been for fewer large stores to replace a greater number of small shops. On the other hand, if total retail capacity did not decline significantly in these two towns then presumably they gained to a comparatively large extent from economies of scale through the construction of larger retail units. However, although sales per shop increased at an above average rate in these two towns, the increase was not abnormally large, whereas the former two towns were ranked 49th and 50th in this respect.

A further possible explanation for the pattern shown by these two towns is that the relationship between sales and productivity is asymmetrical, in the sense that a decline, or lack of growth, in trade may itself stimulate gains in productivity. Thus such a market situation is likely to be much less conducive to the continued survival of the less efficient retailers than one in which the volume of sales is expanding.[2] At the same time, we have to admit that no such asymmetry was evident in Chapter III with respect to the experience of the different kinds of business over the period 1957 to 1966, the businesses experiencing declines in sales also showing the smallest gains in productivity.

The effect of excluding these four towns from the sample is shown by the figures in brackets in Table VII.4 above. As can be seen, the average productivity increase of Group A becomes much the same as that realised by the towns in

1 In the former two towns, sales rose by an average of 25·4 per cent but productivity by only 6·1 per cent, and in the latter two, sales declined by an average of 4·3 per cent whereas the average productivity increase was 15·9 per cent.

2 This is analogous to the argument in Chapter II, which was concerned with the effect on productivity of a sustained period of slow growth at the national level.

Group B, while the productivity rise of Group E is almost reduced to that of Group D, so that a much more systematic relationship between sales and productivity growth emerges.

The result of recalculating the regression equation for the remaining 46 towns is:

$$P = 7\cdot5 + 0\cdot307T \qquad r^2 = 0\cdot34 \tag{2}$$
$$(0\cdot064)$$

where P and T are as before. The value for r^2 is increased markedly while the regression coefficient becomes highly significant. The latter indicates that in a town in which the volume of sales rose by ten percentage points above average over the period, productivity would have tended to increase by about three percentage points above average.

However the validity of excluding four towns from our sample is open to dispute. It may be argued, for example, that it is always possible to justify the exclusion of observations that conform least well to some general pattern on some ground or other. Alternatively, it can be maintained that special factors are likely to be present in each town in varying degrees, the four excluded towns merely representing extreme examples of their influence. In answer to this type of criticism, we can only say that the influence of special factors seems markedly greater in respect of the four towns in question than over the remainder of our sample. What the findings do illustrate, of course, is the potential importance of the points made in our introductory discussion.

5. Changes in Shops and Sales per Shop
The above discussion suggests that an alternative to excluding the four towns showing an atypical relationship between sales growth and shopping capacity from the analysis, would be to take explicit account of changes in the number of shops when examining the influence of changes in sales on productivity growth. The result of doing this for the fifty towns is summarized in the regression equation:

$$P = 7\cdot2 + 0\cdot304T - 0\cdot165S \qquad \overline{R}^2 = 0\cdot17 \tag{3}$$
$$(0\cdot085) \quad (0\cdot055)$$

where P and T are as above and S is the percentage change in the number of shops between 1961 and 1966.

For any given increase in the volume of trade, therefore, an above average rise in the number of retail outlets has a dampening effect on the rate of productivity growth. A point to note is that the value of the regression coefficient in respect of sales – approximately $0\cdot3$ – is almost identical to that in equation (2) above, in which the rise in productivity was regressed on the movement in sales volume alone but the four towns were excluded from the sample. A further feature of Equation (3) is the low value of $\overline{R}^2$, although this was only to be expected from our *a priori* discussion, in which we emphasized the improbability of finding a completely systematic relationship between sales and productivity growth at the town level over the small number of years being considered.

A further step is to consider directly the association between gains in productivity and changes in the sales-size of shop. In the above, we have ignored certain problems

Table VII.5 *Changes in Sales per Shop and Productivity for Town Groups, 1961 to 1966*

Town Group (ten in each)	% Increase in Sales per Shop[a]	% Increase in Productivity[a]
A	34·7	12·5
B	23·8	12·3
C	19·3	12·3
D	14·5	11·0
E	5·2	9·2

Notes: The towns are grouped according to the increase in sales per shop.
a Weighted average movements.

concerning a comparison of changes in the number of shops *vis à vis* movements in sales volume. These are of the same nature as those encountered in comparing inter-town movements in productivity. Thus both the typical turnover-size of shop at any one point in time and the average change over the period under investigation vary between kinds of retail business, which means that both the change in the composition of the goods purchased and the initial pattern have a potential bearing on the observed movement in the number of outlets in relation to the movement in the total volume of trade with respect to individual towns. We can explicitly allow for the differential influence of these two factors by basing the analysis on a weighted average measure of change similar to that adopted to compare productivity increases.[1]

The association between the weighted average movements in sales per shop and productivity is indicated in Table VII.5, in which the towns are grouped according to the increase in the former variable. It is evident that there is some positive relationship between the two variables, but it is not a continuous one, in the sense that the differences in average productivity growth between Group A and Groups B and C is negligible despite the wide variation in the average rise in sales per shop.

The relationship is further summarized in Equation (4):

$$P = 8·8 + 0·134X \qquad r^2 = 0·13 \tag{4}$$
$$(0·050)$$

where X is the percentage increase in sales per shop between 1961 and 1966.

Of course, as we have emphasized already, we cannot necessarily interpret this result to mean that productivity gains have been realised through the concentration of sales on a lower level of retail capacity. Increases in sales per shop embody this effect and the replacement of smaller outlets by larger stores; both however would be expected to work in the same direction as far as productivity is concerned, although clearly the magnitude of the influence may differ according to which element is dominant.

1 The method of calculation is the same as for productivity, the average percentages of shops classified to each kind of business for the fifty towns being used to weight the changes in sales per shop within each town.

6. Changes in Population and Income per Head

(i) Population Changes

We remarked earlier that there is little reason to expect changes in the number of people living within a town's Census boundaries to reflect changes in the number of people using a town's shopping facilities. Nevertheless it is of interest to examine the influence of the former on the growth in productivity. From what we have said, we might expect a *given* rise in sales to be associated with a lower increase in productivity, the greater is the increase in population. The argument here is that population growth would tend to lead to the construction of more shopping facilities, or, more generally, to an increase in the *number* of transactions, and hence produce a dampening effect on the rise in productivity, in contrast to an increase in expenditure per customer which probably, overall, has a positive influence on sales per person engaged. This effect might be offset in some degree as the new shopping capacity would tend to embody the most up-to-date methods of selling which would thus be associated with an increase in productivity, but the latter is unlikely to completely outweigh the former consideration. This expectation is supported to some extent by the evidence of our sample, which is summarized by the regression equation:

$$P = 6 \cdot 5 + 0 \cdot 350T - 0 \cdot 284N \qquad \overline{R}^2 = 0 \cdot 37 \qquad (5)$$
$$(0 \cdot 064) \quad (0 \cdot 121)$$

where P and T are as above and N is the change in population between 1961 and 1966, for 46 towns. The equation indicates that there was some tendency for increases in population to reduce the gain in productivity expected on the basis of a given increase in sales. A further feature to note is that the inclusion of changes in population has the effect of slightly raising the value of the regression coefficient in respect of sales growth.[1]

Despite the qualifications that surround the measure used, the result of making some allowance for variations in population change between towns therefore conforms to our *a priori* expectation — at least as far as the direction of its influence on productivity growth is concerned.

(ii) Income per Head

To the extent that an increase in income per head is associated with a rise in expenditure per retail customer, it may potentially have two conflicting influences on productivity growth. One consequence is likely to be an increase in the average value of goods purchased per shop visit, which may entail little or no increase in sales staff and almost certainly a less than proportionate rise. A second consequence, however, may be a rise in the demand for the services provided by retailers, including for example, a demand for a wider variety of goods and more specialist shops. This

---

1   This is also a feature of the equation calculated for all fifty towns which is

$$P = 9 \cdot 1 + 0 \cdot 156T - 0 \cdot 233N \qquad \overline{R}^2 = 0 \cdot 06$$
$$(0 \cdot 068) \quad (0 \cdot 153)$$

Table VII.6   *Changes in Income per Head and Productivity for Town Groups, 1961 to 1966*

Town Group (ten in each)	% Increase in income per head 1959/60 to 1964/65[a]	% Increase in productivity 1961 to 1966
A	41·3	14·1
B	38·6	12·7
C	36·6	11·5
D	35·3	10·0
E	34·1	9·1

Notes: The towns are grouped according to the increase in income per head.
a *Source: Inland Revenue Reports*, 1962, 1963 and 1967.

may potentially lead to a reduction in productivity as measured.[1] We might expect this second potential effect to become more important at high levels of income per head, as it seems reasonable to suppose that the income elasticity of demand for services itself increases with income.

As we noted in Chapter V above, statistics on income per head are not published in a form that allows the influence of this factor to by analysed with any confidence. The closest approximation to what we require is Inland Revenue information by county and conurbation, and we again assume that the average levels of income per head for these are representative in each case of the levels for the towns located within their boundaries.

The relationship between the change in income per head, calculated on this basis, and productivity growth for our sample of towns is indicated in Table VII.6, in which the towns are grouped according to the increase in the former variable.[2]

The table shows clearly that there is a systematic tendency for the rate of productivity increase to vary with the percentage rise in income per head. This is further described by Equation (6):

$$P = -11·7 + 0·623Y_1 \qquad r^2 = 0·18 \tag{6}$$
$$(0·191)$$

where Y_1 is the change in income per head between 1959/60 and 1964/65. A town in which income per head as measured rose by three percentage points above average over the period would therefore have tended to show a gain in productivity of almost two percentage points above average.

The implication of this result would therefore seem to be that the effect of an increase in income per head on average transaction size more than offset any negative influence on productivity growth arising from an increased demand for retail service. However it is possible to test, again in a very approximate way, the validity of our *a priori* hypothesis from the data, by looking at the relationship between productivity change and the absolute level of income per head. In other words, from what we said,

---

1. While an increase in services may possibly be reflected in the movement of gross margins, it is unlikely to be reflected in the change in the volume of sales. There are, of course, many reasons why retail margins might change, which are completely unrelated to the change in the level or quality of service offered.

2. As income per head statistics are not published annually, we have taken the change between 1959/60 and 1964/65 as the closest approximation to the change between 1961 and 1966.

Table VII.7   *The Initial Level of Income per Head and Productivity Change for Groups of Towns, 1961 to 1966*

Town Group	Income per head, 1959/60[a]	% Increase in productivity
A (10)	763	9·0
B (11)	721	10·7
C (11)	705	12·1
D (10)	695	11·3
E (8)	666	14·9

Notes: The towns are grouped according to the level of income per head in 1959/60; the figures in brackets give the number of towns in each group.

a *Source: Inland Revenue Reports,* 1962 and 1963.

we would expect to find that the rise in sales per person engaged was relatively small in those towns with high levels of income per head, other things being equal. The evidence is summarized in Table VII.7, which groups the towns according to the level of income per head at the beginning of the period and gives the corresponding average changes in productivity between 1961 and 1966.

The pattern shown by the table clearly tends to support our argument, inasmuch as the average productivity gains for the two extreme Groups, A and E, are respectively much smaller and much larger than for the other groups. The relationship between the two variables is further described by the equation:

$$P = 51·6 - 0·056Y_0 \qquad r^2 = 0·22 \qquad (7)$$
$$(0·015)$$

where Y_0 is the level of income per head in 1959/60. On average, a difference of £10 in the initial level of income per head between towns was therefore associated with a difference of 0·6 of a percentage point in the rise in productivity between 1961 and 1966.

At the same time, it should be made clear that there is some tendency for the increase in income per head to have been greater over the period, the lower the initial level, the correlation coefficient being $-0·43$.[1] The relationships described by Equations (6) and (7) may therefore owe something to the correlation between Y_1 and Y_0, in that variations in one reflect, in some degree, similar variations in the other. The result of including both variables in the explanation of productivity growth is indicated by Equation (8)

$$P = 26·6 + 0·402Y_1 - 0·042Y_0 \qquad \overline{R}^2 = 0·24 \qquad (8)$$
$$(0·200) \quad (0·016)$$

This gives a slightly higher degree of explanation of variations in productivity change than when either of the two variables are considered in isolation.

However we must end this section by re-emphasizing the unsatisfactory nature of the data that we have been obliged to use. It has to be accepted that there may well be quite a few towns in our sample, the actual level of income per head of which diverges significantly from the average level for the county or conurbation in which

1   This compares with $-0·46$ implied by the value of r^2 in Table VII.3 above, which covers 41 towns.

it is situated. Nevertheless, having said this, it is interesting that the findings tend to support our *a priori* expectations, as far as the direction of the influence of income per head on productivity change is concerned.

7. Changes in the Importance of Multiples and Coops

In 1961, multiple organisations and cooperative societies were, on average, responsible for 44·6 per cent of the retail sales of our sample of towns. In 1966, their share averaged 48 per cent. But the change in the relative importance of these forms of organsiation varied markedly between towns, ranging from a gain of over 17 points in the percentage of turnover sold, to a fall of five points. Given the higher level of sales per person engaged in multiples and coops as compared with independents, the question arises as to the contribution made by this factor to the variation in productivity growth within the sample. Table VII.8 shows the towns grouped according to the increase (the percentage point rise) in the share of trade going to multiples and coops over the period, together with the corresponding average changes in productivity.

It is very apparent that there is no systematic tendency for productivity to have increased at a relatively high rate in those towns in which multiples and coops increased their proportion of retail sales by a comparatively large amount. Indeed towns which experienced large gains in productivity over the period appear, if anything, to have benefited less from any diversion of sales between forms of organisation than towns in which productivity grew relatively slowly. This is confirmed if we adjust the figures for productivity growth to take account of any such diversion of trade. For example, on the assumption that for each town the percentage of sales made by multiples and coops was the same in 1966 as it had been in 1961, the difference in the rise in total sales per person engaged (the ratio of the change in the former to the change in the latter) between the five towns in which this was highest and the five in which it was lowest, increases from 12·1 per cent to 12·9 per cent. In other words, the evidence suggests that inter-town variations in the change in the relative importance of multiples and coops tended to narrow the disparity in productivity performance between towns, rather than being a factor helping to explain this disparity.

However this result may, in part, arise from the fact that we are unable to take account of variations in the distribution of multiples and coops between business categories or indeed in the relative importance of the two forms of organisation themselves. Thus, for instance, the productivity gain resulting from a relative expansion in the turnover of multiples and coops is likely to be considerably greater if it were concentrated in 'Grocery and provision dealers' as opposed to 'Other non-food shops' or 'General stores', where the productivity 'superiority' of these two forms of organisation is comparatively small.[1]

---

1 With respect to 'Grocery and provision dealers', there is in fact some (slight) tendency for the increase in productivity to be positively associated with the change in importance of multiples and coops. This is described by the regression equation:

$$P_G = 16·7 + 0·329M_G \qquad r^2 = 0·10$$
$$(0·148)$$

where P_G and M_G are respectively the productivity growth and the change in the proportion of sales made by multiples and coops for 'Grocery and provision dealers'.

Table VII.8   *The Increase in the Share of Trade of Multiples and Coops and Productivity Growth, 1961 to 1966*

Town Group (ten in each)	% point change in the share of multiples and coops[a]	% increase in productivity
A	10·1	9·6
B	5·3	12·3
C	3·1	11·8
D	0·8	11·1
E	−2·2	12·4

Notes: The towns are grouped according to the percentage point rise in the share of retail sales made by multiples and coops.

a *Source:* Information especially supplied by the D.T.I., defining multiples as organisations owning ten or more retail establishments in both 1961 and 1966.

8. Intra-Sector Analysis

The preceding analysis has solely been concerned with general tendencies relating to total retailing in our sample of towns. But retailing is, of course, composed of a number of trades which may well have differed markedly in various ways over the period under consideration. Thus for instance, the importance of new products, the scope for introducing new methods of selling, the demand for retail service and the prevalence of restrictive trading practices, especially r.p.m., are all most unlikely to have been similar across the sector as a whole. A possible implication of this is that a given change in a particular variable might not have a uniform effect as between trades, which might further imply that it may be misleading in certain cases to formulate generalisations from the aggregate experience of the sector.

For this reason we examined inter-town variations in the changes shown by individual retail trades. The general conclusion to emerge is that, with notable exceptions, the relationship between productivity growth and movements in the other variables considered in this chapter is much weaker than for all retailing. Thus disaggregation results in almost no correlation between the changes in sales and productivity experienced by certain groups of traders, whether the groups concerned are broadly defined as food shops and non-food shops or whether each of the seven major kinds of business is taken separately. The same is true with regard to the association between productivity growth and the two income per head variables, which in view of the relationship found at a higher level of aggregation seems to imply that the trades most affected in terms of productivity by the income per head variables were not the same ones as between towns.

However a tendency does emerge for the productivity growth shown by food retailers and certain durable goods traders in different towns to vary with the respective increases in sales per shop. The regression equations summarizing the association between these two variables for the categories of business concerned are presented in Table VII.9. It is evident that there is a closer relationship between changes in productivity and sales per shop for food retailers than for the other categories, and indeed than for all retailing. Moreover the regression coefficient has a much higher value in the former case, which signifies that a given increase in sales per shop tended to be associated with a greater gain in productivity in respect of food stores than in respect of non-food outlets. This result is not entirely unexpected in view of the

Table VII.9   *Regressions of Productivity Growth on Changes in Sales per Shop, by Trade, 50 Towns, 1961 to 1966*

Trade	Constant	Regression Coefficient	r^2
Food	7·5	0·272 (0·059)	0·31
Clothing and footwear	11·9	0·118 (0·061)	0·07
Household goods	14·4	0·165 (0·071)	0·10
Other non-food	10·2	0·172 (0·053)	0·18

Notes: For the two trades not included in the table – 'C.T.N.'s' and 'General stores' – no correlation between productivity growth and the change in sales per shop was found.

probability that the replacement of small shops by larger stores took place at a more rapid rate in the former case, and in view of the greater importance of increasing returns to scale in the food trade.

9. Summary of Main Findings

The main findings of this chapter are as follows:

1. There is only a weak correlation between the growth of towns and changes in productivity over the period 1961 to 1966, but this is strengthened if either four towns are excluded from the sample or if changes in the number of shops are included in the analysis.
2. There is no relationship between changes in sales and sales per shop over the period, but there is some tendency for the latter to be positively associated with the growth in productivity.
3. At the aggregate level, increases in population appeared to have an adverse effect on productivity growth, while the reverse was true for increases in income per head. In addition the initial level of income per head was negatively associated with the change in productivity.
4. No correlation was found between changes in the market share of multiples and coops at the town level and productivity growth. Indeed making an allowance for differential changes in the importance of such organisations tends to widen rather than narrow the disparity in productivity growth between towns.
5. There is a much weaker correlation between productivity growth and both changes in sales and the two income per head variables if parts of the retail sector are considered separately rather than in aggregate. However a tendency does emerge for productivity growth to vary with increases in sales per shop, particularly in respect of the food trade but also in respect of 'Other non-food', 'Household goods' and 'Clothing and footwear' retailers.

VIII
Changes in Labour Productivity, 1961 to 1966 – the Influence of Labour Market Conditions

1. A Review of *A Priori* Expectations

In previous chapters we have outlined the *a priori* arguments which would lead us to expect labour market conditions to have some bearing on sales per person engaged in retailing. These can briefly be reviewed under three headings: the effect on the amount of service provided, the effect on methods of operation, and the effect on the number of outlets. Thus, firstly, the ease with which retailers are able to retain and to recruit suitable staff is likely to depend on the job opportunities available in other sectors. If these are relatively abundant, retailers may be obliged to operate with fewer employees than they ideally require, with the result that a deterioration in service to customers occurs.

Secondly, recruitment difficulties may lead to some reorganisation of methods of operation. In the longer-term this may take the form of the introduction of new selling techniques, such as self-service or self-selection, which involve some saving of labour.

Thirdly, to the extent that tight labour market conditions are associated with higher wage costs and to the extent that retailers find difficulty in passing these on to customers, marginal outlets are likely to be eliminated, with a resulting concentration of sales on fewer shops of relatively high efficiency. In addition, some reduction in the number of outlets may occur by virtue of the increased opportunity costs of self-employment or by virtue of the availability of more highly paid jobs in other sectors. In other words, looking at the reverse side of the coin, where labour market conditions are slack, there is some encouragement to be self-employed as an alternative to unemployment or a low wage job elsewhere.

In the preceding analysis, we have seen firstly that, over the period 1954 to 1965, an inverse association exists between abnormally high levels of unfilled vacancies and persons engaged in retailing, other things being equal. Secondly, for both 1961 and 1966, there is a tendency for sales per person engaged to be higher in those towns in which the labour market was relatively tight. It was argued that the first finding tends to illustrate the short-term effects of recruitment difficulties, any increase in sales per person engaged probably involving a deterioration of service, and that the second finding is, at the least, consistent with the existence of 'longer-term' repercussions of labour market tightness on retail productivity. This was particularly so as the use of five-year averages to measure labour market conditions gave a better 'fit' than when the state of labour market in a single year was taken.[1] Furthermore,

1 Clearly, however, we are not able to completely discount the possibility that short-term factors were entirely responsible for the relationship which we found.

some tendency emerged for labour costs to be positively related to the degree of labour shortage, as between towns in 1966, as a result of both the level of wages for any given category of worker and, more especially, the proportion of relatively highly-paid assistants tending to be higher in tight labour market towns. At the same time, little discernible difference was apparent in the level of gross margin within the sample — at least as far as independent retailers were concerned.

Our concern in this chapter is with the influence of labour market conditions on changes in labour productivity over the period 1961 to 1966. The two main aspects which we wish to examine are, firstly, the effect of a sustained period of labour market tightness on productivity growth and, secondly, the effect on the latter of a change in the degree of tightness.

Before looking at the evidence, however, it is as well to re-emphasize the potential importance of such factors as local planning regulations and the extent of urban redevelopment which lie outside the scope of this study but may well play a crucial role in determining the rate of productivity growth over any given period, particularly one as short as the period we are considering. Thus, for example, slum clearance may have produced a dramatic reduction in the number of outlets in a town, whereas labour market considerations might lead us to expect little change. Alternatively, the construction of additional retail capacity may have been restrained by local planning regulations in the period under investigation, which would tend to have imposed a limit to the growth of employment and to disrupt any relation between the expansion of sales and the change in persons engaged. Under such circumstances a deterioration in service might well be of a long-term nature. Certainly a possible implication of this type of consideration is that any association between the state of the labour market and movements in productivity which exists at the town level may be concealed by factors which we are unable to identify.

2. The Influence of a Sustained Period of Labour Market Tightness

It might be argued, on the basis of the points made earlier, that a sustained period of labour shortage would tend to accelerate productivity growth by, for instance, encouraging a more rapid rate of adoption of labour-saving methods of selling, making it relatively difficult for marginal outlets to survive, or by inducing a progressive deterioration in the amount of service provided. However the evidence of our sample of towns shows no systematic association between the prevailing degree of labour market tightness over the period 1962 to 1966 and the movement in productivity. This is described in Table VIII.1 in which the towns are grouped according to the average percentage vacancies less unemployed over this period. Thus the average increase in productivity for the ten towns in which the labour shortage was most acute over the period — those included in Group A — was identical with that for the eleven towns where labour was most abundant — those included in Group E.

It is possible to rationalise this result in the following way. The towns in which the labour market was relatively tight between 1962 and 1966 tended also to be ones which had experienced a comparative shortage of labour in the preceding period. Thus the percentage vacancies less unemployed averages for the years 1962 to 1966 are strongly correlated with the averages for the years 1957 to 1961, the

Table VIII.1   *Productivity Growth and the Degree of Labour Market Tightness, 1961 to 1966*

Town Group	Average % Vacancies less % Unemployed, 1962 to 1966	% Increase in Productivity
A (10)	1·1	12·0
B (9)	0·4	10·5
C (10)	0·2	11·3
D (10)	−0·5	11·3
E (11)	−2·3	12·0

Notes: The towns are grouped according to average percentage vacancies less unemployed over the period 1962 to 1966; the figures in brackets show the number of towns in each group.

coefficient of correlation being 0·88.[1] This being so it is possible to argue that the incentive for retailers to make the most efficient use of labour — or to reduce the level of services — and to adopt labour-saving methods of operation, for example, had existed over a much longer period than the one which we are considering. Indeed we have seen that a close association exists between sales per person engaged in 1961 and the degree of labour market tightness over the preceding five-year period. Consequently it follows that the scope for further raising labour efficiency, or further reducing the amount of service provided with sales, tended to be less in tight labour market towns than in 'slack' towns. Thus, while 'tight' towns tended to have a high *level* of productivity in both 1961 and 1966, they did not necessarily show a more rapid rate of increase between the two years. There was no tendency, in other words, for the difference in productivity between 'tight' and 'slack' towns to be greater in 1966 than it had been in 1961.

3. The Influence of a Change in the Degree of Tightness

To extend the above argument, it might be postulated that towns which had shown an improvement in productivity relative to other towns between 1961 and 1966 would, to some extent, tend to be those in which retailers had experienced a tightening of labour market conditions in the intervening period — again relative to other towns. In other words retailers in such towns may have been faced with a relative increase in the difficulty of recruiting staff, and possibly in labour costs, with consequent implications for the amount of service provided, the rate of adoption of new methods of selling and the pressure on marginal outlets. If this is so, we might expect to find a positive relationship between the change in the degree of labour market tightness over the period and productivity growth in those towns in which labour had become comparatively more scarce, retail sales embodying perhaps less service or being sold in greater proportions through more modern outlets, in 1966 than in 1961.

It is important to emphasize in this context that the (slight) relationship found between average wages per employee in 1966 and the state of the labour market over the period 1962 to 1966, does not necessarily demonstrate that a (relative)

---

1 This correlation is in fact based on 42 towns rather than fifty, as changes in the classification of employment exchanges to towns mean that it is not possible to directly compare the statistics for the two periods with respect to eight towns.

increase in the degree of labour market tightness, for example, would be associated with a (relative) increase in average wages. It might be held to suggest that the latter type of association would be found, but this has to remain an assumption until the necessary data become available.

To test the effect of changes in labour market conditions, we have taken the average percentage vacancies less unemployed over the period 1962 to 1966 for the individual towns and compared this, in each case, with the average for the period 1957 to 1961.[1] There are, however, a number of ways of making such a comparison. The simplest — which is almost always the most attractive starting point — is merely to subtract the latter from the former, and the relationship between the measure of change in the degree of labour market tightness derived by this procedure and the change in productivity is illustrated in Table VIII.2. The towns in the table are grouped according to changes in labour scarcity by this measure and the corresponding average movements in productivity are shown for each of the five groups. A positive association between the two variables is clearly indicated. Thus the eight towns included in Group A which experienced the greatest tightening of the labour market, showed an average productivity gain of 15·2 per cent, whereas the eight included in group E, all of which experienced a reduction in the degree of labour shortage, had an average gain of only 8·1 per cent. It should be noted however that there is only a slight variation in average productivity increase between Groups B, C, and D.

The relationship is further summarized by the regression equation:

$$P = 10·0 + 5·46L \qquad r^2 = 0·36 \qquad\qquad (1)$$
$$(0·59)$$

where P is the weighted average movement in productivity over the period 1961 to 1966 and L is the change in the degree of labour market tightness by our measure, for 41 towns.[2] The equation indicates that there was a tendency for an above average increase in the degree of labour scarcity of one percentage point to be associated with a gain in productivity of over five percentage points above average.

However the above exercise is based, as we have said, on a very simple measure of change in the degree of labour market tightness. It assumes, for example, a linear relationship between the latter and productivity growth, whereas we saw in Chapter VI that a quadratic formulation gave a better 'fit' to the data on inter-town differences in sales per person engaged and the state of the labour market. It might therefore be thought that, for example, a rise of one percentage point between the

1 As we have noted, it is only possible to make such a comparison with respect to 42 of the fifty towns, because of classification changes. It should be mentioned that the eight towns excluded from the analysis are largely those which had relatively slack labour market conditions in both 1961 and 1966, which may have some bearing on the findings, although it is not immediately apparent what precisely this might be.

2 We have excluded one town from the 42 of Table VIII.2, as this showed an increase in percentage vacancies less unemployed between the two periods of 2·4 per cent, or almost twice as much as any other town. This not only had a disproportionate effect on the regression equation, but the actual change from −4·4 per cent to −2·0 per cent is unlikely to have represented a correspondingly greater increase in the degree of labour scarcity than for the other towns.

Table VIII.2 *Productivity Growth and Changes in the Degree of Labour Market Tightness, 42 Towns, 1961 to 1966*

Town Group	% Vacancies less Unemployed Average 1962–66 minus Average 1957–61.	% Increase in Productivity
A (8)	1·2	15·2
B (9)	0·5	11·4
C (8)	0·3	11·7
D (9)	0	10·6
E (8)	−0·3	8·1

Notes: The towns are grouped according to average percentage vacancies less unemployed over the period 1962 to 1966 minus the average over the period 1957 to 1961; the figures in brackets show the number of towns in each group.

averages for the two periods would involve a more than proportionate degree of tightening than, say, a rise of half a percentage point. Various non-linear forms of equation, however, gave a worse 'fit' to the data than the linear form described by Equation (1) above.[1]

Further consideration, however, would lead us to expect the initial degree of labour market tightness to be an important element, insofar as a change in average percentage vacancies less unemployed from +1 per cent to +2 per cent between the two periods is likely to involve a greater degree of tightening than a change from −2 per cent to −1 per cent. We therefore related productivity growth to both the change in labour market conditions and the initial state. The result is indicated by the regression equation:

$$P = 10·0 + 5·36 \, L_1 - 0·141 \, L_2 \qquad R^2 = 0·36 \qquad (2)$$
$$\quad (1·24) \qquad (0·563)$$

where L_1 is the change in average percentage vacancies less unemployed between the two periods and L_2 is the average percentage vacancies less unemployed for the period 1957 to 1961. L_2 is not statistically significant by any test and clearly does not add anything to the overall explanation of variations in productivity change. Moreover the value of the regression coefficient with respect to L_1 — the change in the degree of labour scarcity — is little altered from Equation (1) above.

Table VIII.3 represents a perhaps more tangible illustration of the lack of any apparent influence on productivity growth exerted by the prevailing state of the labour market. The towns in the table are divided into two groups of approximately equal size according to the average degree of labour scarcity over the period 1957 to 1966, as measured by percentage vacancies less unemployed, and the towns in each group are then classified according to the change in the degree of labour scarcity between 1957–61 and 1962–66. It is very clear that there is no tendency for the productivity growth of the 'tight' group of towns to be greater than that of the 'slack' group, but within each group, there is a positive relationship between productivity growth and changes in labour market conditions.

1 Specifically equations of the form $P = a + b_1 \, L + b_2 \, L^2$, $P = a + b \log L$ and $\log P = a + b \log L$, where P and L are as defined in the text, were tried.

Table VIII.3 *Productivity Growth in Groups of Towns Cross-Classified by the Degree of Labour Market Tightness 1957 to 1966, and Changes in Labour Market Tightness, 42 Towns, 1957–1961 to 1962–1966*

Change in Labour Market Tightness, Average 1962–66 – Average 1957–61	% Increase in Productivity 1961–66	
	'Tight' Towns	'Slack' Towns
0·8 and over	16·0 (3)	15·7 (4)
0·4 to 0·7	11·0 (5)	11·8 (5)
0 to 0·3	10·2 (7)	12·7 (6)
Less than 0	7·4 (5)	8·9 (7)

Notes: 'Tight' towns are those in which percentage vacancies less unemployed for the period 1957 to 1966 averaged over 0·1 per cent, and 'slack' towns are those in which the figure was less than this. The figures in brackets refer to the number of towns in each category.

Nevertheless it is important to recognize that we cannot necessarily interpret these results to mean that the measure of labour market change which we have adopted provides a satisfactory indicator of the change in the degree of labour scarcity, or that the prevailing state of the labour market is of no importance. Rather the findings may reflect the influence of differences in the scope for making improvements in labour productivity, or for reducing the amount of service provided, as between towns. Thus in towns where labour market conditions had been comparatively tight over a period of time, it might well have been necessary for a greater degree of tightening to have taken place to achieve a given rise in sales per person engaged than in a town where labour had been comparatively abundant. In other words, there is a likelihood that a given increase in the degree of labour scarcity, if this could be adequately measured, would tend to produce greater gains in productivity in 'slack' towns than in 'tight' towns, by virtue of the greater opportunities available in the former than the latter for making such gains.

As in Chapter VI above, we have made an (unavoidably crude) attempt to assess the importance of 'short-term' effects of changes in labour market conditions on movements in sales per person engaged. Such effects, as we have argued, take the form of compensating changes in the amount of service provided with the sale of goods and arise from the likely association between the difficulty of recruiting suitable staff and the level of unfilled vacancies in other sectors. If this were the only reason for the relationship between productivity growth as measured and changes in the degree of labour shortage, we might expect to find a closer association between the two if the figures for 1961 and 1966 alone were used in the measure of labour market change, instead of the five-year averages used in the preceding analysis. In other words, we might expect the level of service included with sales in any year to be lower, the greater the degree of labour shortage in that year, and for the deterioration from one year to another to be greater, the scarcer is labour in the latter year relative to the former.

In fact, the evidence is that there is almost no correlation between the movement in productivity over the period 1961 to 1966 and the change in percentage vacancies less unemployed between these two years (taking the percentage in 1966 minus that in 1961), the square of the correlation coefficient being 0·004. Some relationship, however, does emerge if we take the change in labour market conditions between

Table VIII.4   *Productivity Growth and the Degree of Labour Market Tightness, by Sector*
1961 to 1966

| Town Group | % Vacancies less Unemployment, 1962–66. | % Increase in Productivity | |
		Food	Non-Food
A (10)	1·1	14·0	12·2
B (9)	0·4	12·4	12·0
C (10)	0·2	15·8	10·5
D (10)	−0·5	10·9	12·9
E (11)	−2·3	10·1	14·2

Notes: The towns are grouped according to the average percentage vacancies less unemployed over the period 1962 to 1966; the figures in brackets show the number of towns in each group. 'C.T.N.'s' are excluded from both sectors.

the two years 1960 and 1961 and the two years 1965 and 1966, but it is much weaker than when periods of five years are compared.[1]

We can therefore conclude that as a longer-term measure of labour market change is much more closely associated with changes in sales per person engaged than a short-term measure, this is at least consistent with the existence of a long-term influence in labour market conditions on productivity growth in retailing. The evidence consequently tends to support the argument that 'fundamental' increases in the degree of labour market tightness are likely to be associated with, for example, the more rapid adoption of new methods of selling or the faster rate of closure of marginal outlets.

4. Intra-Sector Analysis

We can extend the analysis by considering the influence of labour market conditions on the movement in productivity shown by the constituent parts of the retail trade. Firstly, the relationship between the prevailing state of the labour market over the period 1962 to 1966 and the growth of productivity in food shops and non-food shops is depicted in Table VIII.4, in which the towns are grouped according to the former variable. As for all retailing, there is little indication of any positive association between the two variables with respect to the non-food sector — indeed Groups D and E show a greater gain in productivity than Groups A and B — but the increase in the productivity of food shops was greater for Groups A, B and C than for Groups D and E. However the relationship in the latter case clearly does not appear to be a continuous one, and this is confirmed by the linear correlation coefficient between the two variables which is only 0·19. In respect of the non-food sector, it makes little difference if the individual business categories are examined separately.

Secondly, the influence of changes in labour market conditions on the productivity growth of the two sectors is illustrated in Table VIII.5, in which the towns are grouped according to the change in average percentage vacancies less unemployed between the periods 1957 to 1961 and 1962 to 1966. In this case, the average

1   The average percentage vacancies less unemployed in 1965 and 1966 minus the average in 1960 and 1961, but even in this case the square of the correlation coefficient is only 0·10. Non-linear forms of equation were also fitted, but yielded similar correlation coefficients.

111

Table VIII.5   *Productivity Growth and Changes in the Degree of Labour Market Tightness by Sector, 42 Towns, 1961 to 1966*

Town Group	% Vacancies less Unemployed Average 1962–66 minus Average 1957–61	% Increase in Productivity				
		Food	Non-Food	Clothing and Footwear	Household Goods	Other Non-Food
A (8)	1·2	16·0	16·6	19·8	21·7	20·5
B (9)	0·5	11·7	12·1	18·0	12·9	16·8
C (8)	0·3	13·3	13·0	13·3	15·9	13·9
D (9)	0	10·9	11·4	12·0	17·6	15·5
E (8)	−0·3	10·5	9·0	10·3	17·2	7·4

Notes: The towns are grouped according to the average percentage vacancies less unemployed over the period 1962 to 1966 minus those for the period 1957 to 1961; the figures in brackets show the number of towns in each group.

movement in productivity is shown both for the non-food sector and for three kinds of non-food business. It is apparent that there is a positive association between the change in the degree of labour market tightness and productivity growth with respect to both food and non-food shops, although there is a slightly greater variation between the top and bottom groups in the case of the latter. At a further level of disaggregation this association is repeated for both 'Clothing and footwear' and 'Other non-food' shops, but no systematic relationship between the two variables is evident for 'Household goods' shops.

The linear regressions of productivity growth on changes in labour market tightness for the categories included in Table VIII.5 are described in Table VIII.6.[1] It emerges from the latter that a continuous association between the two variables is more apparent for the non-food sector in aggregate than for food shops. The values of the regression coefficients are, however, much the same, which suggests that a given change in the degree of labour scarcity over the period tended to have a similar impact on productivity growth with respect to both sectors. Further disaggregation of the non-food sector serves to weaken the correlation between the two variables, and indeed for both 'Clothing and footwear' and 'Other non-food' shops, the value of r^2 is lower than might have been anticipated on the basis on the variation between groups shown by Table VIII.5. This suggests that the relationship in these cases is not a linear one.

5. Summary of Main Findings

The analysis of this chapter therefore suggests that long-term changes in the state of the labour market had more influence on productivity growth over the period 1961 to 1966 than the prevailing degree of labour shortage. Thus there was some tendency for towns which showed a comparative increase in productivity between these two years to have experienced a relative increase in the difficulty of recruiting suitable staff, and possibly in the costs of employing labour, although the latter must remain a supposition on our part. No tendency was discernible for the towns which had been consistently 'tight' over a long period to have improved labour

---

1 The analysis is again based on the data for 41 towns, the town showing an abnormal increase in percentage vacancies less unemployed again being excluded.

Table VIII.6   *Regressions of Productivity Growth on Changes in the Degree of Labour Market Tightness, by Sector, 41 Towns, 1961 to 1966*

Sector	Constant	Regression Coefficient	r^2
FOOD	11·4	5·03 (2·26)	0·11
NON-FOOD of which:	11·0	5·29 (0·70)	0·28
Clothing and footwear	12·9	7·16 (2·87)	0·14
Household goods	15·8	5·38 (4·14)	0·04
Other non-food	12·6	6·92 (3·80)	0·08

efficiency to a greater extent than towns which had been consistently 'slack'.

Although it is impossible to isolate the 'short-term' implications of an increase in the degree of labour scarcity — or, in other words, the effect of recruitment difficulties on the provision of retail service — the evidence seems consistent with hypotheses which lay stress on the influence of this factor on the rate of adoption of new techniques or the elimination of marginal outlets. At the same time however, we should recognize that the evidence is also consistent with differential rates of decline in service having taken place as between towns, by virtue of variations in the rate of change of average transaction size. Thus it should be recalled that changes in the degree of labour tightness over the period were positively correlated in some degree with changes in income per head.[1] Moreover it is possible — though not necessarily true — that a more satisfactory measure of income change would be more closely correlated with changes in the degree of tightness.

Finally, examination of the experience of different sectors within the retail trade revealed a similar pattern with regard to the respective effects on productivity growth of the prevailing state of the labour market and changes in the state. In addition, changes in the degree of labour shortage tended to be associated with similar changes in productivity with respect to food and non-food shops, although the association was closer for the latter. Further disaggregation revealed certain differences in the influence of labour market change between the businesses included in the non-food sector.

1   R^2 equals 0·20, as is shown in Table VII.3.

IX
An Explanation of Productivity Growth

In this chapter our main object is to examine the extent to which the factors identified during the course of the study as influencing labour productivity in retailing, provide in combination a statistical explanation of inter-town variations in productivity performance. This we hope might give some indication of the process underlying the realisation of gains in labour efficiency in this sector. Firstly, however, we bring together the main findings of the preceding analysis and consider their interpretation in the light of the alternative hypotheses of retail productivity growth which were outlined at the beginning of the study.

1. A Review of the Preceding Analysis
Our concern here is to briefly review the results of the regression analysis so far and to discuss their implications for the hypotheses referred to above, rather than to give a complete summary of all that has gone before.

Firstly, it was seen that employment in retailing in the years 1954 to 1965 was positively related to the volume of sales, though (perhaps) less than proportionately, and inversely related to the level of unfilled vacancies and to a time factor.

Secondly, cross-sectional data on kinds of retail business revealed a tendency for productivity growth between 1957 and 1966 to vary directly with the rate of sales increase and the rise in sales per shop, and inversely with the change in gross margin per unit of sales.

Thirdly, inter-town variations in sales per person engaged in both 1961 and 1966 were found to be positively associated in turn with differences in the market share of multiples and coops, sales per shop, income per head and the degree of tightness in the labour market. In addition some tendency was evident for sales per person engaged in 1966 to vary with retail labour costs, if account is taken of both difference in average earnings per employee and in the sex composition of the work-force.

Fourthly, productivity growth by town over the period 1961 to 1966 appeared to be positively related, in some degree, to the rate of sales increase – provided four towns were excluded from the sample, the rise in sales per shop, the growth of income per head and the increase in the degree of labour market tightness between the periods 1957 to 1961 and 1962 to 1966. It also seemed to be inversely related to the initial level of income per head.

If we consider these findings in terms of what we would expect to observe on the basis of the alternative hypotheses of retail productivity growth, it is clear from our discussion during the course of the study that in virtually every case the results are, at the very least, not inconsistent with each of the views described in our introductory

114

chapter. Thus the time-series analysis for the years 1954 to 1965 might be regarded as giving some support to the view that productivity increases mainly stem from autonomous advances in technical know-how, insofar as year-to-year movements in retail employment for any given volume of sales seemed to be largely a function of a time factor, reflecting the upward trend in productivity. However, as we pointed out, such a trend might, for instance, conceal the long-term effects of labour market conditions or (the possibly associated) changes in retail wage costs on the adoption of labour-saving selling techniques or on the elimination of marginal outlets, or it might conceal a gradual reduction in the amount of service provided with the goods sold.

Similarly, the results of the kind of business analysis clearly give support to the Salter-type hypothesis which ascribes a major role to the influence of sales growth on the spread of innovations through the construction of new capacity. At the same time, however, while the finding of a close relationship between changes in sales and productivity seems to indicate that increases in the latter are not autonomous, it is also consistent with both the Kaldor view of the retail market and the Schwartzman hypothesis which attributes a central role to reductions in the activities performed by the sector. Thus, in the latter case, insofar as average transaction size increases with sales, the work required on the part of retail staff to sell a given volume of goods – and hence employment per unit of sales – would be expected to have declined by the greatest amount in the most rapidly expanding trades. In the former case, relative rates of sales increase are seen as reflecting 'the changing incidence of excess capacity' which Kaldor regards as a prominent feature of the retail trades. More direct support for the Kaldor view is derived from the finding of a close association between productivity growth by kind of business and the increase in sales per shop, the latter being considered, of course, as the major source of gains in labour efficiency over time.

In the same way, the relationships which emerged from comparing the variations in the experience of our sample of towns are not obviously inconsistent with any of the alternative hypotheses, although again each would interpret individual results in a different way. For example, the positive association both between the level of labour productivity in 1961 and 1966 and the degree of labour market tightness and between the change in productivity over this period and the increase in the latter, can be held to support all three major views. Thus the evidence is consistent with recruitment difficulties inducing a search for labour-saving methods of operation and, to the extent that real wages in retailing vary with labour scarcity, with increases in overhead costs causing an elimination of marginal outlets, as in the Kaldor model. In addition, the evidence also conforms to the hypothesis that productivity as measured is closely related to the average size of transaction, inasmuch as the latter tends to vary with income per head which in turn varies with labour scarcity. On this point, it should be recalled that our measure of labour scarcity refers to the whole of that market and not just to the retail sector. Assuming that earnings are related to labour market conditions, then a tightening of the market implies an overall rise in income per head in the town concerned. At the same time, the rise in wages may also be associated with an increase in the cost of supplying retail service relative to goods – insofar as productivity tends to increase by less in the former case than in the latter, which may mean a reduction in the amount of service provided with retail sales. More direct support for this mechanism, which is that advocated by Schwartzman, consists, of course, of the finding of a positive relationship between inter-town variations in productivity performance and differences in income per head.

The conclusions to emerge are therefore that the main alternative views of the process underlying the realisation of productivity gains in retailing can each draw some support from the findings, and that we are not able from the evidence presented so far to say which is the most valid. The most satisfactory way of attempting to determine the relative importance of the alternative mechanisms would almost certainly be to examine individual trades or, more appropriately, individual retail markets in great detail. This would ideally provide a direct guide to the effect on labour productivity of the adoption of new methods of selling and of the exit and entry of shops, as well as to the factors affecting the rates at which these occur. The *sine qua non* of this type of approach is, of course, the availability of the necessary data, and the collection of these represents a formidable obstacle to say the least. However given the data that are available to us, it might be possible to gain some insight into the main process involved in retail productivity growth, by considering the various factors identified at the town level in combination rather than in isolation.

Thus the first hypothesis which emphasizes the gains in efficiency stemming from the adoption of new methods of operation would predict a relationship between labour market tightness and productivity and between the latter and sales growth, but not necessarily between sales per shop and productivity. In addition, we might expect to observe a positive association between the latter and the market share of multiples and coops, to the extent that such organisations tend to incorporate relatively more labour-saving methods of working than independents, although this contention is open to dispute.

The second hypothesis, which is the Kaldor view, would predict, on the other hand, that we should observe a decline in shops per unit of sales in towns where the increase in productivity was greatest. Thus in terms of the static model on which it is based, an increase in overhead costs results in the elimination of marginal outlets and discouragement to new entry, the number of exits exceeding the number of entrants so that sales are concentrated on fewer stores. Under conditions of an expanding market, it should be noted, the number of shops would not necessarily show an absolute decline and may even show an increase if the rate of expansion is sufficiently great, but the number at the end of the period should be less than it otherwise would have been, had not the increase in overhead costs occurred. What we should observe, therefore, with regard to our sample of towns, is that the towns with the biggest increase in labour costs showed the biggest gains in productivity and the largest rise in sales per shop.

The third hypothesis, which emphasizes the role played by decreases in the amount of service supplied with retail sales, would predict that the towns with the highest increase in real wages and income per head should show the largest gains in measured productivity, through experiencing the largest rise in the average size of transaction and in the 'price' of retail service per transaction. However no direct information is available on these latter two factors and we have to rely on the assumption that they vary with income per head and the degree of labour scarcity.

To examine whether these predictions are fulfilled, our intention is, firstly, to

Table IX.1 *Productivity, Labour Market Tightness, Sales per Shop, Income per Head and Market Share of Multiples and Coops, 1966*

Town Group	Sales per Person Engaged (£)	% Vacancies less Un-employed, 1962–66	Sales per Shop (£000)	Income per Head 1964/5–1967/68 (£)	% Multiples and Coops
A	5,594	0·7	29·34	1,095	53·6
B	4,697	−0·7	19·92	1,032	43·7
Mean	5,116	−0·3	25·03	1,052	48·0

Notes: Group A consists of the ten towns in which the level of sales per person engaged was highest in 1966, Group B of the ten in which it was lowest. The mean is calculated for the 50 towns in the sample.

compare the evidence for the 'extreme' towns in our sample in terms of productivity performance, on the expectation that this exercise would illustrate most clearly any inter-town differences in experience. Secondly, we apply multiple regression techniques to the data in an attempt to discern the relative importance of the different variables which we have found to be related to productivity variations in the preceding analysis.

2. A Comparison of 'Extreme' Towns in terms of Productivity

Our concern here is, firstly, to take the ten towns in our sample which had the highest level of labour productivity in 1966 and the ten which had the lowest, and to examine any differences between these two groups in the values for the other variables which we have been able to identify. Secondly, we carry out the equivalent exercise for the two groups of ten towns showing, respectively, the largest and the smallest rises in productivity over the period 1961 to 1966.

Table IX.1 shows the average degree of labour market tightness, sales per shop, income per head and the percentage share of multiples and coops for the two extreme groups of towns in terms of sales per person engaged in 1966. It is clear that each of the mechanisms above receives support from the table, inasmuch as the ten towns with the highest level of productivity in 1966 tended to show considerably greater values for each of the variables included than both the ten with the lowest level and the mean.

Table IX.2 presents the results of conducting a similar exercise on the basis of the change over the period 1961 to 1966. Again it is apparent that the figures are con-sistent with each of the three hypotheses.[1] Thus the increase in the degree of labour scarcity was greatest in the towns showing the biggest productivity gains, as was the expansion of sales which might suggest that such towns benefited to a comparatively large extent from the introduction and spread of improvements in working methods. In addition, as predicted by the 'elimination of marginal shops' hypothesis, these towns experienced the greatest growth in sales per shop. Indeed the support for this hypothesis is especially strong as, despite the bigger increase in the volume of trade

---

1 The table does not include details on changes in the market share of multiples and coops. As we saw in Chapter VII, such changes are not positively related to productivity growth as far as our sample of towns is concerned. Indeed 'low productivity growth' towns appear to have experienced a greater increase in the importance of such organisations than 'high growth' towns.

Table IX.2   *Changes in Productivity, Labour Market Tightness, Sales, Sales per Shop, and Income per Head, 1961 to 1966*

Town Group	% Increase in: Productivity	Labour Market Tightness[a]	Sales	Sales per Shop	Income per Head[b]
A	16·6	0·6	18·3	25·3	39·1
B	6·4	0	12·1	13·9	35·8
Mean	11·4	0·2	13·4	19·8	37·3

Notes: Group A consists of the ten towns in which productivity increased at the highest rate over the period, Group B of the ten in which the productivity gain was lowest. The mean is calculated for 41 towns.

a Average percentage vacancies less unemployed, 1962—66 minus 1957—61.

b The percentage increase over the period 1959/60 to 1964/5.

in the high productivity growth towns than in the low productivity growth towns, the number of outlets declined by more, even in absolute terms, in the former as compared with the latter. Thirdly, the difference in the increase in income per head between the two groups might be held to reflect a similar difference in the rise in expenditure per customer, and therefore perhaps in the growth of the average size of transaction, which would imply that the work-effort required of retail staff per unit of sales decreased by more in Group A than in Group B.

Further discussion is called for, however, with regard to the former two hypotheses. The evidence presented in Tables IX.1 and IX.2 supports the contention that sales concentration is an important part of the explanation of productivity growth. But we cannot necessarily assume that the sales per shop variable is indicative of the strength of 'the elimination of marginal shops' hypothesis. It is perfectly feasible that an increase in sales per shop would also be a result of improvements in efficiency made at the establishment level. Thus whereas the former hypothesis sees the underlying mechanism as one of increases in real wages raising overhead costs and directly causing the elimination of those shops 'at the margin', it may well be that such shops are instead forced out of business by the transfer of customers to those stores which have adopted the most up-to-date working methods. In diagramatic terms, marginal units in the former case experience a shift in their average cost curve above their demand curve, in the latter case, a shift in their demand curve below their average cost curve. Moreover, it may be that the new selling techniques themselves involve a rise in sales per shop, inasmuch as large scale is often a necessary requirement for their successful introduction. This would have the effect, at the same time, of raising the barriers to entry, in the sense of increasing the costs of establishing competitive outlets, which implies a reduction in potential entrants and hence in the degree of competition in the retail market. In terms of our introductory discussion, this would lessen the tendency towards a 'tangency solution' and thus reduce the prevalence of excess capacity. The two hypotheses are therefore interrelated and there is no possibility of distinguishing between the two mechanisms on the basis of the data to hand. Indeed it is difficult to conceive of any information which would enable this to be done.[1]

A further point needs to be made with regard to the picture presented by Tables IX.1 and IX.2. This indicates a positive association between labour market tightness, sales per shop and income per head for the 'extreme' towns, both in respect of the position in 1966 and the changes over the period 1961 to 1966. However as far as the former two variables are concerned, we have seen that the relationship does not appear to be a continuous one. Thus the coefficient of correlation between average percentage vacancies less unemployed for the period 1962 to 1966 and sales per shop in 1966 is only 0·28 for our sample of fifty towns,[2] while with regard to the change in both variables from 1961 to 1966, almost no correlation at all is evident (r = 0·06). A closer association emerged as between labour market tightness and income per head, the correlation coefficient being 0·61 for 1966 and 0·45 for changes over the period 1961 to 1966.

Thus if we consider the sample as a whole, the evidence suggests that, for instance, an exceptional tightening of the labour market was not necessarily associated with an above average rise in sales per shop, or alternatively that the latter was not solely caused by the former. In other words, it would seem necessary to consider these two factors individually rather than as different aspects of the same phenomenon. The application of multiple regression analysis to the town data indicates that both factors are of importance and that in combination they provide much of the explanation for differences in productivity performance as between the towns, although they are not the only factors to be taken into account. These findings are demonstrated in the next section, which is concerned, firstly, with inter-town variations in sales per person engaged in 1961 and 1966, and, secondly, with differences in productivity growth between these two years within our sample of towns.

3. Multiple Regression Analysis

(i) Labour Productivity in 1961 and 1966
It will be recalled that for both the 160 towns in 1961 and the fifty towns in 1961 and 1966, labour productivity was found to be positively associated with the market share of multiples and coops, sales per shop, income per head and the degree of labour market tightness, when each of the latter variables was considered in isolation. Our purpose here is to assess the combined impact of these four variables on productivity.

The 1961 study found that these variables in combination provided a high degree of explanation of inter-town variations in sales per person engaged. The

---

1 One suggestion is that information on changes in gross margins might indicate whether the pricing behaviour of retailers corresponded to that described by the monopolistic competition model. However, as illustrated by our discussion on S.E.T. in Chapter II, there are other reasons why gross margins might be invariant to rises in labour costs. On the other hand, if a positive relationship between these two variables did emerge this would tend to refute the Kaldor hypothesis, always providing that the effect of real wage changes on gross margins could be isolated from other factors, such as purchase tax changes, the abolition of restrictive trading agreements, changes in demand conditions or movements in interest rates. This clearly is a very big proviso.

2 See Table V.6 above. For the 160 towns in 1961, however, the correlation coefficient was a good deal higher at 0·45.

Table IX.3   *Multiple Regressions of Productivity on the Degree of Labour Market Tightness, Sales per Shop, the Market Share of Multiples and Coops and Income per Head, 160 Towns, 1961*

Equation	Constant	Regression Coefficients				R^2
		Labour Market	Sales per Shop	% Multiples	Income per Head	
1.	4,108	164·3 (13·4)				0·49
2.	3,008		0·059 (0·005)			0·45
3.	3,330	120·5 (11·6)	0·041 (0·004)			0·68
4.	2,967	146·1 (11·0)		21·75 (2·35)		0·67
5.	2,903	124·8 (10·9)	0·027 (0·005)	13·38 (2·67)		0·72
6.	800	63·5 (10·8)	0·026 (0·004)	12·52 (2·12)	4·26 (0·45)	0·82

Notes: The 'Labour market' variable refers to average percentage vacancies less unemployed over the period 1957 to 1961, and 'Income per head' to the data for the 1959/60 financial year.

regression equations are repeated in Table IX.3. Thus the inclusion of both labour market conditions and sales per shop raises the degree of explanation of productivity differences from less than 50 per cent to 68 per cent, while the addition of the market share of multiples and coops leads to a further increase to 72 per cent. Taking account of variations in all four variables as between towns yields an R^2 of 0·82. The inclusion of income per head in the equation, however, substantially reduces the size of the regression coefficient in respect of the degree of labour shortage, owing to the correlation between these two variables. Bearing in mind the potential errors surrounding the estimates of income per head for individual towns, the conclusion of the 1961 study was that the state of the labour market contributed most to explaining overall differences in the level of sales per person engaged within the sample of 160 towns.

The results of conducting the equivalent exercise with regard to the fifty towns are presented in Table IX.4. It will be recalled that the association between labour market tightness and sales per person engaged was less close in 1966 than was the case in 1961 – as is shown by Equation 1 – while the relationship between sales per shop and the latter variable was more similar as between the two years – as is shown by Equation 2. The inclusion of both explanatory variables in Equation 3 yields an $\overline{R}^2$ of 0·47, which compares with the R^2 of 0·68 in respect of the 1961 sample. Moreover it should be noted that the value of the regression coefficient with respect to labour market tightness is reduced by much more in 1966 than is that of the sales per shop coefficient, when both variables are considered together. Equation 4 reveals that the inclusion of the market share of multiples and coops with the labour market variable provides a much lower degree of explanation of productivity differences in 1966 than for 1961, although the value of the regression coefficient with respect to the former variable is similar for both years. Taking account of these three explanatory variables serves to raise the value of $\overline{R}^2$ to 0·50, as is indicated by Equation 5, but the coefficient for the market share of multiples and coops is no

Table IX.4 *Multiple Regressions of Productivity on the Degree of Labour Market Tightness, Sales per Shop, the Market Share of Multiples and Coops and Income per Head, 50 Towns, 1966*

Equation	Constant	Regression Coefficients				$\bar{R}^2$
		Labour Market	Sales per Shop	% Multiples	Income per Head	
1.	5,150	126·6 (32·7)				0·21
2.	4,127		0·040 (0·007)			0·40
3.	4,297	88·0 (27·8)	0·034 (0·007)			0·47
4.	4,071	100·0 (29·6)		22·3 (5·7)		0·39
5.	3,947	83·4 (27·2)	0·026 (0·008)	11·2 (6·2)		0·50
6.	1,828	46·3 (31·9)	0·025 (0·007)	8·6 (6·1)	2·1 (1·0)	0·53

Notes: The 'Labour market' variable refers to average percentage vacancies less unemployed over the period 1962 to 1966, and 'Income per head' to the average figures for the 1964/5 and 1967/8 financial years.

longer significant at the five per cent level. Moreover the addition of income per head in Equation 6 results in the labour market variable also becoming non-significant at this level of confidence.

The final outcome is therefore that 53 per cent of inter-town variations in productivity in 1966 can be statistically explained by differences in the four variables identified as the important factors on the basis of the 1961 study; only two of the four variables are significant at the five per cent level with sales per shop clearly contributing most to explaining the overall variation. By contrast, in 1961 about 80 per cent of productivity differences were explained by these variables, all of which were highly significant, with the labour market variable being the important factor.

To pursue this matter further, we have firstly examined the regression equations formulated from the 1961 figures for the '1966' sample of towns. The most relevant equations are presented in Table IX.5. It is evident that the values for the regression coefficients shown in the table are much more similar to those contained in Table IX.3 for the 160 towns in 1961 than those included in Table IX.4 for the same fifty towns in 1966. This would seem to suggest that in this case the difference between the 1961 and the 1966 results does not arise from the change in the composition of the sample, which we found to be a factor of some significance in Chapters V and VI above, but rather that productivity was not influenced to the same extent in 1966 by the variables which were important in 1961.

Secondly, we have examined the effect of including a squared term for the labour market variable in the equations, on the grounds that in both 1961 and 1966 an equation of the form $P = a + b_1 L + b_2 L^2$, where P is productivity and L is percentage vacancies less unemployed, gave a better fit to the data than a linear equation when these two variables were considered in isolation. The results for 1966 are shown in Table IX.6. A comparison of these equations with those contained in Table IX.4 indicates a number of striking differences. Thus the effect of adopting what might

121

Table IX.5   *Multiple Regressions of Productivity on the Degree of Labour Market Tightness, Sales per Shop the Market Share of Multiples and Coops and Income per Head, 50 Towns, 1961*

Equation	Constant	Regression Coefficients				$\overline{R}^2$
		Labour Market	Sales per Shop	% Multiples	Income per Head	
1.	3,487	111·6	0·031			0·57
		(18·6)	(0·007)			
2.	3,141	114·9	0·018	11·7		0·61
		(17·7)	(0·008)	(4·6)		
3.	431	60·6	0·028	7·9	3·8	0·74
		(18·4)	(0·007)	(3·8)	(0·8)	

Notes: The 'Labour market' variable refers to average percentage vacancies less unemployed for the period 1957 to 1961, and 'Income per head' to the data for 1959/60.

be considered a more satisfactory measure of the degree of labour market tightness is: firstly, to raise the values for $\overline{R}^2$ in each case; secondly, to increase the importance of the labour market as an influence on relative levels of productivity; thirdly, to reduce the regression coefficient with respect to sales per shop and to increase the coefficient with respect to the market share of multiples and coops, when both variables are included; and fourthly, to reduce the contribution of the income per head variable. With the exception of the latter, all the coefficients expressed in Equation 5 are significant at the five per cent level. Nevertheless, even with the inclusion of the squared term for the labour market variable, this equation still leaves over 40 per cent of inter-town differences in sales per person engaged statistically unexplained, which is considerably more than is the case for 1961. Moreover there is little question that the adoption of a similar measure of labour market tightness with respect to the 1961 sample would further increase the degree of explanation for that year.

To sum up, therefore, the results of relating inter-town variations in productivity to the four major factors identified in the preceding analysis are less satisfactory with regard to 1966 than for 1961. The main reason for this seems to be a weaker association between productivity and the degree of labour market tightness in the former year, although the inclusion of a squared term for this variable leads to some improvement. Nevertheless we can conclude that, for both years, labour market conditions and sales per shop are important factors underlying differences in labour productivity between towns.

(ii) Changes in Labour Productivity, 1961 to 1966

Turning our attention to the changes that occurred in retailing over the period 1961 to 1966 with respect to our sample of towns, it will be recalled that productivity growth between these two years was found to be related, in turn, to the movement in sales and the number of shops, changes in sales per shop, the growth and initial level of income per head, and changes in labour market conditions. These six variables are all included in Table IX.7, which presents the results of regressing productivity growth on various combinations of these factors, with respect to the reduced sample of 41 towns.[1] Looking at each of the equations in turn, Equation 1

1   That is, the fifty towns excluding the nine for which it is not possible to measure changes in labour market conditions between the period 1957–61 and the period 1962–66.

Table IX.6   *Multiple Regressions of Productivity on the Degree of Labour Market Tightness, Sales per Shop, the Market Share of Multiples and Coops and Income per Head, 50 Towns, 1966*

Equation	Constant	Regression Coefficients					$\overline{R}^2$
		L	L^2	Sales per Shop	% Multiples	Income per Head	
1.	5,078	210·4 (41·0)	57·1 (18·9)				0·36
2.	4,366	142·1 (38·6)	33·5 (17·1)	0·029 (0·007)			0·50
3.	3,991	184·4 (35·3)	57·7 (16·0)		22·5 (5·1)		0·51
4.	3,926	151·2 (36·8)	42·9 (16·6)	0·018 (0·008)	14·7 (6·0)		0·55
5.	2,179	113·3 (42·0)	38·2 (16·5)	0·018 (0·008)	12·2 (6·0)	1·77 (1·01)	0·57

Notes: L equals the average percentage vacancies less unemployed over the period 1962 to 1966. 'Income per head' refers to the average figures for the financial years 1964/5 and 1967/8.

repeats the simple regression of productivity growth on changes in the degree of labour market tightness, using the measure formulated in the previous chapter. Equation 2 indicates that the addition of sales growth leaves the value of $\overline{R}^2$ unaltered, in contrast to Equation 3, which shows that the effect of including instead changes in sales per shop with changes in the state of the labour market results in an increase in the degree of explanation, while leaving the respective regression coefficients similar to those derived from the simple regression equations.[1] However if we take account of changes in the number of shops as well as of the movement in the volume of sales, the regression coefficient in respect of the latter becomes highly significant, as is clear from Equation 4, and the value of $\overline{R}^2$ is increased to 0·53.[2] These three equations demonstrate, therefore, the importance of reductions in the number of outlets per unit of sales as a factor influencing the gain in productivity.

Equations 5 to 7 show the effect of taking account of variations between the towns in both the increase in income per head and the level at the beginning of the period. We would expect, as we have said, the former variable to reflect in some degree the extent to which labour requirements per unit of sales are reduced as a result of increases in the average size of transaction, and the latter to reflect the possible increased demand for retail service, including the demand for more luxurious shopping facilities, at high levels of income. The inclusion of income per head growth with changes in labour market tightness and movements in sales per shop results in a rise in $\overline{R}^2$, a reduction in the regression coefficient in respect of labour market change, and an increase in the 'sales per shop' coefficient. The addition of the initial level of income per head further raises the value of $\overline{R}^2$, and again reduces the 'labour market' coefficient and increases the coefficient with respect to changes in sales per shop.

1   The simple regression of productivity growth on changes in sales per shop yielded a regression coefficient of 0·134 with respect to the latter, on the basis of the data for 50 towns. For 41 towns, the coefficient is 0·145.

2   Again the regression coefficients are similar to those derived in the previous two chapters.

Table IX.7   *Multiple Regressions of Productivity Growth on Changes in the Degree of Labour Market Tightness, Sales, Sales per Shop, the Number of Shops, Income per Head and the Initial Level of Income, 41 Towns, 1961 to 1966*

Equation	Constant	Regression Coefficients						
		Δ Labour	Δ Sales	Δ Sales per Shop	Δ Shops	Δ Income	Income	$\overline{R}^2$
1.	10·0	5·46 (0·59)						0·33
2.	9·0	5·06 (1·22)	0·083 (0·077)					0·33
3.	7·5	5·26 (1·06)		0·131 (0·044)				0·44
4.	6·0	5·21 (1·02)	0·285 (0·081)		−0·184 (0·045)			0·53
5.	−11·7	3·79 (1·09)		0·148 (0·041)		0·515 (0·174)		0·54
6.	19·5	2·89 (1·07)		0·167 (0·038)		0·379 (0·171)	−0·037 (0·014)	0·60
7.	13·9	3·42 (0·99)	0·241 (0·072)		−0·209 (0·039)	0·397 (0·173)	−0·030 (0·013)	0·65

Notes: 'Δ Labour' refers to the average percentage vacancies less unemployed over the period 1962 to 1966 minus the average over the period 1957 to 1961. 'Δ Income' equals the percentage change in income per head between the 1959/60 and 1964/65 financial years, and 'Income' is the level of income per head in the 1959/60 financial year.

While Equation 7 yields the highest $\overline{R}^2$ and suceeds in explaining 65 per cent of inter-town variations in productivity growth, the equation is not entirely satis-factory, inasmuch as the regression coefficients in respect of changes in sales and changes in shops are almost equal in value and of the opposite sign. This implies that it is not possible to distinguish between the influence of a rise in sales and an in-crease in sales per shop, in the sense that given increases in both sales and shops have almost completely offsetting effects on productivity growth. For this reason and because the equation takes no account of inter-town variations in the business composition of retail shops, we prefer to concentrate attention on Equation 6 which incorporates a direct and more satisfactory measure of sales per shop changes. Thus Equation 6 statistically explains 60 per cent of variations in produc-tivity growth between towns, in terms of differences in this factor together with those in the change in the degree of labour market tightness, the rise in income per head and the initial level of income per head. Each of the four explanatory variables is shown to be significant at the five per cent level, which seems to emphasize the multiplicity of factors underlying the gains in productivity at the town level over this period of time. Given the brevity of the latter and the many relevant features that we have not been able to take into account, such as local planning regulations and the extent of urban redevelopment, which are almost certain to have a differential impact as between towns, the degree of explanation provided by these four variables is surprisingly high.

A comparison of the actual productivity growth experienced by the individual towns over the period with that calculated on the basis of Equation 6 is presented diagramatically in Figure IX.1. The percentage change in productivity is shown on

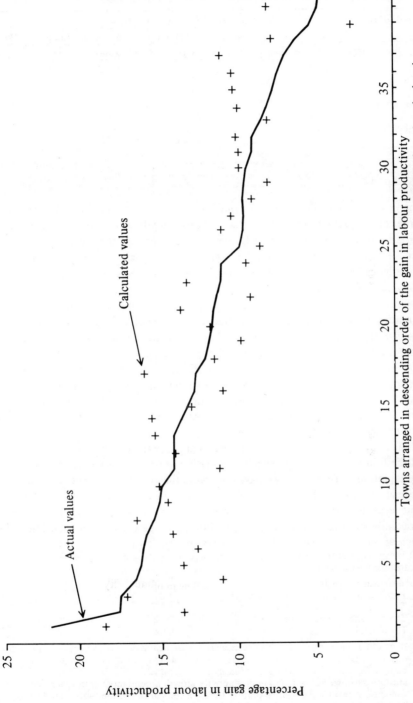

Towns arranged in descending order of the gain in labour productivity

The line shows the actual gain in productivity for each town, ranked from 1 to 41; the crosses show the gain calculated on the basis of the regression equation: $P = 19.5 + 2.89L + 0.167X + 0.379Y_1 - 0.037Y_0$, which is Equation 6 in Table IX.7.

Table IX.8 *Multiple Regressions of Productivity Growth on Changes in Labour Market Tightness and Sales per Shop by Kind of Business, 41 Towns, 1961 to 1966*

Kinds of Business	Constant	Regression Coefficients		$\overline{R}^2$
		Δ Labour	Δ Sales per Shop	
Food	6·4	3·43	0·273	0·36
		(1·90)	(0·063)	
Clothing and Footwear	10·2	7·69	0·128	0·15
		(2·79)	(0·067)	
Household Goods	12·7	7·12	0·197	0·12
		(3·92)	(0·077)	
Other Non-Food	8·4	7·54	0·151	0·16
		(3·55)	(0·057)	

Note: Δ Labour represents the average percentage vacancies less unemployed for the period 1962 to 1966 minus the average for the period 1957 to 1961.

the vertical axis, while on the horizontal axis the towns are arranged in descending order of productivity increase. The actual productivity growth experienced in each case is shown by the solid line, while the crosses represent the value calculated from Equation 6. For example, the town with the highest productivity growth experienced a gain of 22 per cent, whereas the calculated gain was 18·5 per cent; the town ranked second, an actual gain of 17·2 per cent and a calculated gain of 13·8 per cent, and so on. If we examine the diagram it is clear that the equation shows a tendency to 'under-predict' the values at the top end of the scale and to 'over-predict' the values at the bottom end. In other words, the actual variation between the 'extreme' towns exceeds that which we would expect to find on the basis of the differences in the variables included in Equation 6. This might suggest for example that we have omitted a factor which tended to push up the productivity gain in towns where this was greatest and depress the gain in towns where it was lowest, or that the influence on productivity growth of one or more of the variables included in the equation is non-linear.

As a further step, we have attempted to measure the relative contribution of each of the four variables to the overall explanation of productivity growth provided by Equation 6. To do this, we have calculated the deviations from the mean in respect of each variable and multiplied these by the appropriate regression coefficients. The result of taking the averages (without regard to size) over all towns, in each case, indicates that changes in sales per shop make the greatest contribution, although each of the other three variables also plays an important role.[1]

1 The averages of the deviations from the mean for each variable multiplied by the appropriate regression coefficient are:

	Percentage points
The % change in labour market tightness	1·01
The % change in sales per shop	1·39
The % change in income per head	0·92
The initial level of income per head	0·94

It should be made clear that this exercise gives an indication of the average contribution of each variable to the inter-town variation in productivity growth calculated on the basis of Equation 6. It does not necessarily indicate which of the four variables explains most of the *observed* variation in productivity growth if considered in isolation. This would be shown by the relative t-ratios. In fact a comparison of the t-ratios implied by Equation 6 (approximately the regression coefficients divided by their standard errors) results in the same rank order of variables as above.

(iii) Intra-Sector Analysis

To turn to the differences between the trades composing the retail sector, we have seen in the previous two chapters that there is evidence of a positive correlation between productivity growth and changes in labour market tightness in the case of food stores, 'Clothing and footwear' and 'Other non-food' shops, and between the former variable and changes in sales per shop in respect of these three categories plus 'Household goods' stores. No systematic association was discernible between movements in productivity and these two explanatory variables in the case of 'C.T.N.'s' and 'General stores', or indeed between productivity growth and changes in sales volume in the case of each category of retailer examined. Table IX.8 presents the results of including changes in both labour market tightness and sales per shop in the explanation of inter-town variations in productivity movement with respect to the former four trades mentioned above.

If we, firstly, compare the multiple regression equations shown in the table with the simple regressions formulated in the previous two chapters, we find that the effect of including both variables in the equation is to reduce the value of each regression coefficient in respect of the food sector, but to raise the value of each — sometimes significantly — in respect of the three non-food trades. Thus in the former case, the 'labour market' coefficient is reduced substantially (from 5·0 to 3·4) if account is also taken of sales per shop changes, and in fact it becomes non-significant at the five per cent level (though still significant at the ten per cent level). In the latter case, the increase in the 'labour market' coefficient is most marked in respect of 'Household goods' (from 5·4 to 7·1), and it becomes significant at the ten per cent level.

Secondly, comparing the equations in Table IX.8 with each other, it is clear that a given change in the degree of labour scarcity over the period tended to have a substantially greater impact on the productivity growth of the non-food businesses than on that of the food trade, while the reverse was equally true of a given change in sales per shop.

Thirdly, comparing the equations with those calculated for all retailing, it is apparent that disaggregation has the effect of reducing the proportion of inter-town variations in productivity growth that can be explained in terms of the factors identified.[1]

(iv) Changes in Persons Engaged, 1961 to 1966

As a postscript to the analysis, we can approach the problem from another direction and look at changes in persons engaged over the period 1961 to 1966 in the towns included in our sample. Table IX.9 shows the results of relating such changes to changes in labour market conditions, the volume of sales and in sales per shop, for all retailing and with respect to the same four business categories included in Table IX.8. It is clear that in each case, these three variables provide a high degree of explanation of inter-town differences in the movement in employment, the value of

---

1 We should add that we also examined the result of including both the change in income per head and the initial level in the equations. In all cases, these variables contributed nothing to the overall explanation, and the regression coefficients were not significantly different from zero by any test.

Table IX.9 *Multiple Regressions of Changes in Persons Engaged on Changes in the Degree of Labour Market Tightness, Sales and Sales per Shop, for all Retailing and by Kind of Business, 41 Towns, 1961 to 1966*

Business Category	Constant	Regression Coefficients			$\overline{R}^2$
		Δ Labour	Δ Sales	Δ Sales per Shop	
All Retailing	−5·7	−3·97 (1·15)	0·843 (0·072)	−0·119 (0·045)	0·77
Food	−6·2	−2·92 (1·74)	0·960 (0·065)	−0·247 (0·057)	0·84
Clothing and Footwear	−10·3	−6·18 (2·33)	0·940 (0·074)	−0·086 (0·056)	0·80
Household Goods	−10·4	−3·50 (3·42)	0·817 (0·076)	−0·141 (0·069)	0·74
Other Non-Food	−6·0	−6·95 (4·06)	0·911 (0·075	−0·172 (0·062)	0·79

Note: Δ Labour equals average percentage vacancies less unemployed for the period 1962 to 1966 minus the average for the period 1957 to 1961.

$\overline{R}^2$ ranging from 0·74 for 'Household goods' shops to 0·84 for the food trade. If we consider the equation for all retailing, this indicates: firstly, that for any given change in sales and sales per shop, those towns which experienced a tightening of labour market conditions tended to show an above average decline in persons engaged; secondly, that an expansion of sales was associated with a less than proportionate increase in employment, for a given change in sales per shop and labour scarcity; and thirdly that a rise in sales per shop tended to reduce the number of persons engaged, assuming given values for the other two variables. These results clearly tend to support the conclusions drawn on the basis of defining productivity growth as the dependent variable, although it is of interest to note that sales growth appears to have some positive influence on productivity growth other than through increasing sales per shop, in the sense that the regression coefficient for this variable is significantly less than unity if only slightly so.

The pattern for all retailing is repeated in varying degrees for the different categories of business included in Table IX.9. However the influence of changes in labour market conditions shows itself less strongly than with respect to productivity growth, in the sense that this variable is not significant at the five per cent level in respect of all four categories except 'Clothing and Footwear' — although for the food sector and 'Other non-food' shops it is significant at the ten per cent level. In addition, the 'sales per shop' variable is not significant in the case of 'Clothing and footwear', while, with the exception of 'Household goods' stores, the regression coefficient for the movement in sales volume is in each case not significantly different from unity. There was no general tendency therefore for the expansion of sales to have a beneficial effect on productivity change in respect of individual trades, which supports the findings noted in Chapter VII.

4. Concluding Remarks
The conclusion to emerge is that a number of hypotheses are consistent with the evidence available and it is not possible to reach a decision as to which is the most valid. However, this is not primarily because the data are unsuited to the task, although

there is some element of this, but rather because there is great difficulty in distinguishing between the respective hypotheses on the basis of their predictions. Moreover to our mind it is much too simple to regard one particular hypothesis as valid to the exclusion of any other, once consideration is given to the diversity of the businesses which make up the retail trades and to the markedly different features of different market situations both over time and as between various locations. The most plausible view would therefore seem to be that productivity growth in this sector is attributable to a number of sources which may vary in importance between trades, markets and periods of time.

Indeed many different mechanisms may be simultaneously set in motion as a result of a change in any given factor. Thus, if we take an increase in labour market tightness as an example, this may lead through recruitment difficulties to an initial deterioration of service and eventually to the more widespread adoption of labour-saving selling techniques. The latter may well entail a growth in sales per shop — both directly through the construction of larger units and indirectly through the transfer of trade to such units from less competitive outlets — and some shift of retail activity onto customers. At the same time, to the extent that an increase in labour shortage is associated with a rise in real wages, this may cause the elimination of marginal shops and discourage new entry, and it is also likely to involve an income-effect, which may show itself in an increase in the average size of transaction.

Each of these potential repercussions is likely to produce some gain in labour productivity as measured, and it is conceivable that all may be present in varying degrees in any given situation, the importance of each depending upon the particular circumstance which happen to obtain at the time and upon which part of the retail sector is most affected. 'Non-economic' factors, such as local planning regulations and the speed and extent of urban redevelopment especially, may play a central role in this regard. These, as we have argued, underlie the whole of the town analysis and it is impossible to know how they affect the results. Certainly, their potential importance for the level of sales per person engaged, the rate of productivity growth and the service which the sector is able to provide for customers, is undeniable. At the same time, it should be recognized that the effect of such factors in the preceding analysis may be to some extent reflected in the relationship between productivity and sales per shop, insofar as restrictions on development, for example, are likely to mean that the value of both variables is artificially inflated.

The main finding of the analysis is therefore that, whatever the underlying mechanism (or mechanisms) certain factors tend to have a favourable impact on the labour productivity of this sector as measured. The ones that we would emphasize are: an increase in the degree of labour market tightness, an expansion of trade (on the basis of the kind of business analysis), a reduction in the number of individual outlets per unit of sales and a rise in income per head — although the indications are that at high levels of income, the latter might result in an increased demand for retail service and correspondingly in a decline in sales per person engaged.

5. Summary of Main Findings
At the beginning of the chapter we briefly reviewed the evidence of the preceding analysis and considered this in the light of the main hypotheses as to the primary source of productivity growth in retailing. These essentially can be divided into

three groups, the emphasis being placed respectively on improvements in working methods, the elimination of the less efficient shops and the decline in the service provided by the sector. It was seen that certain variants of each of these views receive some support from the evidence, in the sense that the relationships observed to exist between variables are consistent with what we might expect to find on the basis of each. Dividing the towns into 'extreme' groups in terms of their productivity performance produced a similar conclusion.

However the application of multiple regression analysis to the town data seemed to indicate that a number of different factors underlie the observed variation in productivity performance, rather than there being a single source of such gain. With regard to inter-town differences in the level of sales per person engaged, this was more apparent in 1961 than in 1966 when all four variables identified appeared to enter into the explanation. In 1966, on the other hand, we were able to explain a much lower proportion of such differences, although we concluded that sales per shop and labour market conditions were probably the most important elements to be taken into account. With regard to variations in productivity growth between towns over the period 1961 to 1966, changes in labour market conditions, sales per shop, income per head and the initial level of income were all found to make significant contributions to the overall explanation. Moreover a comparatively low degree of inter-correlation had earlier been observed between each pair of variables. In other words, a town which experienced, for example, an above average tightening of labour market conditions did not necessarily tend to show an exceptional rise in sales per shop or income per head — although one must bear in mind the qualifications surrounding the statistics on the latter — but if it did happen to do so, its gain in productivity is likely to have been so much the greater. Thus the high productivity growth towns tended to show significantly higher values for each of these three variables than the remainder of our sample.

At the same time, while the factors which we were able to identify explained much of the inter-town variation in overall productivity growth, they explained considerably less of such variations with respect to individual kinds of retail business, which suggests that other considerations are much more important if we adopt a more disaggregated view. Alternatively, it would appear to indicate that such features as labour market or income per head changes have a general influence on retailing and may well have a differential impact on a given category of trader as between towns, according to the particular circumstances in each, In addition, it was apparent that the factors concerned did not affect individual business categories to the same extent. Thus changes in labour scarcity tended to have a greater influence on the productivity gains made by 'Clothing and footwear' retailers than respect to other traders, while sales per shop growth seemed to be a crucial factor underlying differences in the gains made by food stores.

X
Summary and Conclusions

Our concern here is to briefly summarize the main findings of the analysis chapter by chapter, without attempting to be comprehensive or going into details on the possible qualifications that have been noted at various points. We began the study by setting out the three groups of hypotheses as to the major process underlying productivity growth as measured in retailing. These place primary emphasis, respectively, on an improvement in selling methods, a concentration of sales on fewer stores and a reduction in the activities performed at the retail level. In addition, we stressed that our concern was directly with the factors affecting the reduction in employment per unit of sales and that welfare implications could be drawn from the results only with some trepidation.

In Chapter II, we noted that over the period 1954 to 1970, the growth rate of labour productivity in retailing was the same as in manufacturing. This owed much to the sharp reduction in retail employment between 1965 and 1970, which most plausibly was the result, in the main, of the imposition of S.E.T., although other factors conspired to intensify the effect of this measure. In addition, employment in retailing in the years 1954 to 1965 was found to be positively related to the volume of sales, though (probably) less than proportionately, and inversely related to time — reflecting the upward trend in productivity — and to the level of unfilled vacancies, or the extent of recruitment difficulties.

In Chapter III, it was seen that the variation in productivity growth between kinds of business over the period 1957 to 1966 was largely explicable in terms of the rate of sales increase and the rise in sales per shop, and that it was inversely associated with changes in gross margin per unit of sales. Differences in the former two variables also appeared to be important factors underlying variations in productivity movement by form of organisation. In this regard, no tendency was observable for multiple organisations to show a higher rate of productivity growth than independents by kind of business, although their overall performance was superior. Moreover, the substantial shift in consumer expenditure towards the former contributed only slightly to the increase in the productivity of the sector, the development of self-service in the grocery trade (and probably other areas) being a far more significant factor.

With regard to the town analysis, Chapter V tended to confirm the findings of the 1961 study, insofar as the level of sales per person engaged in 1966 was found to be positively related, in turn, to the market share of multiples and coops, sales per shop and income per head. In Chapter VI, a positive association emerged between the degree of labour market tightness and sales per person engaged, though

131

this was less close than in the earlier year; moreover no systematic relationship was found for the 1966 sample between the latter and the use made of part-time working although this varied — in a non-continuous way — with labour scarcity. An attempt was made to examine differences in average wages in retailing between towns and while this was not very satisfactory, some slight evidence of a positive relationship between this variable and both the degree of labour market tightness and the level of productivity was apparent. More conclusive evidence, however, indicated a systematic tendency for retailers in 'tight' towns to employ a greater proportion of male labour (and part-timers) than was the case in 'slack' towns.

Chapters VII and VIII examined the influence on productivity growth over the period 1961 to 1966 of changes in the variables mentioned above together with that of the movement in sales volume. Inter-town differences in the latter — provided four towns were excluded from the sample — in sales per shop changes, in the rise in income per head and in the change in labour market tightness over the period were all found, when considered separately, to be positively associated with inter-town variations in productivity increase. In addition, an inverse relationship was observed between the latter and differences in the initial level of income per head, while the change in the market share of multiples and coops showed no systematic tendency to vary with productivity growth; indeed if anything the relationship seemed to be an inverse one. Changes by kind of business were also examined and important differences were noted between these and the pattern for retailing as a whole. In particular, the only significant correlations to emerge were between productivity growth and the movements in, respectively, sales per shop and the degree of labour scarcity, with respect to the food sector and certain durable goods shops.

Finally, in Chapter IX, we brought together the variables found to influence labour productivity and attempted to explain inter-town variations, firstly, in the level of productivity and, secondly, in its movement between 1961 and 1966, in terms of these variables combined. With regard to the level of sales per person engaged in 1966, the degree of explanation attained was less than for 1961 and only difference in labour market conditions and sales per shop seemed to be important, whereas the market share of multiples and coops and income per head were also significant in the earlier year. On the other hand, changes in labour market tightness, the growth of sales per shop, the rise in income per head and its initial level all made significant contributions to the overall explanation of inter-town variations in productivity growth over the period 1961 to 1966. For individual business categories, these variables explained a much lower proportion of such variations, the former two being the only ones of any significance. Moreover these did not exercise a uniform effect, changes in sales per shop seeming to be the important factor underlying differences in the productivity gain achieved by food stores as between towns, while for 'Clothing and footwear' retailers changes in labour market conditions was the prominent factor.

The conclusion we reached in Chapter IX was that we were unable to say which was the major process involved in the realisation of productivity gains in this sector on the basis of the evidence, and that this was so largely because the alternative hypotheses are difficult to distinguish from each other in terms of what they predict we should observe. Nevertheless, no matter what the underlying process, the results of the analysis indicate that an expansion of sales, an increase in the difficulty of

132

retaining, or recruiting, labour or in its cost, a rise in sales per shop and an increase in income per head are all likely to accelerate the reduction in employment per unit of sales in the retail sector.

XI
Introduction

1. The Background to the Study

In the preceding analysis we have tended to treat retailing as an independent function rather than as part of the process of distribution. It is clear however that the structural changes that have taken place in the retail sector over recent years have carried certain implications for the method by which manufacturers distribute their goods and for the level and nature of distributive margins. As we have intimated above, the growth of the multiple form of organisation has a potential influence on the volume of trade handled by independent wholesalers, to the extent that it represents a movement towards the integration of the retailing and wholesaling functions. In addition, the concentration of a larger proportion of retail sales among fewer concerns has meant that it has become increasingly important for manufacturers to ensure that their products are stocked by such outlets. There has therefore been an incentive for manufacturers to improve their terms, and a tendency for the balance of bargaining power to tilt in favour of the largest distributors.

We might expect these tendencies to have become more significant since the period covered by the above analysis. Thus prior to the Resales Prices Act of 1964, resale price maintenance (r.p.m.) extended over a large part of the sales of non-food shops, although it had disappeared from the grocery trade in the late fifties and early sixties. While manufacturers were entitled to fix the retail selling price of their products, this meant that competition at the retail level was restricted to the facilities and services provided with the sale of any good, rather than including the price of the good itself. Insofar as it was not possible for a retailer to use a 'low' price to attract custom, the effect may have been to hinder the expansion of multiples, or the more efficient traders in general, and to enable the less efficient shops to remain in business. At the same time consumers suffered a potential loss, to the extent that multiples were unable to pass on to them (except indirectly) any additional revenue arising from an improvement in their buying terms, or from a reduction in their operating costs, resulting from more efficient working methods.

The breakdown of r.p.m., however, enabled retailers to choose precisely which products, and more significantly which brands, to offer to consumers at 'cut' prices. To quote the National Board for Prices and Incomes (N.B.P.I.), 'the final marketing initiative was transferred to retailers'.[1] As well as reinforcing the tendency noted above, we might expect this to have favoured the leading brands of particular

---

1 Report No. 165, *Prices, Profits and Costs in Food Distribution,* H.M.S.O., April, 1971, p. 5.

products, 'whose quality and value in the consumer's eye were assured'.[1] This clearly has implications for competition at the manufacturing level and potentially for the variety of lines between which the consumer is able to choose. Moreover the freedom of retailers to use cut prices as a selling aid may have favoured the more general stores as against specialist retailers, insofar as the former are more able to recoup losses (or rather the revenue foregone) on one type of commodity, through additional sales over the rest of their turnover. In other words, the disappearance of r.p.m. may have affected the business composition of the retail sector as well as its structure.

However these are expectations based on *a priori* reasoning, and the purpose of this part of the study is to throw some light on what has actually happened in this area over recent years. Specifically we are interested in the changes in the channels of distribution, in the pattern of retailing and in distributive margins and retail prices that have taken place in the period since the 1964 Resale Prices Act began to take effect.

The breakdown of r.p.m. and the growth in importance of multiple retailers are not, of course, the only factors that may have influenced these changes over the period in question. In particular, the introduction of S.E.T. in September, 1966 involved the imposition of a new distortion in this field, as it effectively discriminated between wholesalers and manufacturers performing the same distributive function. We might therefore expect the tax to have further weakened the position of the independent wholesaler. In addition, S.E.T. may have had some influence not only on the level of distributive margins, but also on the pattern of retailing, insofar as the tax, being levied at a flat-rate on labour, represented a greater cost to those traders employing a relatively large number of assistants per unit of value-added.

Other factors that are likely to have had an effect on the proportion of home-market sales distributed through wholesalers include any changes that have occurred over the period in the number and size of retail outlets and in the structural characteristics of the production sector. The influence of this type of factor is discussed in the next section.

2. General Factors Influencing Methods of Distribution

An essential point to be recognized is that there are certain distributive activities that need to be undertaken, whichever method of distribution obtains. These include the 'functions of obtaining information about the requirements of consumers and telling consumers of the goods available, of transporting, of providing credit and stockholding against demand, of breaking bulk, of sorting, grading and preparing for sale and of physically selling the goods.'[2] A manufacturer can distribute some or all of his goods direct to retailers, only at the cost of taking on the activities performed by wholesalers, or at the 'cost' of persuading retailers to assume these, the 'cost' in the latter case usually taking the form of a lower selling price. Similarly he can deal direct with consumers only if he is willing to undertake both the

---

1 *ibid.*, p. 5.

2 J.B. Jeffreys, *The Distribution of Consumer Goods*, Cambridge University Press, 1950, p. 34.

necessary wholesale and the necessary retail functions, or if he is able to induce consumers to assume part or all of the responsibility.

In the former instance, we would expect both the cost to manufacturers of supplying retailers direct and the ability of retailers to perform the necessary wholesale functions to increase with the number of outlets supplied and to decrease with the size of order delivered. At the same time, the advantages achieved by manufacturers from direct contact with retailers, in the form, for example, of more detailed and reliable information on sales and of closer control over selling and promotion, are also likely to vary with the size of retail organisation supplied. We would also expect there to be some tendency for the relevant costs and advantages to differ in importance between commodities according to their characteristics, including under this heading such aspects as their perishability, unit value and degree of brand loyalty.

These expectations are supported by the available evidence, which suggests that considerations of retail structure and of the nature of the commodity group in question, together with the structural features of the production sector, largely determine the prevailing method of distribution. This emerges very clearly from the study undertaken by Jefferys for 1938,[1] which remains by far the most comprehensive investigation into this area. The conclusion that he reached was that, in the case of three-quarters of the domestically-produced commodities studied, the decision of producers on how to distribute 'appeared to be scarcely of their making',[2] but was readily explicable in terms of the above factors.

Thus multiples, cooperative societies and department store organisations tended to purchase their supplies almost exclusively direct from manufacturers, irrespective of the nature of the commodity or of the characteristics of the production sector. In other words, the ability of such organisations to perform the necessary wholesale functions or to purchase in bulk dominated the other considerations. This is not to say that in each case manufacturers distributed to a central warehouse, leaving the retailer to undertake delivery to the individual shops, but that where this type of system was not in operation, the organisations usually represented sufficiently large buying units to be able to negotiate terms centrally and to induce the manufacturer to bear the necessary transport costs.

In the case of other retailers, the commodities largely distributed through wholesalers tended to possess at least some of the following features: small-scale production, 'the inability of producers and retailers to hold large stocks', 'a retail demand for a range of goods greater than can be supplied by any single producer', a low unit-value, an insignificant degree of branding and advertising and a high degree of perishability. Commodities largely distributed direct to retailers tended to possess the opposite characteristics.[3] It therefore follows that any changes in the latter direction — in particular, any structural changes that tend to increase the average size of retail purchase — may reduce the proportion of trade distributed through wholesalers. For example, an increase in the degree of concentration among the producers of any

1 *ibid.*

2 *ibid.*, p. 59.

3 *ibid.*, p. 42.

commodity group is likely to reduce the importance of the wholesalers' ability to offer to individual retailers a range of similar lines, or a selection of different brands of the same product. Correspondingly, the size of order which any retailer is able to place with a manufacturer is likely to be increased.

This is not to say that, for 75 per cent of commodities, manufacturers have no choice on the method of distribution to adopt, only that there is a tendency for product groups displaying similar characteristics to be distributed *very broadly* through similar channels. Indeed individual producers of any commodity group are likely to distribute varying proportions of their output through wholesalers according to their assessment of the relevant advantages and costs involved in direct supply. This clearly applies more uniformly to the manufacturers of the other 25 per cent of domestically-produced commodities covered by Jefferys, which possessed similar features, yet some of which were distributed mainly through wholesalers while others were mainly distributed direct to retailers. The basic characteristics of these groups were a higher than average degree of concentration in production, a high degree of branding and a low unit price.

Thus one producer may decide, for example, to forego a potential saving in cost from distributing goods through wholesalers in order to obtain the advantages involved in selling direct to retailers, whereas another producer facing similar circumstances or perhaps engaged in the same trade may attach a higher value to the former consideration. The largely unquantifiable nature of the benefits achieved from direct contact with retailers gives some scope for such variations. In other words, individual manufacturers may hold different opinions on the value of any improvement in marketing information and of a greater degree of control over the final point of sale. These differences are likely to manifest themselves in variations in the minimum size of order that individual producers are willing to supply direct to retailers, which in turn is partly a reflection of the size of outlet to which it is considered beneficial to sell direct.

At the same time, however, a manufacturer's distribution policy at any one point in time is likely to be influenced in some degree by the actions of his competitors and the method adopted in the past. Thus, in a situation where the majority of trade goes direct to retailers, a manufacturer may find that he would lose sales to competitors if he relied on wholesalers to distribute his goods, because of the consequent reduction in the degree of control over the point of sale. This gives rise to the possibility that the competitive behaviour of producers may result in the over-expansion of direct accounts, in the sense that all manufacturers would gain if a common decision was taken to supply the smaller outlets through wholesalers, but any individual manufacturer would lose if he took this course of action unilaterally. This point is closely akin to that of the likely over-expansion of advertising expenditure in a similar environment.

In addition, if, for example, a manufacturer has in the past built up an extensive distribution system and selling organisation it may prove difficult to bring about any significant alteration of policy, even where justified by the estimated opportunity costs. The desire to maintain 'goodwill' among retailers and the reluctance to break traditional ties, or to adopt any radical changes, play a part here. These types of consideration, according to Jefferys, 'often preclude a fully rational approach to the question of the most efficient and economic method of distribution'.[1]

The above discussion presupposes of course that manufacturers can exercise some choice in the method by which they distribute their output. In some instances, this may clearly not be so. Thus we might expect a firm would need to be larger than a certain size in order to be able to develop its own transport organisation and selling activities, and, if it were smaller, would need to rely upon the services of wholesalers. This critical size is likely to vary with the type of product manufactured and the number of outlets served. For example, a small producer might supply a limited number (one, in the extreme case) of large retail organisations with an 'exclusive' line, which might possibly be sold under the retailers' own label. Moreover the possibility of using specialist transport organisations, such as British Rail or National Carriers, for delivery obviously facilitates a policy of distributing direct to retailers.

A further point is that in the above discussion, we have regarded the method of distribution as a reflection of various structural factors, whereas there is some degree of interaction between the two. In particular, the prevailing pattern of distribution may itself influence the process and scale of production. Thus the size of distributive organisations, as measured by the volume of a particular line that can be ordered from individual manufacturers at any one time, clearly tends to affect the operating costs of producers, through its influence on the length of production run, stock-holding and planning in general, as well as on the risk and effort involved in selling the commodity. This type of factor may be equally as important to the manufacturer as delivery cost considerations and may be equally reflected in the discount structure operated, or, in other words, in the variation in terms between different sizes of order.

To conclude this section, we can say that there are numerous factors underlying the method of distribution of any commodity group, and clearly it is likely to prove difficult to predict the effect of a change in any particular one, especially if other factors do not remain constant. However, it would appear that any increase in the share of sales made by multiple or other large organisations is likely to cause a reduction in the proportion of trade distributed through wholesalers, and, more generally, that any change which results in an increase in the average size of order which retailers are able to place with individual manufacturers has a similar tendency.

We turn now to a more detailed description of the study.

3. The Six Commodity Groups Chosen for Study

Rather than attempt to cover the whole range of consumer expenditure on commodities, we intend to discuss recent changes in the distributive process by reference mainly to what has occurred in the case of six categories of product. These consist of tobacco, confectionery, domestic electrical appliances, hardware, carpets and pharmaceutical preparations. The group as a whole has been chosen to include products with widely different characteristics with regard both to their nature and to the conditions under which they are typically produced and sold. As such the findings for these commodities may apply to a broad range of consumer goods.

Moreover, the six categories include five types of good on which r.p.m. was

1   *ibid.*, p. 60.

enforced relatively stringently after the 1956 Restrictive Practices Act (which prohibited the collective enforcement of resale prices, but strengthened, *de jure*, the position of the individual enforcing firm), and two (of the three) classes on which the practice was defended before the Restrictive Practices Court. Indeed the Court found that r.p.m. constituted a net benefit to consumers in the case of one of these, pharmaceutical preparations, and these products, together with books, are the only remaining ones on which manufacturers can legally control the price set by distributors. The sixth commodity group, carpets, is one on which retail prices have never been generally enforced, but it is one in which formal agreements between producers to fix common prices and distributive margins for standard qualities were of importance before 1959, when the Restrictive Practices Court prohibited the Federation of Carpet Manufacturers' Agreement. It is therefore probable that the effects of the breakdown of r.p.m. would be particularly evident from a study of these commodities.

As far as the composition of the groups is concerned, we do not intend to set out any precise rules of classification. They consist in general of products which are readily identifiable, from common usage, as belonging to one of the categories named, or more relevantly, of commodities which are commonly sold together in the same shop, or in the same department of a large store. Indeed most classification problems are of marginal importance, although it should be said that we exclude radios and televisions from our domestic electrical appliance category.

Each group as such does not necessarily consist of commodities which are similar with regard to their characteristics, or the conditions under which they are produced and sold, and hence with regard to the method of distribution employed. In other words, there are significant differences in unit price and structural variations in production and retailing within groups, which often make it misleading to regard each group as if it represented a collection of products subject to the same influences and characterized by similar developments in the distributive process. This being so, the impact of a common change in the environment, such as the breakdown of r.p.m., is unlikely to be uniform across any particular group. Although it is not possible to take account of this problem completely, we have attempted to reduce its importance in some degree, by considering different types of product separately where the relevant information is available. Thus, for example, we have tended to divide some of the groups into sub-categories — confectionery into chocolate and sugar confectionery, electrical appliances into large and small appliances, and pharmaceuticals into ethical and proprietary drugs — where appropriate and as far as it is possible to do so. But even within these sub-categories there will obviously be some lines which do not conform to the general pattern.

4. Outline of Analysis
As we have said, our concern is to assess the changes in channels of distribution, in the pattern of retailing and in prices and margins, that have occurred in the period since the 1964 Resale Prices Act began to take effect. This immediately raises one problem, insofar as the measures contained in the Act were implemented over a period from the end of 1965 to the middle of 1970, when the pharmaceutical case was heard.

To be specific, the Act required any supplier who supplied 'goods under arrangements for maintaining minimum prices on resale' to register such goods with the Registrar of Restrictive Practices, and prohibited the enforcement of r.p.m. on any categories of good not appearing on the register. The Restrictive Practices Court was then empowered to remove from the register those classes of product, the manufacturers of which were unable to satisfy the Court of the benefit to the public of the continued existence of r.p.m.[1] The register was compiled during 1965, and from the end of that year until the beginning of 1969, the products included were progressively removed. During this period, all the producers concerned, apart from those of confectionery and footwear, agreed to abandon r.p.m. as their cases came to be heard, and at the end of the period, as we have said, only pharmaceuticals remained on the register.

Of the commodity groups which we have selected for study, the hardware products registered were removed by stages between the beginning of 1966 and the end of 1967, domestic electrical appliances were removed in January, 1967, confectionery in June, 1967 and tobacco in September, 1968. But we cannot necessarily assume that the whole of the impact of the breakdown of r.p.m. occurred after these respective dates in each case, as it is quite possible that r.p.m. was enforced less stringently after the 'mood' of the Court, and its interpretation of the Act, became apparent. In other words, some manufacturers may have anticipated the Court's decision by turning a blind eye to price-cuts made by retailers, and may also have reconsidered, and perhaps modified, their distribution policy prior to the official ban on r.p.m. This implies that we need to consider the experience of each commodity group individually to some extent.

It thus makes for some difficulty in identifying an '*ex ante*' and '*ex post*' position in each case. Our intention, however, is to take the period around 1965 as our 'base' and to examine the changes that have occurred in the distributive process since then. We begin by looking at the relevant features of the process at the start of our period. Firstly, we examine the main structural characteristics of the manufacturers and retailers of the six groups in '1965', relying for the most part on the details contained in the Censuses of Production and Distribution. Although these are for 1963 and 1966, respectively, they suffice in most respects for our purpose, insofar as it is unlikely that there were many significant changes in manufacturing between 1963 and 1965 or in retailing between 1965 and 1966, for most of the products covered — besides which, we have little alternative but to use the statistics available. Secondly, we look at the distribution of each of the groups through wholesalers at this time, in the light of the structural features and the nature of the product. Thirdly, we examine the level of distributive margins and their constituent parts for the groups in '1965', the latter being a particularly important aspect as it indicates variations in potential gross profit between the distributors of the same commodity. As we have discussed above, such variations should tend to reflect differences in the cost-saving to

1 Five 'gateways' were stipulated, the producers having to satisfy the Court that the removal of r.p.m. would cause the public to suffer through its effects on one of the following: the quality and variety of goods, the number of retail outlets, retail prices, the necessary services provided, or that it would lead to the good being sold under conditions likely to cause danger to the health of the public. Furthermore the Court had to weigh such benefits arising from the existence of r.p.m. against the detriment to consumers from its continuation, particularly that resulting from the restriction on competition.

manufacturers of distributing *via* the alternative channels, and, more generally, they should tend to be a reflection of the distribution policy pursued. In other words, the price structure imposed by manufacturers can be regarded as a means of achieving the desired pattern of distribution. However this is a rather over-simplified view, insofar as there may be a considerable degree of interaction between the two elements. Thus, for example, a rise in the proportion of sales made by multiple retailers may enable these to improve their buying terms relative to other traders, which strengthens their competitive position and hence may cause a further increase in their share of the market. Moreover, the initial impact of the ban on r.p.m. is likely to be on retail prices and on the margins earned by distributors, any change in the pattern of distribution being a consequence of changes in these.

Such changes, of course, form the central theme of the study, and having discussed the main features of the situation in '1965', we turn to an examination of these. This consists, first of all, of an attempt to identify the major developments which may be expected, on the basis of our previous discussion and of what emerges from considering the position in '1965', to have influenced the distribution of the groups over the period since 1965. Included under this heading are, firstly, the long-term structural changes, or 'trends', in the relevant retailing and production sectors that were evident before 1965, and which are likely to have continued to operate after 1965, other things remaining equal. Secondly, we include the two legislative influences – the end of r.p.m. and S.E.T. – that ensured that other things did not remain equal during this period, and which are likely to have affected the pattern of distribution as well as prices and margins.

Lastly, we consider the evidence that we have on what has actually happened in this area since 1965, and try to assess, in particular, the influence of the breakdown of r.p.m. on the distribution of those commodities which were affected. In the absence of any official statistics for this period, we have been forced to adopt a rather 'piecemeal' type of approach. The evidence takes the form, primarily, of information collected from a number of manufacturing companies in each of the relevant trade groups. In all, 26 concerns, fairly evenly divided between the six groups, supplied us with details of their distribution activities over recent years, both by completing questionnaires and, in the majority of cases, by allowing us to interview them. Although this represents a small sample, an important part of the turnover of each commodity group is covered, and moreover, as well as recounting their own experiences, the companies also gave their impressions, often supported by statistics, or estimates, of the changes that had occurred generally in the particular trades in which they were engaged. While we found some differences between companies in their view of the situation and of the importance of current developments, these tended to be relatively minor, and a fair amount of agreement emerged. This information, combined with details from various published sources, have enabled us to build up what we believe to be a fairly representative picture of the most significant recent changes in the distributive process with regard to each of the six commodity groups. It has to be admitted, however, that our level of confidence varies somewhat between these, and it goes without saying that the estimates we make are subject to a degree of error that has to remain unknown until such time as more satisfactory data become available.

XII
The Structure of Manufacturing and Retailing

Our concern here is with the structural features of the manufacturers and retailers of the six groups which are most likely to have influenced the pattern of distribution prevailing in each case, in '1965', on the basis of our discussion above.

1. Manufacturing

With regard to manufacturing, the most relevant factors to consider are the number of individual concerns engaged in the production of each commodity group, the size-distribution of these and the proportion of total output produced by the largest concerns. As we have said, the main source of information in this connection is the Census of Production for 1963. This, for the most part, compiles statistics on an establishment basis and classifies establishments to industries on the basis of the 'principal products' manufactured. As details are presented in terms of Census industries, the composition of which is largely determined by supply factors, the breakdown does not correspond exactly to our particular groupings. However some information relating to sales concentration is given for certain products forming more satisfactory aggregations from the point of view of demand factors. These generally are more narrowly defined than the categories which we have chosen to study, but they do provide an indication of the structural variation within groups. In the main, our intention here is to present a broad description of the structural features of the Census industries which correspond to our six groups.

The most serious problem in this regard arises with respect to hardware, the manufacturers of which are classified to a number of different industries, consisting principally of: 'Miscellaneous Metal Manufactures', 'Tools and Implements' and 'Bolts, Nuts, Screws, Rivets, etc.,' but including others such as 'Plastic Moulding and Fabricating' and 'Wire and Wire Manufactures'. In addition, the major part of the output of these industries consists not of consumer goods but of products which are sold to other producers for use in the production process. This makes it impossible to build up any coherent picture of the structure of manufacturing of this group from the Census.

For the other commodity groups, the problem is far less acute and in each case there is a corresponding Census industry. However each of these excludes some production of the particular commodity group taking place in other 'industries' and includes the output of some products which do not belong to the group in question. These two considerations were of negligible importance in 1963 in the case of tobacco, confectionery and carpets, but almost 13 per cent of the sales of pharmaceutical preparations was produced in establishments classified to other industries, and about 30 per cent of the output included in the pharmaceutical preparations industry in fact consisted of 'other' products. Moreover the domestic electrical appliances industry excluded the production of domestic refrigerators, which represent a significant part of the major appliances sold by retailers. A related difficulty arises to the extent that a certain part of the output of the Census industries goes to other industries or users for further processing, rather than to final consumption. This is of greatest significance with regard to pharmaceuticals and, to a lesser degree, confectionery (about five per cent of the output of which consisted of 'cooking chocolate' in 1963), but is a very minor consideration with regard to the other three groups.

Despite these qualifications, the Census details are, in most respects, reasonably adequate for our purpose. Table XII.1 shows the distribution of enterprises according to numbers employed, and the proportion of gross output[1] produced within each size category, in 1963, for the industries corresponding to five of our groups. As we have said, it is not possible to present similar details for hardware, but the note to the table provides some information on the most important Census industries covering this group.

The table indicates that the number of enterprises in each industry varied from 29 in 'tobacco' to 454 in 'confectionery' and 510 in 'tools and implements'. In each case, a large proportion of the total number were extremely small firms, about half or more employing less than 25 people and about two-thirds or more employing less than 100. Indeed 85 per cent of confectionery enterprises fell into the latter category as did almost 94 per cent of those engaged in the production of tools and implements. However, apart from in the last-named industry such enterprises were responsible for a very small part of output.

At the other end of the scale, six enterprises accounted for 99 per cent of tobacco output in 1963; in fact, virtually all of the domestic market was divided between the three largest concerns, Imperial Tobacco, Gallaher and Carreras. The degree of concentration was also relatively high in the production of confectionery and domestic electrical appliances, in which the largest eight enterprises were responsible for 65 per cent and 60 per cent of gross output respectively. In the former, moreover, five of these accounted for almost 58 per cent of gross output. Large firms were less important in the production of pharmaceutical preparations, carpets and tools and implements. In the case of the former two trades, the largest four concerns controlled only a quarter of gross output, while 'medium-sized' enterprises — those employing between 400 and 2,000 — were responsible for about half. This contrasts with the situation in 'confectionery' and 'domestic electrical appliances' where such firms accounted for less than 16 per cent and less than 26 per cent of gross output, respectively, the actual number of enterprises in this size-category being the same for these two trades as for 'carpets'.

Turning to the Census information on sales concentration for selected products within the six groups, this indicates, firstly, a marked difference between the

1 Gross output is the value of goods produced and other work done; it equals the value of sales and work done plus the value of stocks and work in progress at the end of the year minus the value at the beginning of the year. Although sales would be more appropriate for our purpose, the Census does not give the necessary information.

Table XII.1 *Structure of Production: 1963*

Numbers employed by the enterprise in the industry	Confectionery			Domestic Electrical Appliances			Pharmaceutical Preparations			Carpets			Tobacco		
	Enterprises		Gross Output %	Enterprises		Gross Output %	Enterprises		Gross Output %	Enterprises		Gross Output %	Enterprises		Gross Output %
	No.	%		No.	%		No.	%		No.	%		No.	%	
Less than 25	312	68·7	5·2	98	50·5	1·8	162	56·6	3·3	67	47·5	2·9	13[b]	44·8	0·4
25 to 99	79	16·4	3·7	35	18·1	2·5	43	15·0	4·0	24	17·0	5·4	10[b]	34·5[b]	0·6[b]
100 to 399	35	7·7	10·3	33	17·0	10·0	49	17·1	16·5	26	18·4	17·4	6[b]	20·7[b]	99·1[b]
										11[a]	7·8[a]	17·8[a]			
400 to 999	14	3·1	7·7	17	8·8	19·5	20	6·9	27·5	5[a]	3·5[a]	14·3[a]			
1,000 to 1,999	6	1·3	8·1	3	1·5	6·3	8	2·8	23·8	4[a]	2·8[a]	15·3[a]			
More than 2,000	8	1·8	65·1	8	4·1	60·0	4	1·4	24·9	4[a]	2·8[a]	26·9			
of which:															
More than 3,000	5	1·1	57·7												
Total	454	100·1	100·1	194	100·0	100·1	286	100·2	100·0	141	99·8	100·0	29	100·0	100·1

a The size classes in these cases are 400 to 749, 750 to 1,499 and 1,500 to 1,999 employees, respectively.

b The size classes in these cases are 25 to 199 and Over 200 employees, respectively.

Source: Census of Production: 1963

Note on Hardware: The Census shows 70 enterprises employed 25 or more persons engaged principally in the production of domestic holloware and these accounted for 85 per cent of the total output of this type of product. 478 employed less than 100, and these accounted for 37 per cent of gross output. 510 enterprises were engaged in the 'Tools and implements' industry. The largest five enterprises were responsible for 33 per cent of gross output. 367 enterprises were engaged in the 'Bolts, nuts, screws, rivets etc.' industry. 310 each employing less than 100 accounted for 14 per cent of total gross output, while 20 enterprises produced 72 per cent of the total and the largest four about 50 per cent.

chocolate and sugar confectionery parts of the confectionery group, the largest five enterprises accounting for 82 per cent of sales in the former case but only for 36 per cent in the latter. Secondly, there is evidence of a high degree of concentration for particular products in the domestic electrical appliance group, the largest five manufacturers of washing machines being responsible for 85 per cent of the sales of such goods and the largest five vacuum cleaner manufacturers for 95 per cent of such sales. Thirdly, the five-firm concentration ratio for woven carpets was 42 per cent, for tufted carpets 51 per cent, and for other types 55 per cent, which compares with a four-firm ratio for the group as a whole of approximately 27 per cent as indicated in Table XII.1.[1]

2. Retailing

The basic factor that determines whether a manufacturer supplies a particular retail outlet direct or through wholesalers is, as we have said, the size of order involved. The proportion of any commodity group distributed through wholesalers is therefore likely to be influenced not only by the characteristics of the production sector but by the total number of retail outlets, their size and the importance of multiple organisations, cooperative societies and other large retailers. These features represent our principal concern in this section.

There are, however, certain difficulties involved in identifying the retailers of our six groups. Our main source of information is the Census of Distribution for 1966, which like the Census of Production, classifies retailers according to the principal products sold. But retail outlets tend to be far less 'specific' establishments than manufacturing plants, in the sense that most retailers are considerably less restricted with regard to the goods they sell than are producers. Thus, although the six groups consist of commodities which are commonly sold together in the same shop, few shops are devoted exclusively to the sale of any particular group. Moreover only a part of consumers' expenditure takes place in shops specialising in their sale – indeed a certain proportion in many instances does not take place in shops at all.

This means that we are not able to isolate a group of retailers in each case, and that if we rely on the Census data for the shops defined as specialising in the six groups, we exclude a varying proportion of retail sales. For example, confectionery is sold not only by confectioners and tobacconists but also by grocers, variety stores and public houses, and we clearly need to consider the latter three types of retailer along with the former. In some respects, however we are forced to rely on the information contained in the Census for specialist shops, particularly with regard to the size distribution of retailers. Although this is not completely satisfactory, it should be said that such outlets account for the majority of sales of four of the commodity groups, and for most of the sales of retail shops in the case of tobacco and confectionery. Moreover they are most likely to reflect the characteristics of the group of products in question and be most affected by changes in factors influencing

1 These figures and those included in Table XII.1 do not make any allowance for the sale of imported goods, nor indeed do they take account of exports. In each case, however, less than ten per cent of domestic sales was composed of imports in 1963, while the same was true of exports as a proportion of domestic production, except in the case of electrical appliances for which the export share was about 20 per cent and pharmaceuticals for which it was about 25 per cent.

Table XII.2   *The Estimated Number of Outlets for the Commodity Groups '1965'*   *('000)*

Commodity Group	Total Outlets	Retail Shops	Specialist Retailers
Tobacco	400−450	200	60
Confectionery	250	210	60
Domestic Electrical Appliances	20−25	Almost all	13
Hardware	30−35	Almost all	15
Carpets	25−30	Almost all	12
Pharmaceutical Preparations	100−150	80	14

Source: For tobacco, the estimates are taken from the Monopolies Commision, *Report on the Supply of Cigarettes and Tobacco and of Cigarette and Tobacco Machinery*, H.M.S.O., July, 1961, pp. 67−68; for confectionery from H. Crane, *Sweet Encounter*, Macmillan, 1969, p. 20. For domestic electrical appliances, hardware and carpets, they are based on the Census of Distribution, 1961, Table 9. For pharmaceutical preparations, the estimates are derived from N.B.P.I. Report No. 80, *Distributors' Margins on Paint, Children's Clothing, Household Textiles and Proprietary Medicines*, H.M.S.O., August, 1968, p. 16.

the distribution of that group.

Nevertheless we are able to make some estimates of the total number of outlets involved in the sale of each group and of the distribution of sales between types of retailer, at the beginning of the period being studied. Table XII.2 contains some details on the former aspect. The figures should be regarded merely as indications of the orders of magnitude involved.

Thus the total number of retailers (in the broad sense) selling the six commodity groups in '1965' varied from over 400 thousand in the case of tobacco to between 20 and 35 thousand in the case of the durable goods included in our sample. With regard to the former group, however, less than half the outlets were retail shops, and only about a third of these could be included in the 'C.T.N.' category. The most numerous outlets were licensed premises and grocery stores which together represented about half of the total. A similar situation existed for confectionery and pharmaceutical preparations, although in the former case, outlets other than retail shops were of far less significance than for tobacco. With regard to the latter, the products sold outside chemist shops were limited to a narrow range of proprietary medicines, mainly including the leading brands of analgesics and antacids. In the case of domestic electrical appliances, hardware and carpets, virtually all the outlets were retail shops — although with regard to electrical appliances, electrical contractors were of some importance — and of these about half could be regarded as specialising in the sale of the respective groups.

To a large extent, however, the numbers of the various types of outlet selling the commodities are a poor reflection of their relative importance in terms of sales. This is shown by Table XII.3 which gives some indication of the percentage distribution of the sales of the groups between categories of retailer in '1965'. Again we should emphasize that the figures are intended as approximations to the true percentages. As we intimated above, the major part of consumers' expenditure on four of the six groups occurred within specialist shops (including Electricity Board Showrooms in this category), while for the other two groups specialist confectioners and tobacconists accounted for a much greater proportion

Table XII.3 *Estimated Percentage Distribution of Commodity Sales between Types of Outlet: 1965*

Commodity Group	Specialist Shops[a]	Grocery and Food Stores	Department and Variety Stores	Other Shops	Mail-Order	Miscellaneous[b]
Tobacco	37	23	2	–	–	38
Confectionery	48	28	10	2	–	12
Domestic Electrical Appliances	36/25[c]	–	15	7	7	10
Hardware	55	2	25	8	10	–
Carpets	63	–	24	6	7	–
Pharmaceutical Preparations	90	3	1	3	–	3

Source: The estimates for tobacco, domestic electrical appliances, hardware and carpets are based on Table 16 of the Census of Distribution for 1966. For tobacco, the Census figures are modified by reference to the Monopolies Commission, *Report on the Supply of Cigarettes and Tobacco, etc.,* p. 68 together with supplementary information. For domestic electrical appliances, the figures are partly based on N.B.P.I. Report No. 97 *Distribution Costs and Margins on Furniture, Domestic Electrical Appliances and Footwear,* H.M.S.O., December, 1968, p. 5. For confectionery, the estimates are taken from H. Crane, *Sweet Encounter,* p. 20. For pharmaceutical preparations, we have used the estimates of N.B.P.I. Report No. 80, *Distributors' Margins on Paint, Children's Clothing, Household Textiles and Proprietary Medicines,* pp. 16–17, in conjunction with the figures on Chemists' turnover in *Nielsen Researcher,* November–December, 1969, p. 3.

Notes:

a Specialist shops are those kinds of business defined by the Census of Distribution as specialising in the sale of each of the six commodity groups.
b This includes such outlets as public houses, restaurants and garages in the case of confectionery, tobacco and pharmaceuticals (for the latter, hospitals and doctors are excluded), and electrical contractors in the case of domestic electrical appliances.
c 36 per cent of sales through Radio and Electrical Goods shops, 25 per cent through Electricity Board Showrooms.

of sales than of total outlets. Most notably, chemist shops represented less than 15 per cent of the total outlets selling at least some products included in the pharmaceutical category, but were responsible for 90 per cent of sales. This of course results from their virtual monopoly of ethical drug supplies, if we exclude those dispensed by hospitals and doctors, together with the fact that ethicals accounted for over two-thirds of the sales of this group (including chemists' receipts for prescriptions dispensed, but excluding drugs dispensed outside the retail sector).

With regard to domestic electrical appliances, Electricity Board Showrooms accounted for almost as large a proportion of sales as specialist retailers in the 'private sector', yet they were far fewer in number. Of the 13 thousand outlets estimated as specialising in the sale of this commodity in 1965, only about 1,330 were Board showrooms.

For the sales not classified to specialist retailers, the most important outlets were grocery stores in the case of tobacco and confectionery and department and variety stores in the case of the durable goods. Grocery stores were responsible for about a quarter of the sales of the former two groups, while department and variety stores sold about the same proportion of hardware and carpet sales and controlled around 15 per cent of the domestic electrical appliance market. For the latter three groups, mail-order sales were also of some significance.

We estimated above that over half of the innumerable outlets selling tobacco were not classified to the retail sector, as defined by the Census of Distribution. The table indicates, however, that these accounted for less than 40 per cent of the market for this product. Moreover the 100 thousand or so licensed premises were only responsible for between 10 and 15 per cent of sales. Similarly, in the case of confectionery, the outlets included in the miscellaneous category — consisting of public houses, filling stations and cinemas, for example — were more important in terms of numbers than in terms of sales. In other words, for both product groups, these types of retailer generally represented relatively small purchasing units, although this is not so for a number of works canteens which occupied a prominent position in the case of tobacco in particular.

The latter point clearly has a bearing on the method of distribution adopted by manufacturers in these cases. Other aspects of Table XII.3 which are immediately relevant in this respect are the sales through department and variety stores and those *via* mail-order companies, since, as we have noted, such organisations tend to represent sufficiently large buying units to be able to purchase direct from manufacturers. With regard to the other shops included in the table, however, it is clearly of importance, from this point of view, to consider the proportion of sales made by multiple organisations and cooperative societies, together with the size-structure of other retailers. The Census provides details on these for specialist shops, but in the case of confectionery and tobacco it is of some interest to know the distribution of sales between forms of grocery organisation, as such retailers control a significant part of the market of both groups.

Fortunately information gleaned from various sources enables us to give a reasonable indication of the position in 1965. Table XII.4 shows the estimated percentage of *total* tobacco and confectionery sales made by multiples, coops and independent retailers included under the 'grocery and food stores' heading of Table XII.3 above.

Table XII.4   *Estimated Percentage Distribution of Total Tobacco and Confectionery Sales between Forms of Grocery and Food Organisation: 1965*

| Commodity Group | Grocery and Food Retailers | | | |
	Multiples[a]	Coops	Independents	Total
Tobacco	2	6	15	23
Confectionery	7	5	16	28

a Retail organisations with ten or more branches.

A notable feature to emerge is that independent outlets accounted for a higher percentage of the sales of the two groups in question than they did for grocery and food sales as a whole. The same is true for cooperative societies, while the multiple share of the two groups was correspondingly much less. Thus independent grocery and food retailers were responsible for slightly more than a half of the sales of this kind of business, whereas their share of the tobacco sales of such shops amounted to 65 per cent and their share of the confectionery sales to almost 60 per cent. Similarly coops accounted for over a quarter of the tobacco sales of this kind of business as opposed to 15 per cent of overall sales. On the other hand, multiple grocery and food organisations were responsible for about a third of 'food' sales, but for only a quarter of the confectionery sales of these shops and for less than ten per cent of the tobacco sales.

We turn now to the structural characteristics of the retailers specialising in the sale of the six commodity groups. As we have said the Census of Distribution for 1966 represents our principal source of information; the classification of retailers to kinds of business, however, only approximates, almost inevitably, to what we ideally require. For example, shops specialising in hardware are included with those mainly selling wallpaper and paint, and shops specialising in carpets with those selling furniture. While it is true that the products covered by a particular category are often sold together, this is not invariably so. Thus we estimate that about 40 per cent of the outlets included under 'Hardware, china, wallpaper and paint shops' sold little or no hardware and about the same percentage of those included under 'Furniture and allied shops' did not sell carpets.[1]

Nevertheless the census data should provide some indication of the main points of interest underlying the percentages shown in the first column of Table XII.3 above. Table XII.5 shows the total number of establishments and the total value of turnover, together with the distribution of these between forms of organisation, in 1966, for the relevant specialist types of retailer, as defined by the Census, and for retailing as a whole. The average sales-size of shop, both overall and for each of the three forms of organisation, is also shown.

As far as the structure of the trades is concerned independent retailers accounted for 80 per cent or more of the total number of outlets in each case (if we exclude Electricity Board showrooms from the 'Radio and electrical goods shops'), and, with the exception of chemists, for 70 per cent or more of turnover, which was considerably greater than their share of total retail sales. Conversely, only 12 per cent of the turnover of hardware shops and less than 15 per cent of that of C.T.N.'s went through

1   These estimates are derived from the Census of Distribution, 1961.

150

Table XII.5   Retail Structure: 1966

Kind of Business	All Retail Establishments			Co-operative Societies			Multiples[a]			Independents		
	Establishments	Turnover	Turnover per Establishment	Establishments	Turnover	Turnover per Establishment	Establishments	Turnover	Turnover per Establishment	Establishments	Turnover	Turnover per Establishment
	No.	£m	£000	%	%	£000	%	%	£000	%	%	£000
Confectioners, Tobacconists, Newsagents	63,333	1,045·6	16·5	0·2	0·5	39·5	9·9	14·5	24·0	89·8	85·0	15·6
Radio & Electrical (including Electricity Board showrooms)[b]	16,691	327·7	19·6	1·5	2·8	36·4	17·3	27·0	30·7	81·2	70·2	17·0
	(18,023)	(392·5)	(21·8)	(1·4)	(2·3)		(23·4)	(39·1)	(36·4)	(75·2)	(58·6)	
Hardware, China, Paint	25,809	306·5	11·9	1·5	2·1	16·4	9·6	12·1	15·0	88·9	85·8	11·5
Furniture and allied	19,539	530·2	27·1	2·9	4·8	45·5	11·2	25·5	61·8	85·9	69·6	22·0
Chemists, photographic dealers	17,959	501·3	27·9	5·6	4·6	22·9	14·9	37·5	70·3	79·6	58·0	20·3
Total Retail Trade	504,412	11,131·8	22·1	5·3	9·1	38·1	14·6	34·5	52·0	80·1	56·4	15·5

Source: Census of Distribution: 1966
a Organisations owning ten or more branches.
b The relevant figures for Electricity Board Showrooms in 1966 are: Establishments: 1,332, Turnover: £64,824 thousand, Turnover per Establishment £48·7 thousand.

multiple outlets in 1966, as compared with a figure of 35 per cent for all retail trade. The multiple share of the sales of radio and electrical goods shops (excluding Electricity Board showrooms) and furniture shops represented about a quarter of the total, while for chemists it was almost 38 per cent. If, however, Electricity Board showrooms are included with multiple retailers in the former case, the share of such organisations in the turnover of the trade increases to almost 40 per cent.

Cooperative societies were of minor importance with regard to each of the five specialist kinds of business, most of their sales of tobacco and confectionery being made through grocery stores and most of those of durable goods through department stores.

The table also indicates that the number of retail establishments for any given level of turnover varied widely between the trades, the average sales-size of shop being considerably greater for chemist and furniture retailers than for the hardware category and C.T.N.'s. This pattern was repeated for both multiples and independents taken separately. In general, the shops belonging to the former tended to be significantly larger than those of the latter, although the difference varied markedly between the five kinds of business. It was relatively small in the case of C.T.N.'s and the hardware category, while in that of chemist and furniture retailers, multiple shops were, on average, about three times the size of independent outlets. As far as electrical retailers are concerned, the outlets in the private sector tended to be relatively small in comparison with furniture shops and also in comparison with Electricity Board showrooms.

However while the sales-size of shop is likely to have some influence on the prevailing pattern of distribution, it is probably a less important consideration than the size of retailer. We would expect the organisations included under the multiple heading in Table XII.5 to be sufficiently large purchasers of the six commodity groups to be able in most instances to deal direct with the manufacturers concerned. But this may equally apply to some retailers included as independents, and in this context, the number of outlets under common ownership is clearly of relevance. In fact for each of the five kinds of business, unit retailers (those owning one shop only) accounted for the major part of the turnover of independents. We estimate (on the basis of the 1961 Census information) that these were responsible for about 90 per cent of the sales through independent C.T.N.'s, for over three-quarters of those of independent hardware and chemist retailers, for about 70 per cent of independent furniture sales and for over half of the turnover of independent radio and electrical goods shops.

A further point of interest, at the opposite end of the scale, concerns the multiple organisations and the proportion of turnover controlled by the largest of these, as this has an important bearing on the balance of bargaining power between manufacturers and distributors, and hence on the level and composition of distributive margins. Again we have to rely on estimates of the position, but it is apparent that the degree of concentration at the retail level was highest in the case of chemist shops, about a third of the turnover of which — or almost all of the multiple sales — was accounted for by the largest five organisations. By contrast, the largest seven C.T.N. enterprises were responsible for only around seven per cent of the total trade of this kind of business, although this represents about half of multiple sales, and a very similar situation probably existed in the case of hardware shops. It is difficult to make approximations for furniture and electrical retailers, but it is almost certain that the largest concerns were more important than in the latter two kinds of business.[1] We can say, however, that, with regard to Electricity Board showrooms, these were under the control of 14 Area Boards, each of which thus represented a relatively significant buying unit.

Finally, as a partial summary of this section, we can incorporate the figures for the distribution of sales between the specialist forms of organisation, with the estimates on the total home market sales of the six groups contained in Tables XII.3 and XII.4 above. From this it emerges that multiple organisations, cooperative societies, department and variety stores and mail order companies accounted for approximately 60 per cent of the sales of domestic electrical appliances (if we include Electricity Board showrooms),[2] almost half the sales of carpets and hardware, about 35 per cent of those of pharmaceuticals, 30 per cent of confectionery sales and 16 per cent of the tobacco market. In addition, a further 12 and 13 per cent of the sales of each of the four groups excluding tobacco and confectionery was made by specialist retailers owning more than one shop, which leaves only 30 per cent of domestic electrical appliance sales and 40 per cent of hardware and carpet sales to unit specialists and other retailers.

3. Summary

The structural characteristics of manufacturers and retailers are likely to have an important bearing on the method by which each of the six product groups chosen for study is distributed. With regard to the former aspect, the Census of Production indicates that the number of manufacturing enterprises in 1963 was greatest for hardware and confectionery and lowest for tobacco, while for each group the vast majority of firms were small but produced a negligible part of total output. Concentration was extremely high in respect of tobacco production and low for hardware, carpets and pharmaceuticals, although marked differences were evident within groups, especially as between chocolate and sugar confectionery.

With regard to retailing, the number of outlets in 1965 approached half a million in the case of tobacco, a quarter of a million for confectionery and over 100 thousand for pharmaceuticals of all varieties, while there were between 20 and 30 thousand shops selling the three types of durable goods. For the former three groups, specialist retailers accounted for a comparatively small proportion of these but represented the most important single source of supply, especially in the case of pharmaceuticals, almost all of which were sold through chemist shops. For the latter three groups, specialist shops were responsible for the majority of sales, while most of the remainder took place in department and variety stores and *via* mail-order companies. In the case of tobacco and confectionery, shops included in the grocery and food category accounted for about a quarter of all sales, with the bulk attributable to independents. Within the specialist sectors, the multiple share of turnover varied from almost 40 per cent with respect to 'Radio and electrical goods' shops (if

1   The 1961 Census indicated that 28 organisations accounted for about a quarter of all sales through 'furniture and furnishings shops', or again for most of the sales through multiples.

2   The actual figure was almost certainly greater than 60 per cent because of the relative concentration of independents on non-appliance sales and repair work.

Electricity Boards are included as multiples) and 'Chemists' to less than 15 per cent with respect to 'C.T.N.'s' and 'Hardware'; coops were relatively unimportant in each case and unit retailers accounted for most of the sales of independents. Finally, our overall estimate from the Census data was that the proportion of sales made by large retail organisations of every type amounted to at least 60 per cent in the case of domestic electrical appliances and to almost half in that of carpets and hardware, but to less than a third in the case of confectionery and to only 16 per cent in that of tobacco.

XIII
Wholesalers and the Pattern of Distribution

Our task here is to relate the observations made in the previous chapter to what we know of the pattern of distribution prevailing in 1965 for the commodities included in each of the six groups.

1. Overview

From our introductory discussion, we would expect the proportion of goods distributed through wholesalers in each case to be inversely associated with the share of the market controlled by multiple retailers, department stores, mail-order companies and other such organisations, other things being equal. These, we observed, are likely to represent sufficiently large buying units, in most instances, to be able to receive their supplies direct from manufacturers. The size of order involved is also likely to be important in determining the method of distribution adopted by manufacturers for sales to other retailers, and hence the characteristics both of these and of the manufacturers themselves are of some significance with regard to the wholesale share of trade. In addition to the structural features outlined in the previous chapter, however, there are other elements to be considered, as is clear from what we said earlier. These include, in particular, the nature of the product, which has a bearing on the costs to manufacturers of distributing a given size of order as well as on the advantages associated with supplying retailers direct. But they also include less 'rational' factors, such as the traditional practice of the trade or of individual concerns.

We also pointed out in the introduction that there are significant variations in the characteristics of the manufacturers and retailers of the different products included in each of the groups, as well as in the nature of the products themselves. These were not referred to in much detail in the previous chapter, but they clearly imply that the method of distribution is unlikely to be uniform within any particular group. Furthermore, the less 'rational' factors referred to above, together with the fact that the net advantages associated with supplying retailers direct are of a kind which permit manufacturers to hold differing opinions as to their magnitude, raise the possibility of even similar products being distributed by dissimilar methods.

These considerations mean that there are certain difficulties involved in presenting a summary view of the position of wholesalers in the distribution of the six groups. In particular, any single figure for the percentage of sales distributed through wholesalers in each case is likely to conceal as much as it reveals. The figures contained in Table XIII.1 should therefore be regarded merely as a starting point to the subsequent discussion. Moreover it must be emphasized that they represent very

155

Table XIII.1   *Estimated Percentage of Home Market Sales Distributed through*
Wholesalers: 1965

Commodity Group	Estimated percentage of home market sales going through wholesalers in 1965
Tobacco	35–40
Confectionery	40–50
Domestic Electrical Appliances	30–35
Hardware	30–40
Carpets	25–30
Pharmaceutical Preparations	40–50

Source: The estimates are derived from the figures supplied by our sample of
manufacturers and from supplementary information received. For domestic electrical
appliances, the figure is partly based on N.B.P.I., Report No. 97, *op. cit.* p. 5 and for
pharmaceuticals on N.B.P.I. Report No. 80, *op. cit.* pp. 17–18.

approximate indications of the true percentages, being derived from information of
a rather piecemeal nature.

2. The Six Commodity Groups

(i) Tobacco

However a single figure is more meaningful for tobacco than for the other groups,
as the major companies pursued essentially similar distribution policies and as their
outlets largely consisted of much the same type of product. The estimate of the
wholesale share of trade shown in the table indicates that a significant proportion
of the retail outlets not owned by multiple organisations were supplied direct, as the
latter accounted for only about 16 per cent of the market, as we have seen. This is
surprising in view of the relatively small scale of the retailers concerned, but is
clearly explicable in terms of the extremely high degree of concentration in the production of this commodity group. Thus the fact that virtually all of home market sale
was produced by three concerns evidently meant that even relatively small retailers
were able to place sufficiently large orders to justify direct accounts.

In practice each of the major companies operated the same type of distribution
system imposing a minimum size of order requirement, which specified that retailers
had to take a certain number of cigarettes or weight of tobacco at regular five-
weekly intervals in order to qualify for a direct account.[1] The price structure which
was enforced by the manufacturers meant, as we show in the next chapter, that the
wholesale share of home market sales was largely, but not entirely, confined to the
retailers that were unable to comply with the minimum order requirement. We would
therefore expect a large number of C.T.N.'s to receive supplies from manufacturers,
and for wholesalers to be more important in the distribution of tobacco to non-
specialist shops and to outlets outside the retail sector as defined by the Census. In
fact, it has been estimated that about two-thirds of the total retail outlets selling
tobacco received supplies entirely through wholesalers in 1960.[2]

1   The minimum number of cigarettes to be taken every five weeks was 10,000 in 1965,
    which represents 5,200 packets of 20 every year, or sales of about £1,040 from each
    company.

2   Monopolies Commission, *Report on the Supply of Cigarettes and Tobacco*, p. 171.

156

However this is a rather over-simplified view, insofar as any individual retailer is likely to have purchased at least some of his supplies from wholesalers. For example, the latter provide a much faster delivery service and could be resorted to for 'topping up' purposes if stocks ran low before the end of the five-week period. This is an illustration of the general point, which applies to all the groups, that a retailer's choice on source of supply is determined by the price—service combination offered by manufacturers as opposed to wholesalers. In certain circumstances, in other words, the service element assumes priority.

(ii) Confectionery

In the case of confectionery, the degree of concentration in production was lower than in that of tobacco, though still relatively high; similarly the outlets selling the product though numerous were less so than in the case of tobacco, with a higher proportion of sales being made by multiple retailers and variety store organisations. These two considerations pull in opposite directions with regard to the relative importance of wholesalers, but the former tends to dominate, as is indicated by the estimate of the wholesale share shown in Table XIII.1.

However, there is much justification for considering chocolate sales and sugar confectionery sales separately. The market for the former is largely divided between a very small number of manufacturers and between a relatively small number of leading lines while that for sugar confectionery is far more differentiated and supports a great many small producers. Thus in 1965, the four largest concerns accounted for about three-quarters of domestic sales of chocolate,[1] producing all but four of the 48 lines which represented about 70 per cent of all chocolate sold, in value terms.[2] By contrast the same four concerns were responsible for only a quarter of sugar confectionery sales[3] while the estimated 20,000 different confectionery packs on sale largely consisted of sugar confectionery lines, manufactured to a great extent by the very many small firms which characterise this trade.[4]

We would therefore expect wholesalers to be more important in the distribution of sugar confectionery than of chocolate, although it should be said that many of the smallest manufacturers — those employing less than 25 in Table XII.1 in the previous chapter sell exclusively direct to consumers through their own shop or market stall. We estimate that over half of sugar confectionery sales was distributed through wholesalers in 1965, while these accounted for about 40 per cent of chocolate sales.

With regard to the latter type of product, there was a considerable amount of

---

1 N.B.P.I. Report No. 75, *Costs and Prices of the Chocolate and Sugar Confectionery Industry*, H.M.S.O., July, 1968, Appendix B.

2 Harold Crane, *Sweet Encounter*, Macmillan, 1969, pp. 30—36.

3 N.B.P.I. Report No. 75, *op. cit.* The five-firm concentration ratio in 1963 was only 36 per cent, as we noted above.

4 See Harold Crane, *op. cit.* Although 14 sugar confectionery lines accounted for about 21 per cent of such sales, nine of these were produced by the four major 'Chocolate Houses'.

variation in the use made of wholesalers between the companies concerned, with broadly similar manufacturers choosing to distribute in one case virtually all non-multiple sales through wholesalers and in another, a large proportion of unit retailer sales direct. This, however, is partly explicable in terms of a practice known as 'detailing', which serves to combine some of the advantages of employing wholesalers with some of those which arise from selling direct to retail shops. Specifically, while the bulk of deliveries are made *via* wholesalers in such cases, the manufacturer employs a merchandising team to buy small quantities of his products from wholesalers and pay visits to local retail outlets, improving the display position and 'topping up' any lines which happen to be low in stock.[1] This policy illustrates the importance to manufacturers of control over the point of sale in respect of confectionery, the sales of which are largely characterised by 'impulse' rather than 'planned' purchases, in the sense that the decision to buy on the part of the consumer often arises from seeing a particular line displayed or advertised. The implication is that individual manufacturers have considerable interest in the positioning of the products in the shop and in the amount of window space devoted to them, since total sales are likely to be closely related to such factors. At the same time, the returns to be gained from supplying retailers direct, in terms of the enhanced control over the point of sale, are difficult to quantify, and hence the weight placed on them by manufacturers is liable to vary. This consideration may well underlie a further part of the difference in distribution arrangements noted above.

With regard to sugar confectionery, there was some tendency for the largest manufacturers specialising in its production to own important wholesale organisations, which, by and large, operated as independent traders, in the sense that there was little evidence of any marked concentration on stocking the products manufactured by the parent companies. The policy almost certainly developed as a result of the prominent position of wholesalers in the distribution of this section of the market and it is not generally a feature to be found among the leading chocolate concerns.

(iii) Domestic Electrical Appliances

In the case of domestic electrical appliances, Table XIII.1 estimates that the wholesale share of home market sales amounted to between 30 and 35 per cent, which is close to what we might have predicted on the basis of the proportion of sales made by large retail organisations in 1965 or so. This we estimated at about 60 per cent, with a further 12 per cent going to independent specialist retailers owning more than one shop. However, in a similar way to confectionery the typical method of distribution employed tended to differ broadly between two sections of the market.

Thus wholesalers were much more important in the distribution of small than of large appliances. Most manufacturers of the former distributed the greater part of their output through such traders, while the wholesale share of major appliance sales amount to only about 20 per cent or so. This variation is partly explicable in terms of the lower unit value carried by small appliances, the fact that their production tended, overall, to be less concentrated among a few producers (although there were exceptions, such as electric irons, the majority of which were manufactured

---

1 Merchandising is, of course, not restricted to 'detailing' arrangements, but represents an important aspect of the marketing policy of all the major manufacturers.

by two concerns), and the difference in the pattern of retailing. With regard to the latter, Electricity Board Showrooms in particular were more important in the major appliance market, and purchased a large part of their small appliance sales from wholesalers. Within the former market, they were responsible for about 70 per cent of all electric cookers sold and for about the same percentage of storage radiators, but for only about 20 per cent of washing machine and refrigerator sales. In consequence, the method of distribution varied in some degree between types of major appliance. Moreover there was some variation between manufacturers of similar appliances; one of the leading concerns for example, had a policy of distributing all goods direct to retailers. The figure for the wholesale share of this end of the market cited above is therefore an estimate of the overall position and is not representative of any particular product or manufacturer.

(iv) Hardware

With regard to hardware, it is especially difficult to make any kind of generalisation at all, simply because of the very wide range of products covered by the term. The variation in unit price and the characteristics of manufacturers and retailers between types of commodity hence tends to be more significant than in the case of the other groups studied. We would expect the small, low unit-value, and often unbranded articles such as nuts, bolts and screws to be distributed predominantly through wholesalers, and for the larger products, such as lawn-mowers, to be distributed to a greater extent direct to retailers. This in fact appears to have been generally true.

The same type of distinction broadly applied within the different sections of the market. For example, in the case of hand tools, some manufacturers relied almost entirely on wholesalers, while other used them hardly at all, the method of distribution employed tending to reflect the unit price of the 'brand' and the number and type of outlet supplied. Thus although the majority of hardware retailers were relatively small in 1965, a significant proportion of sales was made by large organisations, as we have seen, which facilitated a policy of direct supply.

Because of the difficulty of covering the whole of the hardware group through a small sample of manufacturers, we have concentrated upon one section of the trade, comprising domestic appliances, holloware and kitchen- and table-ware. For the products included in these categories, department and variety stores and mail-order companies were at least as important as specialist hardware shops. Again, however, there were some marked variations between different lines of the same type of product which partially accounted for the different methods of distribution prevailing. In general terms, firms manufacturing kitchenware, cutlery and gadgets, typically operated a policy of supplying the large retail organisations direct and others through wholesalers; in the case of holloware and kitchen and bathroom scales, perhaps the major part of trade went through wholesalers, while manufacturers of cleaning implements, such as carpet sweepers and brooms tended to distribute direct to retailers (or in a few cases, direct to consumers, through door-to-door salesmen), as did those producing the more expensive lines of tableware, which were sold through a limited number of retail outlets.[1] In addition, an important part of

1 In contrast to the general pattern, one of the biggest manufacturers with interests in all these fields pursued a policy of distributing virtually all retailer sales through wholesalers.

the manufacturers' output of these types of product was taken by trading stamp companies and gift catelogue operators, and, as such, was not sold on the retail market. These generally represented extremely large purchasing units and took delivery direct from manufacturers.

(v) Carpets

As far as carpets are concerned, Table XIII.1 estimates that between 25 and 30 per cent of sales were distributed through wholesalers. We saw in the previous chapter that large retail organisations were relatively important in the market for this product group and moreover that specialist furniture shops were, on average, comparatively large establishments. The relatively high proportion of direct-to-retailer sales is therefore to be expected on the basis of these considerations. In addition, however this method of distribution is facilitated by the customary practice of the trade and the nature of the product. Thus the use of pattern books as selling aids and the willingness of consumers to wait a period of time before taking delivery together obviate the need for retailers to hold a high level of stocks, and indeed reduce the level which the trade as a whole needs to carry at any one time. Moreover rolls of carpet are relatively easy to transport and are virtually damage-proof, which means that transport contractors, such as British Rail or National Carriers, can be used. All these factors reduce the importance of the service which wholesalers are able to offer.

However the proportion of sales distributed through wholesalers differed somewhat between types of carpet. Our estimate is that the wholesale share amounted to about 15 per cent in the case of tufted carpets, which accounted for around 40 per cent of the market, in volume terms (but for substantially less in value terms) in 1965, and to about 30 per cent in the case of woven carpets. But there were some variations to be found between manufacturers in the use made of wholesalers. While these were employed by the majority of companies for at least part of their output, a very few manufacturers distributed virtually all their sales through wholesalers, while a greater number sold only to retail outlets or large consumers.

The difference between the two sections of the trade is partly explicable in terms of historical factors. Thus prior to 1959, a fairly rigid and extensive code of practice existed between the majority of the manufacturers of woven carpets, with regard to their distribution activities, and particularly with regard to discounts.[1] This had the effect of restricting the wholesale discount essentially to 'bona fide' wholesalers, and meant that the best terms available to retailers buying direct were represented by the 'trade' price, or the same price as offered by wholesalers. There was consequently little advantage to be gained by retailers through buying direct, which is likely to have caused the overall wholesale share to have been greater than it otherwise would have been, or indeed was warranted by the nature of the trade.

No such restriction existed in the case of tufted carpets. Moreover, a large part of the output of this type of product initially come from new entrants to the carpet trade, particularly engineering companies. These were attracted by the low capital costs and the possibility of employing unskilled labour, and, at the same

1 See the description of the Federation of British Carpet Manufacturers' Agreement in *Restrictive Practices Reports*, Volume 1.

time, encouraged by the reluctance of a great many established carpet manufacturers to expand into tufted production. Potentially at least, they were able to adopt the most efficient method of distribution, unhampered by past arrangements, although at first there was some reluctance on the part of retailers to stock the lower priced type of carpet and manufacturers were obliged to initiate their own distribution system, which involved direct sales to consumers. Such sales have declined in importance over time as retailers become more willing to stock and promote tufted carpets.

A further part of the explanation might lie in the fact that the technique of tufted production restricts the range of possible patterns, which means that one manufacturer's lines are far more similar to another's than in the case of woven carpeting. In consequence, retailers may be able to take supplies from one or a few manufacturers, which eliminates part of the *raison d'etre* of wholesalers as far as this section of the market is concerned.

(vi) Pharmaceutical Preparations

The major part of the pharmaceutical preparations group consists of ethical drugs, which, in the main, are only available to consumers if prescribed by doctors, their supply within the retail sector being confined to dispensing chemists. To this extent they differ from the other products included in the study, and also from proprietary medicines, which make up the rest of the pharmaceuticals group; these are sold 'over-the-counter' and are not restricted to any one type of retail outlet. Moreover, in contrast to carpets for example, the speed of the delivery service can be of primary importance with regard to certain classes of ethical drug. Indeed there are instances when prompt supply is essential to save a person's life, and consequently a distribution system has to exist which is capable of meeting such contingencies. This factor is likely to outweigh, in some degree, considerations of manufacturing or retail structure, as far as the method of distribution is concerned.

It is estimated that there are approximately 2,500 different drugs classed as ethicals[1] and there were probably not much fewer in 1965. As a pharmacist, unlike any other retailer, is committed to supplying any particular type *and* brand of these − and at short notice − it would obviously be both costly and inefficient for each individual chemist outlet (or hospital) to keep a comprehensive stock. Indeed there are substantial economies to be gained from holding stocks collectively rather than individually, particularly in the case of the slow-moving items, for which the transport costs implied by the maintenance of a frequent delivery service are offset by a reduction in the level of total stocks that need to be held at any one point in time. Thus the probability that a number of chemists will need to dispense a given drug at a given time is obviously less than the probability that any one of them will need to do so.

The function of holding stock for the trade and of guaranteeing prompt delivery is performed, in some degree, by wholesalers, although it is true that manufacturers are usually willing to supply a particular drug direct to retailers very quickly and in minimum quantities, if so requested. In general, manufacturer-direct-to-retailer sales

---

1   This figure was presented in evidence to the Restrictive Practices Court in 1970, by the manufacturers defending the practice of r.p.m. on this class of product.

are largely confined to those products with a relatively rapid rate of stock turn. However it has been estimated that 200 or so lines (eight per cent of the total numb account for about 73 per cent of all sales,[1] and again the situation has probably not altered dramatically since 1965. Even the largest retail organisations therefore relied on wholesalers for some of their supplies, but received the major part direct from manufacturers, and broadly speaking the proportion of purchases from wholesalers was closely related to the size of chemist concerned.

The distribution pattern was very similar for proprietary medicines, insofar as most manufacturers tended to deal direct with retailers for the larger orders, while sending the others through wholesalers. The latter included grocery distributors, which probably accounted for about the same proportion of this type of trade, in value terms, as those specialising in pharmaceuticals.

As far as independent retail chemists are concerned, a sample survey carried out by the N.B.P.I. in 1968, found that small pharmacists (those with a turnover of less than £20,000) purchased about 75 per cent of their *total* sales from wholesalers, while those with a turnover of over £40,000 obtained over 40 per cent from such suppliers.[2]

3. Postscript on Wholesaling

In the foregoing we have outlined the position of wholesalers with regard to the distribution of the six groups. Although their importance in each case is largely a function of the structural features of the relevant manufacturers and retailers and of the nature of the commodity group concerned, it does not follow that their characteristics have no part to play in the matter at all. For example, the method of distribution adopted by manufacturers is likely to be influenced in some degree by the volume of goods that individual wholesalers are able to take relative to the volume that retailers are able to take, and hence by the typical size of the former customer as against that of the latter.

The inquiry into the wholesale trades undertaken by the (then) Board of Trade in 1965, although unsatisfactory in many respects (particularly with regard to the coverage), shows that there were a large number of individual wholesale businesses specialising in the distribution of five of our groups, at least, and that the majority were relatively small. Table XIII.2 reproduces the estimates made by the inquiry on these two aspects and also gives an indication of the importance of the largest companies, for the relevant four kinds of business as distinguished by the Board of Trade.[3]

Thus it is evident that, in 1965, there were many more wholesalers than manufacturers in each trade, with the exception of confectionery. Their average receipts were smaller than the turnover of a number of retail organisations specialising in the sale of the same commodities, while the degree of concentration of sales among a few

1 These figures are again taken from the Restrictive Practices Court proceedings.

2 See N.B.P.I. Report No. 80, *op. cit.,* p. 18.

3 The classification adopted by the inquiry aggregates those wholesalers specialising in the distribution of hardware and electrical goods into a single kind of business and conceals floorcoverings wholesalers within the clothing and textile category.

Table XIII.2 *Wholesale Businesses in 1965*

Kind of Business	Business Units	Average Receipts (£000)	The largest business units:[a]	
			Number	% of Total Receipts
Cigarettes and Tobacco	923	457·6	6	24·8
Chocolate and Sugar Confectionery	439	129·6	14	18·5
Hardware and Electrical Goods	2,400	160·4	5	9·8
Chemists' Wares	480	300·7	7	45·5

Source: *Board of Trade Journal*, 26th July, 1968
a This section shows the percentage of the estimated total receipts of each kind of business accounted for by the largest business units as distinguished by the inquiry.

traders was relatively low. The exception to the latter is the 'Chemists' wares' category, almost 46 per cent of the total receipts of which was accounted for by the largest seven businesses, which clearly might be a factor underlying the comparatively extensive reliance on wholesalers in this trade.

Summary
The proportion of the home market sales of our six commodity groups distributed through wholesalers in 1965 ranged from almost half in respect of confectionery and pharmaceuticals to just over a quarter in respect of carpets. For the other three groups, the overall wholesale share was between 30 and 40 per cent. In the case of tobacco, this means that even comparatively small retailers had direct accounts, which is a reflection of the high degree of concentration in production. This factor also underlies the variation within the confectionery group, wholesalers accounting for a much higher proportion of sugar confectionery sales than of chocolate, although marked differences existed even between similar manufacturers. Moreover most producers of large domestic electrical appliances distributed much the greater part of their output direct to retailers, while wholesalers were the most important source of retail supply for the less concentrated small appliance end of the market. With regard to hardware, it is difficult to make any overall estimate of the wholesale share and we were only able to make a number of general observations as to its variation between types of product. Within the carpet group, wholesalers were responsible for a greater part of woven sales than of those of tufted, the difference being partly explicable in terms of past trade restrictions and the much greater design range of the former. In the case of pharmaceuticals, it is again natural to divide the group into two parts, the importance of wholesalers being especially obvious with respect to ethical drugs, for which the speed of delivery and the holding of comprehensive stocks are crucial factors, although a similar distribution system prevailed for proprietary medicines.

Finally a brief examination of the structural features of the wholesale trades served to highlight the generally large number of individual units and low degree of concentration, against which the fact that only seven wholesalers accounted for 46 per cent of the total receipts of the 'Chemists' wares' business was particularly prominent.

XIV
Distributive Margins

1. General Considerations

It is broadly possible to classify the practices of manufacturers in fixing price into two methods. Manufacturers either set a retail selling price − the price at which retailers are recommended to sell the product, or the price at which they are obliged to do so, if r.p.m. is enforced − and quote prices to wholesalers and retailers in terms of percentage discounts off this price, or they directly quote prices to distributors. In the latter case, the 'benchmark' used is generally the 'trade price', which represents the basic retail buying price on small orders, or the 'worst' terms; if a retail selling price is specified, it is usually determined by the addition of a percentage mark-up to this 'benchmark'. It is clear that where resale prices are enforced, manufacturers explicitly control the gross margin which any distributor earns; where they are merely recommended, there is still an implicit margin allowed to trade customers.[1] In general terms, the margin allowed in each case should tend to recognize the activities or services performed by individual distributors; alternatively, the differentials between terms should reflect the opportunity costs to producers of distributing a given commodity in varying quantities via the alternative channels. Indeed an implicit assumption underlying the discussion of the previous two chapters is that such a rational price structure obtained in the year under consideration. Thus in the final analysis the proportion of goods distributed through wholesalers depends on the terms that they can offer to retailers as opposed to what the latter can obtain from manufacturers. In other words, the difference between the wholesale buying price and the manufacturers' terms to the various retailers is the critical factor and forms the concern of the present chapter.

There are three aspects of the above paragraph to be considered: firstly, the variation between the six commodity groups in the practice adopted by manufacturers in setting prices to trade customers; secondly, the differences in the margin allowed between the distributors of each group; thirdly, the variation in the level of distributive margin both between groups and between the commodities included in any one group.

2. The Method of Pricing for the Six Groups

The characteristic method of pricing employed by the manufacturers of each of the

---

1 This is true even if only the retail selling price is specified, the implicit wholesale margin allowed then being the difference between the manufacturer's price to wholesalers and that to retailers.

six groups, and often the standard margins allowed to distributors, have tended to show remarkable resilience to change. Consequently, the procedure used in 1965 was, in many instances, similar to that prevailing at an earlier period, and may not in fact differ overmuch from that employed at the present time.

To take a broad view, manufacturers either recommend or (mostly) controlled the retail selling price of the majority of the products included in the groups, with the exception of carpets, for which retailers were largely free to determine their own mark-up. In the case of tobacco and ethical drugs, manufacturers also controlled the wholesale selling price. With regard to the buying price of distributors, terms on tobacco and confectionery were generally related to the quantity purchased, the same price structure applying to both wholesalers and retailers alike. This was also broadly true of proprietary medicines and of the small items included in the hardware group, such as nuts and bolts. On the other hand, the producers of domestic electrical appliances and the majority of those of hardware and pharmaceuticals quoted terms in the form of standard percentage discounts, retailers receiving a discount off the recommended or maintained retail selling price and wholesalers a further discount off the retail buying price. A similar procedure was adopted by most carpet manufacturers, except that the trade price represented the basic terms to retailers, and wholesalers received a discount off this. This method also applied to some hardware products, for which no retail selling price was specified.

Thus it is possible to divide the groups into two categories, those whose manufacturers largely made no distinction between wholesale and retail purchasers, which would include tobacco and confectionery, and those for which there was some tendency to recognize the service performed by wholesalers, in the form of a standard discount. However this is too superficial a view, as it does not take account of the existence of quantity discount structures or rebate schemes, which applied to retailers in the case of the groups included in the latter category. The effect of these, in some instances (by no means all), was to reduce the buying price of the large organisations to a level comparable to that of wholesalers.

3. The Wholesale and Retail Margins for the Six Groups

Table XIV.1 represents a summary view of the 'standard' margins allowed to trade customers by the manufacturers of the six groups in 1965, and also gives an indication of the potential gross margin which retailers could achieve by buying in bulk direct from the manufacturer. It shows not only the variation between trades in the level of distributive margin, but also that existing within commodity groups, both between sizes of retailer and between the different types of product included. In addition, however, there was some difference in the practice adopted by manufacturers of similar products, and at the same time, there are certain elements of the total margin which, because of their nature, are difficult to summarize in any table. These include discounts given for display or promotional purposes, which are not included in Table XIV.1. Because of these variations it is necessary to consider each group individually.

(i) Tobacco
In the case of tobacco, the low levels of margin shown in Table XIV.1 are a

Table XIV.1   *The Margins on the Commodity Groups, 1965*

Commodity Group	Basic Wholesale Margin as % of Wholesale Selling Price[a]	Retail Margin as % of Retail Selling Price:	
		'Basic'[b]	'Best'[c]
Tobacco:			
Cigarettes	3 – 4	8	11
Confectionery:			
Chocolate	7	16	22
Sugar	8 –14	21–30	26–40
Domestic Electrical Appliances:			
Major	10	20–22½	28–30
Small	15 –20	25	36–40
Hardware	15 –20	25–33⅓	36–47
Carpets[d]	11 –12½	(28)	n.a.
Pharmaceuticals:			
Ethical	15	33⅓	40–43
Proprietary	12½–15	18–33⅓	28–43

Source: The figures are derived from details received from our sample of manufacturers. In the case of proprietary medicines, the figures are taken from N.B.P.I. Report No. 80 *op. cit.*, p. 18.

Notes:

a The wholesale gross margin, assuming that the whole of the standard discount is retained

b The standard retail discount, or the difference between the recommended retail selling price and the wholesale selling price, under the assumption that Note (1) obtains, expressed as a percentage of the former. In the case of domestic electrical appliances, hardware and proprietary medicines, the retail selling price *excludes* any purchase tax payable, as this is the customary 'base' for these trades.

c The retail gross margin, assuming that recommended retail selling price is adhered to and that retailers obtain the maximum quantity discount from suppliers.

d The figure in brackets represents the approximate average retail gross margin in 1965. As no selling price was specified, manufacturers had no control over the actual margin achieved.

See text for a fuller explanation of the figures.

consequence of the fact that excise duty constitutes a significant part of both whole-sale and retail selling (and buying) prices. As a result of this, and the periodic increases manufacturers have come to assess the margins allowed on a cash rather than a per-centage basis.

Since 1960, and the publication of the Monopolies Commission report on the industry, terms to trade customers on the majority of sales have been solely related to the quantity purchased.[1] Before 1968, resale prices were strictly maintained on both wholesale and retail sales.[2] With regard to the former, two selling rates applied

1   The Monopolies Commission was critical of the bonus schemes operated by the manufac-turers, and by Imperial Tobacco in particular. In the case of this company, bonuses, which were additional to the basic discounts, were paid in return for the distributors' undertaking, in writing, to promote and display the company's products in prominent positions. The size of the bonuses and the high market share controlled by Imperial Tobacco (63 per cent in 1959) meant that distributors were obliged to conform to the agreement and therefore the company's lines were assured of a high degree of promotion relative to those of its competitors. In 1959, in fact, 99½ per cent, by value of Imperial's trade passed through distributors who were signatories to the agreement. See Monopolies Commission, *Report on the Supply of Cigarettes and Tobacco.*

2   Gallahers, for example, took steps to prevent trading stamps from being given with tobacco sales in the mid-1960s.

166

to cigarettes (one for delivery of less than 7,500, the other for those larger than this), the 'small parcel' rate yielding wholesalers a gross margin of about half a percentage point more than the 'large parcel' rate, assuming that wholesalers purchased at the best terms, which was always the case. (The best terms applied to an order of 50,000 cigarettes or more.) A retailer buying in the former quantity would have obtained a gross margin of slightly less than eight per cent in 1965 (and slightly more than eight per cent if he purchased more than 7,500), as compared with a margin of about $9\frac{1}{2}$ per cent if he had purchased direct from the manufacturer in the smallest quantity possible (5,000 cigarettes) and of almost 11 per cent if he had been able to buy at the best terms. The margins on tobacco were generally slightly less than on cigarettes, while on cigars they were twice as large, in percentage terms. In both cases only two buying rates applied and only one selling rate was stipulated for wholesalers, but the difference between margins was broadly similar to that for cigarettes.

Consequently, as the margins on cigarettes indicate, there was a clear incentive for retailers to purchase direct from any individual manufacturer, if they were able to satisfy the minimum size of order requirement, rather than to combine their purchases of this company's lines with those of others and to buy instead from wholesalers, at the 'large parcel' rate. In other words, the difference between the two wholesale rates was much less than that between the 'worst' terms offered by manufacturers and the best price available from wholesalers. This may have had the further result of encouraging retailers to concentrate on stocking the most popular brands in order that they might meet the necessary minimum requirement. Indeed this was the argument that was expounded to the Monopolies Commission by the Wholesale Tobacco Trade Association.[1]

(ii) Confectionery

The method of pricing employed by confectionery manufacturers was similar to that for tobacco, at least as far as the larger companies were concerned, prices to trade customers varying according to the number of 'outers' ordered.[2] Resale prices were enforced at the retail stage only, and the maximum distributive margin that these implied, in conjunction with the best buying price, was much the same for comparable manufacturers but varied a good deal across the trade and between products. As we indicated in Table XIV.1, the best terms on chocolate – taking the products of the major companies – generally represented a discount off the retail selling price of about 22 per cent in 1965, while those on the most popular sugar confectionery lines traditionally represented a discount of five percentage points above this. On the latter type of product, however, the distributive margin could be as high as 40 per cent or more, the actual level closely reflecting the rate of stock turn of the line in question and the amount of promotion undertaken by the manufacturer concerned.

---

1 See Monopolies Commission, *op. cit.*, p. 149. Moreover the largest manufacturers other than Imperial Tobacco said that they encouraged retailers to open direct accounts in order to be able to compete with the Imperial companies, even though this added to distribution costs (*ibid.*, p. 147).

2 An 'outer' consists of a varying number of packs of a particular line.

The price structure applying to wholesalers was the same as that for retailers buying direct. The wholesale selling price although not specified by manufacturers was until 1960 controlled by an agreement among wholesalers themselves, which stipulated a fixed division of the total distributive margin between wholesalers and retailers. Effectively the agreed rates gave wholesalers 25 per cent of the margin on 'weigh-out' lines (jars of sweets) and 28 per cent on others, which implied a gross margin of about seven per cent for chocolate and between eight and 14 per cent for sugar confectionery depending upon the total margin allowed.[1] This implied, in turn, a retail margin on purchases from wholesalers of 16 per cent on the leading chocolate lines and between 21 and 30 per cent on sugar confectionery. It is difficult to compare these figures with those on direct purchases at the smaller end of the scale, as there was a good deal of variation between manufacturers on the minimum size of order that they were willing to supply direct to retailers, reflecting the difference within the trade on overall distribution policy.

In addition to the basic price structure, a number of manufacturers operated over-riding discount or quantity rebate schemes, which were based, sometimes not very precisely, on the annual turnover of distributors, or on the growth in turnover. These were particularly important with regard to sales to multiple organisations. Moreover a few companies gave additional discounts periodically to finance or encourage the promotion of particular lines. More generally, settlement discounts of the order of $1\frac{1}{4}$ per cent for payment within 30 days applied throughout the trade and were earned by virtually all distributors.

(iii) Domestic Electrical Appliances

As we have said, the terms on domestic electrical appliances were quoted as percentages off the retail selling price, excluding purchase tax, in the case of retailers and off the trade price in the case of wholesalers. The basic retail discount varied, with slight differences between companies, from 15 per cent on cookers, to 20 per cent on refrigerators, and $22\frac{1}{2}$ per cent on washing machines and vacuum cleaners, to 25 per cent on most other appliances. The basic wholesale discount was ten per cent on the former four products and between 15 and 20 per cent on others. In addition, most manufacturers operated quantity discount schemes, which could often reduce the retail buying price to wholesale terms, in respect of large multiple organisations and Electricity Boards. Quantity discounts to wholesalers, however, were by no means general, and, where they existed, usually consisted of an additional five per cent. Some manufacturers also gave annual rebates to large customers.

R.p.m. only applied at the retail stage, and competition between wholesalers meant that the basic discounts quoted above exceed the gross margin actually earned by wholesalers in a number of cases, and correspondingly are lower than that achieved by some retailers. Similarly any quantity discounts or rebates given to wholesalers were often passed on to retailers.

Settlement discounts of $2\frac{1}{2}$ per cent, for payment within the month after that in which the invoice was issued, were customary not only in this trade but also in the

---

1 In 1960, the Restrictive Practices Court found against the Wholesale Confectioners' Alliance agreement and forced its dissolution, at least from a legal standpoint. For details of the agreement, see *Restrictive Practices Cases, Volume 2.*

hardware and carpet trades.

(iv) Hardware

The method of pricing used for most products included in the hardware group was identical to that described above. The standard discounts varied from 25 per cent to retailers and 15 per cent to wholesalers on lawn mowers to $33\frac{1}{3}$ per cent to retailers and 20 per cent to wholesalers on most domestic hardware, with hand and garden tools occupying an intermediate position.

For the products in which we are specifically interested (domestic appliances, holloware and kitchenware), quantity discount schemes were by no means general for wholesalers; where they existed, additional discounts were given up to a maximum of about five per cent, or took the form of retrospective rebates based on a trader's annual purchases, with a maximum of around two per cent. In the case of retailers, such schemes were more widespread, but differed somewhat between manufacturers. In some cases, the maximum additional discount was one of ten per cent, in others, retailers could obtain wholesale or special terms on large orders; this was so particularly where retail organisations took delivery at central warehouses. The actual details of the quantity discount scheme operated tended to reflect closely the policy of the manufacturer concerned, with regard to direct supplies to retailers.

Again wholesale reselling prices were not enforced by producers, although they were suggested explicitly in some cases, and implicitly in others, where list or retail prices were combined with a standard discount structure. In general, wholesalers operated quantity discount schemes, and it was possible on some products for retailers ordering in bulk to obtain better terms from these than from some manufacturers.

(v) Carpets

Carpet manufacturers have never generally adopted the practice either of recommending or of enforcing retail selling prices.[1] Instead they operated on the basis of trade or list prices, which represented the standard prices at which retailers could buy, and quoted terms to wholesalers as a percentage discount off this price.

The wholesale margin of between 11 and $12\frac{1}{2}$ per cent shown in Table XIV.1 was the range specified by a trade agreement between manufacturers, which was operative until 1959 (the Federation of British Carpet Manufacturers' Agreement). This not only fixed a common wholesale discount for certain qualities of carpet, but prevented the giving of quantity discounts on normal sales. Moreover wholesale terms were restricted to those distributors recognized as '*bona fide*' wholesalers by the Federation, and these had to conform to similar trading arrangements as manufacturers.[2]

It can be argued, as we have above, that the main effect of the agreement combined with the approved wholesale list was to prevent retailers from being able to press for quantity discounts, and after the agreement was abandoned, it was a

1 According to the Monopolies Commission, *Recommended Resale Prices*, H.M.S.O., February, 1969, p. 26, in 1968 no woven carpet manufacturers recommended retail selling prices, while only a few tufted producers did so.

2 For details of the agreement, see *Restrictive Practices Cases, Volume 1.*

number of years before such schemes became at all widespread. These then took the form of either discounts off the list price or rebates assessed on annual turnover, or in some cases terms were negotiated centrally with large multiple organisations. In general, wholesalers continued to receive the same percentage discounts as stipulated by the agreement, although the very few wholesale groups were usually able to negotiate special terms.

As far as the retail mark-up is concerned, the evidence is that this varied a good deal between retailers and between different lines. Moreover any assessment needs to take account of whether fitting and laying are included in the price to the consumer or whether an additional charge is levied. We estimate that the average retail gross margin was about 28 per cent in 1965,[1] which represents a mark-up of about 39 per cent, although for some retailers the average mark-up was only about 25 per cent, while for others it was close to 50 per cent.[2]

(vi) Pharmaceutical Preparations

Resale prices were — and still are — maintained both on ethical drugs and proprietary medicines. For the former type of product, the N.H.S. represents the main final buyer and compensates retail chemists on prescriptions dispensed, by valuing the drugs at the manufacturers' recommended prices. The enforcement of r.p.m. therefore applies essentially at the wholesale stage rather than at the retail stage, as in the case of proprietary medicines.

For ethical drugs, the basic retail margin in 1965 was $33\frac{1}{3}$ per cent, while wholesalers generally received a discount of 15 per cent off the trade price, as indicated in Table XIV.1. In a few cases, wholesalers were able to earn quantity discounts in addition, but these were mainly confined to companies which distributed a large part of their output through such traders. Retailers could usually obtain discounts on bulk purchases, which occasionally reduced the buying price of the largest chemist chains to wholesale terms, or mostly, slightly above. Such discounts were sometimes used to encourage stocking during slack periods. R.p.m. prevented wholesalers from themselves giving quantity discounts to customers, except insofar as permitted by manufacturers; in some cases, large parcel rates were stipulated, althoug the extent to which they were actually given was limited by the small size of order typically delivered by wholesalers.

With regard to proprietary medicines, the method of pricing was similar to that described for confectionery, except that discounts were quoted in percentage terms. The amount of the basic retail margin was generally less than for ethical drugs and varied in large measure with the rate of stock turn, as indicated in Table XIV.1 above

1 This figure is based on data collected from a sample of retailers by the D.A.E., during the course of the enquiry into the economic effects of S.E.T., and from trade association information.

2 Individual lines are likely to have shown a much wider variation. A survey conducted at around this time by one manufacturer interviewed discovered an instance where the mark-up applied by a retailer was as high as 320 per cent, and in another case was as low as ten per cent.

3 According to the N.B.P.I. Report No. 80, *op. cit.,* p. 18, the basic retail discount off the tax-exclusive retail selling price, varied between 18 and 25 per cent on 'the nationally advertised products of leading manufacturers' and from 25 to $33\frac{1}{3}$ per cent on 'unadvertised or slow-moving products'.

The same quantity discount structure in most cases applied to both retailers and wholesalers, up to a maximum of between $12\frac{1}{2}$ and 15 per cent off the trade price, which thus represents the wholesale gross margin. In addition, the larger manufacturers gave periodic promotional bonuses to encourage retailers to 'push' a particular line; these often took the form of an extra unit with no extra change. However, unlike the other groups, with the exception of tobacco, settlement discounts were not generally given.

4. The Variation in Distributive Margin between Commodities

From our discussion of the individual commodity groups, it would appear that the difference in the level of distributive margin between products is related in some degree to three factors: the rate of stockturn, the amount of brand advertising undertaken by manufacturers and the unit price. Thus, for example, the margin allowed on both confectionery and proprietary medicines tended to be higher on those lines on which advertising expenditure was relatively low and which had a slow rate of stock turn. Similarly, the level of unit price and the extent of promotion may account for part of the difference in basic discounts between types of electrical appliance. This association can be ascribed to the fact that these three factors have an important bearing on the costs to traders of distributing any commodity – expressed as a percentage of their turnover. Thus the inverse of the rate of stockturn – the costs of holding stock in relation to turnover – in many cases represents a significant element of total operating costs, while the selling effort required on the part of the distributor is clearly reduced with a rise in the advertising expenditure of manufacturers. In addition, there is little reason to suppose that the absolute level of costs is proportionately greater for those products carrying a relatively high unit price.

However the view that the distributive margin allowed on any commodity is at all closely associated with the costs involved in its distribution is open to dispute. We have seen that the percentage discounts given to trade customers are traditional for many products and have remained unchanged over a long period of time. To quote the N.B.P.I., 'the ratio between the recommended price and the ex-factory price is not based on any calculation of distributors' costs and is seldom changed despite the changes that occur in manufacturers' prices'.[1] In other words, the distributive margin, in terms of cash, would appear to vary directly with the retail selling price, rather than with distribution costs; consequently, even if there were initially some relation between the latter and the margin allowed for a particular class of product, it does not follow that this is so for a later period. Thus it is unlikely that distribution costs change in line with production costs, or ex-factory prices.

However, if there is no relationship between the two, the implication is that net profitability to distributors varies between the commodities traded. Given the ease both of entry into the distributive trades and of diversification on the part of existing traders, we would not expect any significant variation to obtain for any length of time. But if resale prices are controlled by manufacturers, this may hinder the ability of new entrants to gain a share of the market, and may allow some

1 Report No. 55: *Distributors' Margins in Relation to Manufacturers' Recommended Prices*, p. 3.

variation to persist. On the other hand, it is possible to argue that distribution costs in this situation come to reflect the customary margin available rather than vice versa. If, for example, margins become too 'slack', the costs of distribution may tend to rise as a consequence of the entry of new traders and their attempt to gain a share of the market, or possibly as a result of the action taken by existing businesses with the object of preventing such entry or of expanding their own sales. Either way, the increase in distribution costs is likely to arise from an increase in the services provided with the sale of the good, including under this heading the number of retail outlets and wholesale warehouses as well as the more obvious elements, as this represents the only area of competition open to distributors and their sole means of expansion.[1]

We have attempted to assess the level of retail and wholesale margins for the six commodity groups, in relation to the functions performed. As we have mentioned, the costs of holding stock often represents a significant part of total operating costs, and much of the variation in the level of margin between the groups can in fact be ascribed to differences in the importance of this factor relative to turnover. This is hardly a novel finding. Thus Jefferys found that his results for 1938 confirmed 'the generally accepted axiom that the relative rate of stock turn, or in other words the holding cost, is the strongest factor in determining the relative wholesale and retail gross margins earned on different commodities, but at the same time the exceptions make it clear that this is not the only factor operating'.[2]

The data which we have used to test the validity of this relationship for a more recent period are derived for retailing, from the 1966 Census of Distribution and, for wholesaling, from the 1965 enquiry carried out by the then Board of Trade.[3] The latter is supplemented by information collected from a sample of traders during the course of the enquiry into the effects of S.E.T. There are a number of qualifications surrounding the use of these figures. In particular, they are averages for individual kinds of retail and wholesale business, rather than for commodity groups; on the one hand, they refer to the gross margin actually earned, rather than to the basic margins allowed by manufacturers and therefore include such elements as bulk purchase and promotional discounts; on the other hand, they refer to end-year stocks rather than the average level held over the year. Nevertheless they should provide an indication of the degree of association between the two variables in question.

Table XIV.2 summarizes the relationship between gross profit and end-year stocks, both expressed as a percentage of turnover, for the kinds of retail and wholesale business as defined by the two official sources mentioned above.

Equation 1 indicates that the association between the two variables in 1966 was not particularly close for all retail businesses. These, however, include outlets selling

1   This argument is akin to that of Professor Kaldor which was described in detail in Chapter 1 of the study. As we saw there, the Kaldow view is that the retail mark-up on the cost of goods purchased is determined by the elasticity of demand for the retailers' output, rather than directly by operating costs – although it should be noted that the costs of holding stock are regarded as the one cost element which does form part of the mark-up imposed. However competition and ease of entry into the retail trades tend to ensure that excess profits do not persist for any length of time, which is equivalent to saying that operating costs come to reflect the gross margin available.

2   *The Distribution of Consumer Goods*, p. 101.

3   Published in the *Board of Trade Journal*, 26th July, 1968.

Table XIV.2   *Regressions of Percentage Gross Margin on Stocks as a Percentage of Turnover, for Retailers in 1966 and Wholesalers in 1965*

Trade	Equation	Constant	Regression Coefficient	r^2	n
Retailing	1	25·1	·361 (·251)	·13	21
Retailing	2	12·8	·909 (·237)	·57	13
Wholesaling	3	8·6	·571 (·152)	·44	20
Wholesaling	4	7·0	·665 (·160)	·53	17
Wholesaling	5	7·7	·708 (·236)	·41	15

Notes:
Equation 1 is based on all retail businesses.
Equation 2 excludes perishable food shops and general stores.
Equation 3 covers all wholesale businesses.
Equation 4 excludes perishable food trades.
Equation 5 is based on the D.A.E. sample data, excluding perishable food trades.
Source: See text.

perishable foods, for which the financing of stocks represents a very small part of total operating costs, and for which the costs of wastage and the associated uncertainty element involved in trading assume a dominant role. They are also not confined to specialist retailers, but include department and variety stores and other shops selling a wide range of products, so that the figures for margins and stocks are not close approximations to those obtaining for individual commodity groups. Moreover this type of business tends to concentrate on the faster moving lines of any product group and to undertake a greater part of the wholesaling function than do other kinds of retailer, with the result that the relationship between the two variables is likely to differ from that prevailing elsewhere in the retail sector.

If these two kinds of business (the 'Other Food' category apart from 'off-licences' and 'General Stores' category plus 'other non-food shops') are excluded, the association becomes much closer. This is summarized by Equation 2, which indicates that a ratio of stocks to turnover of ten percentage points above average is associated with a gross margin of nine points above average. Furthermore 57 per cent of the variation in gross margin between the remaining 13 kinds of retail business was statistically explained by differences in the costs of holding stocks.

Equation 3 is based on the 20 kinds of wholesale business as distinguished by the Board of Trade within MLH 810 of the S.I.C. (wholesalers trading in consumer goods other than industrial products). The exclusion of perishable food trades makes comparatively little difference to the relationship, as is revealed by Equation 4. This indicates that, on average, a rise in the stocks/turnover ratio of five percentage points was associated with an increase in gross margin of about three percentage points in 1965.

Equation 5 summarizes the relationship for the D.A.E. sample of wholesalers, again excluding perishable food traders; although fewer kinds of business are covered, the traders are classified into narrower categories which more closely approximate to individual commodity groups. Nevertheless the regression coefficient is very similar to that of Equation 4.

Thus the conclusion which emerges from Table XIV.2 is that there is a positive and fairly close relationship between the gross margin earned by distributors and their relative costs of holding stock. However there are clearly other factors to be considered, inasmuch as about half of the variation in margins is not 'explained' by the stock/sales ratio. These two points are illustrated by our six commodity groups. Table XIV.3 shows the stocks/sales ratio and the level of gross margin for the relevant retail and wholesale businesses, in 1966 and 1965 respectively, together with the gross margin calculated on the basis of the appropriate equations described above. (Grocery traders are included because of their significance with regard to the sales of the non-durable goods.)

For more than half of the categories shown in the table, the difference between the actual and calculated margin is three percentage points or less; for the remainder other considerations apart from the cost of holding stock are clearly of some importance. However in the case of traders dealing in tobacco, we have mentioned the fact that excise duty represents a substantial proportion of the value of sales; as the duty is levied upon the raw material it also enters into the value of stocks held. But because distributive margins are determined in cash terms, excise duty is excluded from gross profit in some degree. Consequently, we would expect gross profit as a percentage of sales for both wholesalers and retailers, to be lower than calculated from our regression equations. In fact, as is shown in Table XIV.3, the gross margin earned by tobacco wholesalers was about seven points lower than the calculated value, while the difference for retailers (C.T.N.'s) was less (4·4 points), probably as a result of the greater importance of non-tobacco sales. In addition, much of the difference between the gross margin earned by the D.A.E. sample of confectionery wholesalers and the average level derived from the Board of Trade enquiry, is explained by the variation in tobacco sales as a proportion of turnover between the two groups, the proportion being higher for the former than for the latter.

This leaves radio and electrical goods retailers, furniture shops and grocery wholesalers as showing significant deviations of the actual margin from that calculated. With regard to the former, almost 14 per cent of turnover in 1966 consisted of receipts from repair and maintenance work.[1] This by its very nature carries a much higher gross margin than on appliance sales, as the cost of goods bought tends to be small in relation to labour charges. In the case of Electricity Board showrooms, this type of work accounted for 23 per cent of turnover in the same year, which helps to explain why their gross margin was over 47 per cent as compared with the 37 per cent of 'private sector' retailers, while their stocks as a percentage of turnover were lower. Moreover transport costs were a more significant element of the total operating costs of retailers selling domestic electrical appliances than for most other shops, because of the bulky nature of the product. These represented over three per cent of the turnover of radio and electrical goods shops in 1966, which was more than twice the average for the retail trades as a whole.[2]

1 *Report on the Census of Distribution, 1966, Volume 1,* H.M.S.O., 1970, Table 15.

2 *Op. cit.,* Volume 2, Table 7.

Table XIV.3 *Stocks–Sales Ratios and Actual and Calculated Gross Margins.*

Kind of Business	Stocks/Sales Ratio	Actual Gross Margin	Calculated Gross Margin	Differences between Actual and Calculated
Retailing: 1966[a]				
Grocery and Provisions	6·6	16·1	18·8	−2·7
C.T.N.'s	8·3	15·9	20·3	−4·4
Radio and Electrical Goods	17·5	36·9	28·7	8·2
Hardware	21·3	29·2	32·2	−3·0
Furniture and Allied	16·2	32·8	27·5	5·3
Chemists and Photo-graphic Dealers	17·3	30·3	28·5	1·8
Wholesaling: 1965[b]				
Grocery and Provisions	6·4 (7·7)	6·9 (6·9)	12·2 (12·2)	−5·3 (−5·3)
Cigarettes and Tobacco	5·7 (5·9)	4·6 (5·0)	11·7 (11·0)	−7·1 (−6·0)
Chocolate and Sugar Confectionery	7·9 (7·3)	10·0 (11·1)	13·2 (11·9)	−3·2 (−0·8)
Electrical Goods[c]	12·9	15·9	16·8	−0·9
	(14·9)	(18·5)	(16·9)	(1·6)
Hardware[c]	15·6	17·5	18·7	−1·2
Floorcoverings[d]	9·5 (n.a.)	13·4 (n.a.)	14·4	−1·0
Chemists' Wares	13·4 (13·4)	14·5 (18·4)	17·1 (15·9)	−2·6 (2·5)

Notes:
a The stock–sales ratios and gross margins are taken from the Census of Distribution, 1966. The calculated gross margin is derived from Equation 2 of Table XIV.2.
b The stock–sales ratios and gross margins are calculated from the financial data provided by the D.A.E. sample of wholesalers; the figures in brackets refer to the Board of Trade enquiry. The calculated gross margin is derived from Equation 5 of Table XIV.2, and from Equation 4 in the case of the Board of Trade enquiry.
c The Board of Trade combined these two kinds of business.
d The Board of Trade included these traders in the category of Clothing and Textile wholesalers, of which they formed a small part only.

The latter point also applied to furniture retailers, for which transport costs were of similar importance. In addition, such retailers are likely to have provided a fitting and laying service with their carpet sales, which carries similar consequences for the gross margin earned on the repair work undertaken by electrical goods shops. On the other hand, carpets are generally sold with the aid of pattern books (and furniture often through the use of catelogues), which means that retailers need to hold relatively low stocks; consequently the costs associated with this function tend to be comparatively small in relation to total operating costs.

Finally, in the case of grocery wholesalers, part of the explanation for the actual margin being so much lower than that expected, might lie in the importance of the cash-and-carry method of operation in this trade. This is analogous to self-service in retailing, in that the customer is able to obtain better terms, in exchange for undertaking a certain amount of the work involved in his being supplied. The wholesaler thus forfeits part of his potential gross margin, but at the same time is more than compensated by the reduction in operating costs, which tend to rise sharply with a decrease in the size of order delivered under normal methods of operation. A further part of the explanation might be that wholesalers is this trade are, on average, more efficient than those dealing in other goods. Thus the Board of Trade enquiry indicates that they tended to be larger (in terms of numbers engaged) than other traders and that the degree of concentration was relatively high (the largest 30 business units were responsible for over half of total receipts in 1965). Moreover wholesale-sponsored voluntary groups of retail shops accounted for a significant proportion of grocery sales in 1965,[1] whereas they were of negligible importance in other trades. We might expect the closer link between wholesalers and retailers fostered by such groups to lead to some saving in distribution costs, particularly through larger and more regular deliveries.

Summary

For the majority of commodities included in the six groups — carpets being the major exception — manufacturers exercised a high degree of control over the gross margin earned by distributors in 1965, although the division between retailers and wholesalers, for example, was not fixed with respect to tobacco and ethical drugs. On these two products, r.p.m. applied to wholesale sales, whereas for the most of the other goods r.p.m. was only enforced at the retail stage. In the case of tobacco, confectionery, some items of hardware and proprietary medicines, the level of such margins was directly related to the quantity purchased, while in the case of the other products wholesalers tended to receive a standard discount. For these latter goods, retail organisations were in many instances able to obtain comparable terms to wholesalers by purchasing in sufficient bulk. The total distributive margin earned ranged from almost 50 per cent on certain hardware lines to only 11 per cent on cigarettes, the low level of the latter resulting from the importance of excise duty. In general, however, the difference in percentage gross margin between commodities appears to bear some relation to the rate of stockturn, the extent of brand advertising and unit price, which are likely to be significant factors underlying distribution costs as a percentage of the retail selling price. This relationship seems to hold in broad terms with regard to variations within product groups, while regression analysis indicates that the first item — or rather its inverse, the cost of holding stock — is capable of explaining much of the variation in margin between Census trades, if perishable food businesses are left out of account. As far as the distributors of our six groups are concerned, other considerations appear to be of importance in a number of cases, particularly in respect of 'Radio and electrical goods' and 'Furniture' retailers, for which repair, installation and transport costs may well be significant. This, however, does not necessarily imply that the direction of causation runs from costs to margins; indeed under a regime of r.p.m. and conventional margins, it is perhaps more plausible to suppose that the margin available determines the total costs of distribution rather than the reverse, through the entry and exit of retail shops and wholesale warehouses.

---

1   About 20 per cent according to *Nielsen Researcher*, March–April, 1969. This represented about 40 per cent of the sales made by independent grocery outlets.

XV
Structural Changes in Manufacturing and Retailing, R.p.m. and S.E.T.

In previous chapters we have presented an analysis of the pattern of distribution and of retail and wholesale margins prevailing in 1965 for the six commodity groups chosen for study. We have seen that the method of distributing the products varied both between and within the groups. Thus wholesalers accounted for about half of the domestic sales of confectionery and pharmaceuticals, but for between a quarter and a third of those of carpets and domestic appliances. At the same time, significant differences were seen to exist, for example, between the distribution of chocolate and sugar confectionery and small and major electrical appliances. While a good many factors underlie such variations, to a large extent they seem to be related to the structural features of the manufacturers and retailers concerned and to the nature of the product in question.

1. Factors underlying Changes in the Distributive Process
The remainder of the study is concerned with the changes in the distribution process that have occurred since 1965. We would clearly expect these to be influenced by any long-term tendencies to structural change which were evident before 1965, and which are likely to have continued to operate during the period under consideration. These include, for example, the increasing proportion of retail sales made by multiple organisations which was evident between 1957 and 1966, and which we discussed in some detail in the first part of the study. In addition, it is likely that the progressive abolition of r.p.m., following the Resale Prices Act of 1964, and the imposition of S.E.T., from September, 1966, also had some influence on developments. We would expect both these factors to affect the pattern of retailing and the methods of distribution through their impact on the prices and margins of different traders. However it is likely that any structural changes at the retail level, whether consequent upon these two factors or not, will tend to be reflected in the pricing policy pursued by manufacturers and in the discounts given to trade customers. This might in turn influence the relative prices of distributors and thus further affect the pattern of distribution. Consequently it is possible for a cumulative process to be initiated. For example, the abolition of r.p.m. may have enabled multiple retail organisations to reduce their prices relative to other traders and thereby to gain a larger share of a particular market. The associated improvement in their bargaining position *vis à vis* manufacturers might have produced a reduction in their buying terms and thus further strengthened their competitive position against other retailers. The latter would tend to be the customers of wholesalers, so that the proportion of sales distributed through the traders is likely to have declined. At the

Table XV.1   *Changes in Enterprises, Output and Concentration, 1958 to 1963*

| Census Industry | % change in number of enterprises 1958 to 1963 | % change in volume of gross output 1958 to 1963[a] | Percentage of Output produced by the largest enterprises: | | | |
			1958 No of units	% Output	1963 No. of units	% Output
Tobacco	−32·6	7·8	10	98·3	6	99·1
Confectionery	−31·6	−4·5	8	49·6	8	65·1
Domestic Electrical Appliances	36·6	84·0	6	57·5	8	60·0
Carpets	4·4	39·0	4	31·1	4	26·9
Pharmaceutical Preparations	−10·6	48·6	4	26·4	4	24·9
Tools and Implements	−24·8	0·1	5	29·0[b]	5	33·8[b]

Source: Census of Production, 1958 and 1963
Notes:
a The change in the value of gross output between 1958 and 1963, deflated by the appropriate wholesale price indices, published in the *Annual Abstract of Statistics*. In the case of domestic electrical appliances, we have estimated the change to exclude refrigerators, which are not included in the Census industry.
b The percentage of sales made by the five largest enterprises as shown in Table XV.2.

same time the imposition of S.EtT. may have weakened the ability of wholesalers to compete with manufacturers, as it effectively discriminated in favour of the latter performing wholesale functions, and may therefore have caused a further decline in their share of trade. On the other hand, it is possible that the abolition of r.p.m. combined with the introduction of S.E.T. represented an inducement to wholesalers to increase their efficiency in order to maintain their turnover. A similar incentive may also have applied at the retail level, particularly in respect of independent traders.

Our intention is to consider these influences in turn before looking at the evidence which we have on the changes that have occurred in the pattern of distribution and in the level and composition of distributive margins.

2. Structural Changes, Manufacturing

We begin by trying to identify any long-term changes in the structural characteristics of the manufacturers of the six commodity groups. There is some difficulty here as there is a lack of suitable census data for the period after 1963 and the only statistics which are directly comparable with 1963 relate to the situation in 1958. Table XV.1 shows the change in the number of enterprises and in the volume of gross output between these two years for the Census industries included in Table XII.1 above; it also indicates the change in the importance of the largest enterprises over this period.

The only trade to experience any significant rise in the number of participant companies between 1958 and 1963 was Domestic Electrical Appliances, the output of which grew at a far greater rate over the five years than that of the other industries covered. In Tobacco, Confectionery and Tools and implements, the number of enterprises fell substantially — in the former two by over 30 per cent, or at an

Table XV.2 *Concentration of Sales of Selected Commodities, 1958 and 1963*

Census Product Group	Five-firm concentration ratio[a]		No. of enterprises in 1958 with same ratio as in 1963
	1958	1963	
Sugar confectionery	22·7	35·9	10
Washing machines	70·4	85·2	7
Tools and implements	29·0	33·8	7
Domestic and industrial holloware	25·2	33·5	9
Woven carpets	41·2	42·3	6
Tufted carpets	72·0	50·7	less than 5
Other carpets	65·6	55·0	less than 5
Pharmaceutical preparations[b]	29·1	29·2	6

Source: Census of Production, 1963
Notes:
a The five-firm concentration ratio represents the percentage of domestically produced sales (excluding those produced by firms employing less than 25) controlled by the five enterprises with the largest sales of the product concerned.
b Excludes surgical and medical dressings and some other products included in the Census industry of Table XV.1

annual rate of almost six per cent — while output remained fairly constant. Carpets and Pharmaceutical Preparations showed similar rises in output, but whereas the number of enterprises increased in the former, in the latter it declined by almost 11 per cent.

The second part of the table indicates that the variation between the trades in the change in concentration over the period, was related in some degree to the change in output. Thus Confectionery and Tools and implements experienced increases in the importance of the largest concerns, significantly so in the former case, while in the case of Carpets and Pharmaceuticals, the proportion of output produced by the largest four enterprises decreased slightly and in the case of Domestic Electrical Appliances, it is almost certain that the degree of concentration was lower in 1963 than in 1958. Tobacco also conforms to this pattern, the number of units in the largest size-class falling from ten to six between the two years, with little decrease in the percentage of output produced. In fact, by 1958, virtually the whole of the domestic tobacco market was divided between two manufacturers, Imperial Tobacco and Gallaher (these accounted for 94 per cent of U.K. sales in that year)[1] and by 1963 most of the remaining companies were under common control (of Carreras).

Turning to the Census information on changes in the sales concentration of products included within our groups, Table XV.2 presents the five-firm concentration ratios in 1958 and 1963 for those commodities on which details are given for both years. As can be seen the market share of the five largest enterprises increased substantially in respect of sugar confectionery, washing machines and holloware, and decreased substantially in respect of tufted and other carpets. For the other products included little significant change is evident. The picture revealed by the table is largely consistent with that shown in Table XV.1, although the overall

1 Monopolies Commission, *Report on the Supply of Cigarettes and Tobacco, etc.*, p. 56.

179

decline in the concentration of domestic electrical appliance production conceals a marked increase in respect of washing machines at least, while large differences are apparent within the carpet group. In the former case, the almost continual development of new products and refinements to old was probably a major factor underlying the divergence between the aggregate change and that for particular appliances. In the latter case, the figures reflect the extremely rapid growth of tufted sales over this period at the expense of those of woven carpeting, which led to new entry and the diversification of established firms into tufted production.[1]

The Census of Production for 1968 does not at the time of writing provide the information necessary to assess the size-structure of the industries in that year, but it does give an indication of the changes in output and in the number of enterprises between 1963 and 1968.[2] In the case of Tobacco and Confectionery the volume of sales remained much the same over the period and the number of enterprises fell by 21 per cent and 26 per cent respectively, while in the case of Carpets and Pharmaceuticals sales increased by about 50 per cent with little change in the number of companies. With regard to domestic electrical appliances, sales rose by approximately 28 per cent in volume terms and the number of enterprises expanded by almost 16 per cent — although if plants employing less than 25 are excluded, the number declined slightly.

Although it is not possible to come to any firm conclusions as to the change in the importance of the largest concerns since 1963, the relationship between output changes and the change in concentration noted above does enable us to say something about likely developments, if considered along with the other relevant information available. Thus we know that the three major tobacco manufacturers have continued to account for virtually all of domestic market tobacco sales, with little significant alteration in their respective market shares.

With regard to confectionery, the tendency towards increasing concentration in production has continued. There has been a high degree of merger activity involving the larger concerns (culminating in 1969 with the Rowntree–Mackintosh merger), which has affected the production of sugar confectionery in particular — the chocolate market being highly concentrated, as we have noted. As a result, by 1967 the four largest manufacturers were responsible for about 26 per cent of sugar confectionery sales and the largest ten for 46 per cent, whereas the relevant proportions in 1961 had been 18 per cent and 36 per cent respectively.[3] However there is some evidence that the rate of decline in the number of manufacturers has decreased since 1968, probably partly as a consequence of an upward trend in sugar confectionery sales after a long period of decline. Thus between March 1969 and March 1971, the number of individual firms fell by less than two per cent in both

1 The Census shows a four-fold increase both in tufted sales and the number of enterprises specialising in its production over the period 1958 to 1963, while woven carpet sales and the number of enterprises in this area both declined.

2 There were some minor changes in the S.I.C. between the two years, so that the 'industries' in 1968 do not exactly correspond with those of 1963. However, the changes between 1963 and 1968 on the 1968 classification are given.

3 N.B.P.I. Report No. 75, *Costs and Prices of the Chocolate and Sugar Confectionery Industry*, Appendix B.

years, whereas the annual average rate of decline was about five per cent over the previous six-year period.[1]

The market for domestic electrical appliances, although growing over the long-term, has been subject to quite severe periodic declines, particularly since 1963. Indeed sales in 1967 were about ten per cent lower than they had been in 1963, although there has been some increase since then. Moreover sales of certain appliances have shown much wider fluctuations than the total; the domestic output of washing machines, for example, fell by almost 50 per cent between 1963 and 1967. This type of market situation may of itself have produced a tendency towards increasing concentration, but it is difficult to discuss the manufacture of domestic appliances in isolation. A number of the larger concerns in particular have always been engaged in the production of a wide range of electrical engineering products, which in some cases constituted a much greater part of output than domestic appliances. Consequently, while it is true that mergers have been extremely important in this trade, especially since 1966, the increasing concentration of the production of appliances, which has undoubtedly occurred, has been largely incidental to the rationalisation of the heavy electrical industry. We are here thinking in terms primarily of the G.E.C. acquisition of A.E.I. in 1967 and the subsequent merger of the enlarged group with English Electric in 1968. On the other hand, British Domestic Appliances was formed in 1966 with the specific object of merging the domestic appliance interests of A.E.I. and E.M.I. However irrespective of the reasons underlying the mergers that have taken place, the result is that a very small number of companies have come to dominate the market for the most important types of appliance. In addition, there is evidence of a recent tendency towards vertical integration, through the acquisition of retail groups (and whole-salers) on the part of a few major manufacturers.

The large rise in carpet sales since 1963 has almost entirely been a result of the rapid expansion of tufted production, which more than doubled between 1963 and 1970. By contrast, the output of woven carpeting declined by about ten per cent over the same period. These two tendencies have been associated with the increasing diversification of traditional carpet manufacturers into tufted production and subsequently with the manifestation of excess capacity in this market. Again it is probable that concentration has tended to increase as a result of the mergers that have occurred.

There is less evidence of increasing concentration in the case of pharmaceuticals, the output of which has also expanded substantially since 1963. Nevertheless there are a few examples of important mergers during this period, such as the Glaxo acquisition of B.D.H.

3. Structural Changes, Retailing

The structural changes occurring in retailing between 1957 and 1966 were considered in some detail in the first part of this study. However, it is worth re-examining briefly the main developments for those kinds of business specialising in the sale of our six commodity groups. Table XIV.3 shows the change in the number of shops, volume of turnover and share of multiple organisations for these categories and for

---

1   See Cocoa, Chocolate and Confectionery Alliance, Annual Reports.

Table XV.3 Changes in Establishments, Turnover and Multiples: 1957 to 1966

Kind of Business	% Change in Establishments			% Change in Volume of Turnover[a]			Multiples: % Point Change in % of Establishments			Multiples: % Point Change in % of Turnover		
	1957–1961	1961–1966	1957–1966	1957–1961	1961–1966	1957–1966	1957–1961	1961–1966	1957–1966	1957–1961	1961–1966	1957–1966
C.T.N.'s	−8·8	−9·7	−17·7	1·5	2·9	4·5	0	1·6	1·6	0·5	2·5	3·0
Radio & Electrical[b]	22·8	1·1	24·1	28·6	22·6	57·7	6·2	3·7	9·9	8·8	5·7	14·5
(Electricity Board Showrooms)	(6·0)	(−0·1)	(88·3)	(19·0)	(124·8)							
Hardware	9·9	2·8	13·0	21·5	19·2	44·8	1·2	0·5	1·7	−0·4	0·4	0
Furniture and Allied[c]	7·7	18·4	27·5	24·4	22·7	52·5	1·4	1·7	3·1	−2·2	3·4	1·0
Chemists	0·9	−0·8	0·1	21·3	22·7	48·9	0·1	0·5	0·6	1·6	1·2	2·8
Total Retail Trade	−0·5	−7·0	−7·5	13·0	8·7	22·8	1·6	2·2	3·8	4·1	5·3	9·4

Source: Census of Distribution: 1961 and 1966

Notes:

a Turnover deflated by price indices supplied by the Board of Trade.

b The changes in the multiple share of turnover and establishments are estimated to allow for the inclusion of television hire shops in 1957 and 1961.

c The changes in the multiple share are estimated to allow for the transference of soft furnishings shops from this category in 1966.

182

the sector as a whole, over this period (and over two sub-periods). In addition the corresponding changes in the number of Electricity Board showrooms and in their volume of turnover (excluding receipts from repair work) are shown in brackets. Thus the growth in sales of the three durable goods kinds of business and chemists shops, at an annual rate of over four per cent, was significantly higher than the average for all retailers. However whereas the number of outlets of the former three trades (excluding Electricity showrooms) also increased substantially, the number of chemist shops remained constant over the period. Correspondingly the average sales-size of the latter increased markedly — by almost 50 per cent, in comparison with a rise of around 25 per cent for the three durable goods trades and C.T.N.'s, which in turn was less than the sector average. By contrast with the other specialist retailers included in the table, the volume of sales of C.T.N.'s rose at an annual rate of less than half of one per cent over the nine years; this was associated with a decline in the number of outlets of almost 18 per cent.

The second part of the table shows the respective changes in the importance of multiple organisations. In the case of four of the five kinds of business, the multiple share of turnover increased by three percentage points or less between 1957 and 1966, in sharp contrast to the rise of over nine percentage points for the sector as a whole. Indeed their share of Hardware sales remained unchanged over the period (at about 12 per cent), although it increased slightly between 1961 and 1966. Similarly there was a tendency for multiples to take a larger proportion of the sales of C.T.N.'s and Furniture shops over the later years of the period, particularly in the case of the latter. Thus for this trade, the multiple share declined by two percentage points between 1957 and 1961, but rose by over three percentage points over the subsequent five years.

In the case of Radio and electrical goods shops, multiples increased their proportion of turnover from an estimated figure of less than 13 per cent in 1957 to 27 per cent in 1966. This represents a trebling of the volume of sales. Moreover the sales of Electricity Board showrooms more than doubled over the period, although almost all of the increase came in the first four years, and between 1961 and 1966 the rise in their turnover was similar to that of Radio and electrical goods retailers.

We can therefore conclude that, for these kinds of business, with the exception of electrical goods retailers, there is less evidence of the increasing concentration of sales in multiple organisations which is such a marked feature of the sector as a whole. But this, of course, gives us only part of the picture. As was made clear in Chapter XII, specialist retailers account for only part of the sale of the six commodity groups, and it is consequently of some significance to consider the change over the period in their sales as against the change in those made by other types of outlet. Details contained in the Census of Distribution provide an indication of this, although the definition of product groups corresponds only approximately to our classification. Moreover the Census information is confined to retail shops (and Mail-Order companies), and we can make only general observations on the change in the proportion of sales made outside the retail sector as defined. With the exception of tobacco, however, this proportion tends to be small, as we have seen.

Table XV.4 shows the percentage distribution of the sales of the relevant Census

Table XV.4 Percentage Distribution of Commodity Sales between Kinds of Retail Business, 1957, 1961 and 1966

Commodity Group	Specialist Retailers[a]			Grocery and Food Stores			Department and Variety[b]			General Mail-Order			Co-ops			Other Shops		
	1957	1961	1966	1957	1961	1966	1957	1961	1966	1957	1961	1966	1957	1961	1966	1957	1961	1966
Cigarettes, tobacco	61	54	60	24	28	26							14	15	12	1	3	2
Confectionery, ice cream[c]	61	54	55	25	32	30							4	5	5	10	9	8
Electrical appliances and supplies	65	64	65				(17)	13	12	n.a.	4	9	8	8	6	10	11	8
General ironmongery[d]	58	54	61	6	5	3	(25)	21	18*	n.a.	6	9	6	6	4	5	8	5
Floorcoverings	54	53	63				(30)	26	17*	n.a.	6	6*	9	9	7	7	6	7
Drugs, toilet preparations	78	75	78	2	4	4	11	12	9				8	9	7	1	1	2

Source: Census of Distribution 1957, 1961, 1966.

Notes: All the figures include a certain amount of estimation as for 1957 and 1966 in particular they are based on only a sample of traders.

a Specialist retailers include Electricity Board showrooms in the case of electrical appliances and supplies; these accounted for 25 per cent of the retail sales of this commodity group in 1957, and for about 27 per cent and 25 per cent in 1961 and 1966 respectively.

b Includes General Mail-Order Houses in 1957.

c Soft drinks are included in 1966 but not in 1957 and 1961.

d Household cleaning materials are included in 1957 and 1961, but not in 1966. In all three years the group includes china and glassware and builders' and decorators' supplies as well as general ironmongery and household appliances.

* We have partially estimated these percentages as the Census withheld one of the relevant figures owing to the danger of disclosure.

groups between kinds of retail business in 1957, 1961 and 1966.[1] There are certain difficulties involved in a direct comparison of the figures for the three years, which are explained in the notes to the table. Specifically there were some minor changes made in the classification of product groups between Censuses, but more importantly the figures particularly for 1957 and 1966, are derived from only a sample of retailers. However despite these qualifications it does seem that there was no significant diversion of trade away from specialist shops over the period, with the possible exception of the confectionery group, for which the specialist share fell from 61 per cent to 55 per cent (although there was some change in the classification). Indeed in the case of three of the groups, the proportion of retail sector sales sold by specialist retailers was the same, or almost the same, in 1966 as it had been in 1957. In the case of the other two groups, this percentage increased over the period, although for general ironmongery the exclusion of household cleaning materials in 1966 is likely to have contributed to the rise. Indeed our impression is that the fall between 1957 and 1961 is much more representative of the trend for this group.[2] No such bias exists for floorcoverings, the specialist share of the sales of which increased from 54 per cent to 63 per cent between 1957 and 1966, the entire rise apparently coming in the last five years of the period.[3] However because of the sampling problems we would hesitate to attach too much significance to the relative magnitude of the percentage in 1961 as compared with the 1957 and 1966 figures.

The decline in the proportion of confectionery sales made by specialist retailers over the period corresponds with an increase in those made by grocery stores, including coops in this category. On the other hand these have apparently not increased their share of tobacco sales, although within this kind of business there is evidence of some diversion of sales from coops to other grocery stores. For the non-durable goods covered, department and variety stores, including coops, almost certainly experienced a reduction in their share of trade, while General Mail-Order Houses clearly increased their proportion of electrical appliance sales and possibly those of hardware. Again coops appear to have lost some trade to other retailers. These latter two tendencies can be regarded as a reflection of the comparative growth of these two forms of organisation between 1957 and 1966. Thus whereas the turnover of Mail-Order Houses increased by almost 250 per cent (in comparison with a rise of 48 per cent for 'traditional' retailing as a whole), the turnover of co-operative societies rose by only 12 per cent.

1 Because the composition of the Census groups differs from that of our groups, the percentage shown for 1966 only correspond approximately to the estimates which we made on the distribution of total sales between types of outlet in Table XII.3.

2 This is supported by information contained in Distributive Trades E.D.C., *Voluntary Group Trading, 6 Case Studies*. H.M.S.O., 1971, p. 4. Although this is rather confusing and the estimates should clearly not be taken at their face value, it does nevertheless appear that there was a large rise in mail-order sales of hardware and some increase in those of variety stores between 1961 and 1966. In addition, mention should also be made of the expansion of trading stamp and gift catelogue companies outside the area of retail sales as such.

3 For this group, the bias if anything operates in the opposite direction. Specialist retailers in this case refer to the 'Furniture and allied' kind of business and 'Soft furnishings shops' were excluded from this category in 1966 whereas they had been included in the two previous Censuses. If these sold any floorcoverings at all, this would clearly have involved a reduction in the specialist percentage shown in the table between 1961 and 1966.

Despite the problems of directly comparing the figures for the three years, there was an apparent tendency for specialists to gain a *higher* percentage of the retail market between 1961 and 1966 for two of the six groups (tobacco and carpets), while their share in respect of the other four groups was probably much the same in each of the three years.

One odd feature to emerge from Table XV.4 is that Electricity Board showrooms do not appear to have increased their share of electrical appliance sales, which seems to be at variance with what we have seen from Table XV.3 above. There we estimated that the volume of their turnover had more than doubled between 1957 and 1966, in comparison with the rise of less than 60 per cent experienced by Radio and electrical goods shops. We would therefore have expected to find a significant diversion of electrical appliance sales from the latter to the former over this period. It is difficult to reconcile the movements shown by the two tables. One possible explanation is that there was a change in the composition of the turnover of the two types of outlet, which would tend to conceal the size of the increase in the sales of appliances. For example, it is likely that the receipts of Radio and electrical goods retailers from repair and maintenance work became less important over the period, as a result of manufacturers assuming more responsibility for after-sales service. Alternatively, our use of the same price index to deflate the rise in the value of turnover of the two types of outlet may be somewhat less than justified, insofar as there are marked differences in the composition of turnover of the two. Thus, as we have mentioned, Electricity Boards tend to concentrate much more heavily on the major appliance market than do other shops. However it is unlikely that these two points provide the full explanation for the difference, and we are left with the impression that the figure shown in Table XV.4 for the percentage of appliance sales made by Electricity Boards in 1966 is perhaps an underestimate of the true proportion.

As we have said Table XV.4 refers only to the sales taking place within the retail sector, as defined by the Census of Distribution, and the question arises as to the relative change in the sales made by other outlets. In fact a negligible proportion of the consumer sales of hardware, floorcoverings and pharmaceuticals actually occurred outside the retail sector, although in the case of hardware account should be taken of the substantial increase in the importance of 'non-monetary' sales, through such organisations as trading stamp companies and gift catelogue operators. With regard to the other three commodity groups, it is unlikely that there were any significant changes over this period in the share of other outlets, although their tobacco and confectionery sales may have shown some increase relative to those of retail shops.

In summary, therefore, we can conclude that, with the exception of domestic electrical appliances, there is little evidence for any marked tendency towards the sales of the groups becoming more concentrated among large retail organisations in the years before 1965, although at the same time the average size of outlet increased significantly in each case and multiples classified to non-specialist trades − grocery in particular − increased their market share significantly.

4. Resale Price Maintenance

The Resale Prices Act was passed in 1964 and implemented over the period 1965 to

1970,[1] during which time r.p.m. was progressively prohibited on all classes of product, with the exception of books and pharmaceuticals. Some of the likely consequences of this move were discussed in the introduction to this part of the study; our *a priori* expectations are considered more fully in this section.[2]

The inherent characteristic of r.p.m. is, of course, that distributors are prevented from determining the prices of the goods which they sell, but have to accept the prices as specified by manufacturers. The two main propositions stemming from this are that distributive margins and the level of services provided by the distribution sector both tend to be higher than if there were no restriction to price competition. Thus final consumers (or the customers of wholesalers where relevant) have no choice on the price which they pay for any particular commodity, except, of course, insofar as this differs between producers, and are able to choose only between different amounts, or types, of service offered with the sale of the product. In other words, they are unable to exercise their potential preference for a lower price coupled with less service, or indeed, for the higher level of service which a higher price might allow. The other side of the coin is that the distribution sector as a whole is prevented from catering for such preferences.[3] Moreover prices cannot reflect variations in efficiency between distributors, or in their location — the price of a commodity will be the same in the outer reaches of Scotland as in London even though transport costs and the rate of stock turn may vary enormously. This may be fine from the equity point of view, but it may have the effect of limiting the provision of distributive services in the remoter parts of the country.[4]

Consequently, the only area of competition open to distributors is the service provided with the product sold, and this represents the only means through which the more efficient organisations can gain a larger share of the market. While the higher rate of profit earned by these may finance their growth, such growth is likely to be associated with the expansion of distribution facilities, such as an increase in the number of shops and warehouses. At the same time the ban on price competition restricts their ability to attract new custom and may hence protect the market position of less efficient businesses. One of the implications of r.p.m. is therefore the existence of more retail outlets and wholesale depots than if prices were free to vary between traders; in particular, small shops will tend to benefit

1 Implemented in the sense that all classes of product registered under the terms of the Act were considered by the Registrar of Restrictive Practices over this period and were ordered to be removed, with the exception of pharmaceuticals.

2 The likely effects of this measure on productivity were considered in Chapter II.

3 Although it may be possible to meet a demand for more service by charging for services separately from the product itself, the ability to do this is limited by the nature of the distributive function. It is difficult, for example, for a shop to levy a separate charge for the time spent by an assistant on advising a customer on his purchase.

4 To the extent that the retail price specified by manufacturers enables a commodity to be supplied in the remoter areas as well as in the more populous regions, there is an element of subsidy from the inhabitants of the latter to those of the former. If this is desirable, which it might well be, it does not necessarily follow that such a mechanism is the most efficient way of achieving the transfer. To make the subsidy explicit would at least focus attention, and discussion, on its size and specific incidence. This type of cross-subsidation is, of course, not only inherent in r.p.m., but also applies to many retail chains which adopt a centralised pricing policy.

from competition among wholesalers, through their access to relatively extensive delivery and credit facilities.

This argument loses none of its validity even if manufacturers consciously assess the operating costs involved in the distribution of their goods and set resale prices accordingly. The calculation has to be based on averages and the traders of above average efficiency therefore earn 'excess' gross profits.

The expectation is therefore that the removal of r.p.m. would tend to lead to the following consequences: a decrease in the services offered by the distribution sector as a whole, including a reduction in the number of retail outlets and wholesale warehouses; a switch in sales towards the more efficient traders and hence an overall increase in the productivity of the distributive trades; a reduction in the average price paid for particular commodities, as traders exercise their option of substituting lower selling prices for part of the service provided; and a fall in the average gross margin earned by distributors, as a result of the former tendency and the decline in less efficient traders. Moreover the end of r.p.m. would be likely to encourage the development of new methods of selling which are based on distributors offering customers lower prices in return for less service in certain areas of their operation. Specifically, we would expect self-service to become more important at both the retail and wholesale levels.

However the effects may not be confined to the distributive trades. Price competition at the retail and wholesale level is almost certain to lead to increased pressure on suppliers for additional discounts, both to maintain net margins and to enable more attractive price reductions to be offered. At the same time, the possible diversion of trade towards the larger distributors means that such pressure becomes more difficult to resist. In other words, the end of r.p.m. is likely to be associated with an improvement in the bargaining position of the larger distributors vis à vis manufacturers, and with selective reductions in the latters' prices. For this reason it becomes more difficult for producers to maintain any price agreement among themselves. This difficulty is further compounded if the increase in competition at the distributive level leads to greater fluctuations in the sales of individual traders, as this carries similar implications for the market shares of individual manufacturers. Thus any decline in the stability of market shares is likely to reduce the willingness of manufacturers to abide by a common price policy.[1]

It therefore follows that the ban on r.p.m. may increase the extent of price competition among manufacturers. On the other hand any movement in this direction may stimulate an increase in merger activity, as might any shift in the balance of power towards distributors.

The above discussion has been conducted in terms of general tendencies. There are a good many reasons, however, for supposing that the aftermath of the breakdown of r.p.m. would not be uniform as between commodity groups, and indeed, that it would vary basically according to how important a restriction on price competition the enforcement of resale prices had actually represented. Thus merely because a formal constraint exists to prevent distributors from competing in terms of price, this does not necessarily imply that they would do so if no restriction were

1 Reference was made to these two points by the Monopolies Commission in its reports on dental goods and cigarettes and tobacco, for example.

188

enforced. The realisation and significance of the tendencies noted above therefore depend crucially, as far as any particular commodity group is concerned, upon the strength of the underlying competitive forces in its distribution. This, of course, is difficult to discern directly, but we expect it to bear a close relationship to such factors as the nature of the product and the structural characteristics of the manufacturers and retailers in question. More precisely, the relevant considerations are likely to include the unit price of the good, the extent of brand advertising, the state of the market, the degree of concentration in production and distribution, and the number of participating concerns and the differences in their size. These are the factors which also determine, in large measure, the method of distribution prevailing and which we have discussed in some detail with regard to the six commodity groups selected for study. The analysis of previous chapters therefore provides an indication of the likely effects of the abolition of r.p.m. in respect of these products.

5. The Selective Employment Tax

S.E.T. was introduced in September, 1966, at the rate of 25 shillings per full-time male employee and was increased by 50 per cent in September, 1968 and by a further 28 per cent in July, 1969; following the change of government in 1970, the rate was halved in July, 1971 and the tax finally abolished in April, 1973 with the advent of V.A.T.

The possible effects of the tax on labour productivity were discussed in some detail in the first part of the study,[1] and as we noted there, it is extremely difficult to distinguish such effects from those of the abolition of r.p.m. In particular, the efforts of distributors to restore their net profits, which are reduced as a result of the increase in labour costs associated with S.E.T., are likely to lead to a rise in the volume of sales per person engaged, but possibly also to a decline in the amount of service provided with sales. Indeed these two consequences are almost impossible to separate as most sources of reduction in labour per unit of turnover, including the introduction of new methods of selling, can be looked upon as decreasing service, if an appropriate definition of this concept is adopted. Similarly, the reduction in available profits may force marginal shops out of business and discourage new entry, thus producing a gain in labour productivity, as conventionally measured, by concentrating sales on fewer shops, but this can equally be regarded as reducing the service supplied by the sector, if the total number of outlets are included as an element of retail service. It is clear that these features are the same as those which we would expect to observe following the ending of r.p.m., and as S.E.T. was imposed during the same period as the Resale Prices Act took effect, there is no unambiguous way of isolating the consequences of the two measures.

However it is to be expected that the efforts on the part of distributors to restore their net profits following the introduction of S.E.T., may be channelled into increasing revenue, and it is therefore likely that gross margins, if anything, would rise rather than fall, as expected on the ending of r.p.m. The ability of distributors to follow this course of action is likely to vary a good deal between them. For example, we might expect the larger traders to be in a better bargaining position to

1 See Chapter II.

improve their buying terms than smaller concerns, and in this sense the tax can be regarded as discriminating in favour of the former. In addition, of course, much depends on the extent of competition and the pricing policy pursued by distributors.

The aspect of S.E.T. which is perhaps of most relevance to recent changes in the pattern of distribution arises from the anomalous treatment of wholesalers *vis à vis* manufacturers. The operation of the tax effectively means that the distribution of goods is taxed when undertaken by a wholesaler, whereas it is not subject to tax when carried out by the manufacturer, or even by the manufacturers' own wholesale organisation in certain instances. The latter is true as long as the sales of the organisation consist of more than 50 per cent of the manufacturer's own goods, and as long as more than 50 per cent of the employees are engaged in 'not non-qualifying' activities. The majority of manufacturing companies appear to have been able to satisfy this condition.[1]

The implication of this is that wholesalers are placed at a disadvantage when competing with manufacturers, in the sense that the price-service package which they are able to offer retail customers is likely to deteriorate relative to that offered by the latter. Thus, as described above, the initial incidence of S.E.T. is on wholesalers' net profits, which implies, for those at the margin, that either revenue has to be increased or operating costs reduced by the amount of the tax, if they are to remain in business. Either course of action is likely to weaken their competitive position *vis à vis* manufacturers, as the former tends to involve an increase in price (if they are unable to improve their buying terms), and the latter a reduction in their services to retailers, *unless* manufacturers take compensatory action. Equally any attempt made by intra-marginal (or the more efficient) traders to restore their net profits would tend to result in a similar deterioration in their competitive position. There is therefore likely to be some diversion of trade from wholesalers to manufacturers, although, at the same time, we would expect the relatively efficient wholesalers to gain sales from the less efficient. However any trade diverted in the latter direction is likely to be the less profitable business, otherwise it would probably have gone to manufacturers. In other words, there may be a tendency for wholesale sales to large retailers to decline. On the other hand, insofar as the sales of the traders remaining in business increase on average, they may be able to improve their buying terms, or alternatively they may benefit from any economies of scale realised.

It follows from the above paragraph that the maintenance of the wholesale share of trade depends in large measure on the action taken by manufacturers. If the wholesale share is not to decline, manufacturers need to either increase the difference between their prices to wholesalers and those to retailers, or reduce their services to retailers, or take on part of the function previously performed by wholesalers (thus reducing their operating costs) — all sufficiently to offset the effects of the tax. It is therefore not sufficient for manufacturers to adopt a passive role and to pursue the same policy with regard to these variables as before S.E.T. was introduced.

It is clear that the overall efficiency of the distribution system may be reduced by the anomalous treatment of wholesalers. S.E.T. implies that the private

1 W.B. Reddaway, *Effects of the Selective Employment Tax, First Report*, p. 159.

opportunity costs of distribution do not equal the social opportunity costs, and therefore that the least-cost method of transporting goods from factory to final consumer would not be employed. But it is hardly conceivable that the most efficient method obtained before the tax was imposed, so that there is some difficulty in coming to any conclusion, not only on the magnitude of the change but even on the direction. For example the introduction of S.E.T. may have 'jolted' manufacturers into reassessing their policy on distribution and possibly into making improvements, as a result, for instance, of the increased pressure applied by distributors for better terms to offset the tax burden. Moreover manufacturers may have discovered that there were economies of scale to be realised in the operation of their own distribution organisations as the volume of goods handled increased. These possible effects should of course be considered together with the likely increase in the efficiency of wholesalers and the demise of marginal traders, in order to make fully clear the problem of coming to any sort of conclusion on this matter.

As in the case of the breakdown of r.p.m., the imposition of S.E.T. is very unlikely to have had uniform effects across the economy. The considerations which we would expect to be important in determining its precise influence in particular instances, include the extent of competition within both the retail and wholesale trades, the nature of competition between manufacturers and wholesalers and the behavioural norms applying with regard to the pricing policy pursued. Again the discussion of previous chapters has provided some insight into such factors in respect of the six commodity groups with which the study is directly concerned.

6. Summary

It is likely that any changes in the structure of the manufacturing and retail sectors, the abolition of r.p.m. and the imposition of S.E.T. were important factors underlying changes in the distributive process in the years after 1965. With regard to the former, there is a lack of official statistics for this period and to some extent we are obliged to rely on tendencies that were evident before 1965. In respect of manufacturing, it would appear that the confectionery trade has shown the most significant long-term change, in the form of a tendency for the degree of concentration to increase and the number of firms to decline. In the case of domestic electrical appliances, it is almost certain that the degree of concentration in production increased markedly after 1965, despite the tendency for the number of firms to expand, and it is probable that there was also some increase with respect to carpets, despite the decrease between 1958 and 1963. For the other groups, there is little evidence of any significant change.

In respect of retailing, there was a tendency for the number of specialist electrical appliance, hardware and carpet shops to increase and for the number of C.T.N.'s to decline, while the market share of specialist multiples remained almost constant in each case, apart from electrical appliances, in the period prior to 1965. Moreover no tendency is discernible for specialist retailers to lose sales to more general stores in this period, and in the case of carpets in particular they seem to have gained trade from the latter. With respect to the change in importance of multiple organisations, it is clear that our group is not representative of retail sales as a whole, the proportion of which sold by multiples increased from a quarter to over a third between 1957 and 1966 as we saw in Part I of the study.

The progressive breakdown of r.p.m. following the 1964 Resale Prices Act is likely, on *a priori* grounds, to have been associated with an increase in price competition among distributors, a reduction in the level of distributive margin and a decline in the amount of service provided with sales. These may have led in turn to a decrease in the number of retail outlets and wholesale warehouses, a shift of business towards the more efficient traders, the more rapid development of new methods of operation and an improvement in the bargaining position of distributors *vis à vis* manufacturers. Such effects, however, are likely to vary in their incidence as between commodity groups according to the strength of underlying competitive forces, which may be reflected in the nature of the product and the conditions of its manufacture and distribution.

The imposition of S.E.T. would be expected to have had similar repercussions as the end of r.p.m., inasmuch as it may have resulted in a decline in service, the introduction of new methods of selling and fewer shops and warehouses. The discrimination of the tax against wholesalers may have led to changes in the method of distribution, unless manufacturers improved their terms to wholesalers relative to those on direct sales to retailers. Again the actual effect of the measure on our sample of products is likely to depend in some degree on those features discussed in connection with the pattern of distribution prevailing in 1965.

XVI
Changes in Retail Prices and Distributive Margins

Having discussed the factors likely to have influenced the distributive process in the period since 1965, we turn to the evidence which we have on the developments that have occurred. In this chapter, we are concerned with the changes in the pricing policy pursued by the distributors of the six groups and in the margins allowed by the manufacturers. The impact of the abolition of r.p.m. on these is examined, together with the influence of S.E.T. and other factors. In the following chapter, we look at the changes that have taken place in the method by which the six categories of consumer good are distributed. These are considered in the light of our discussion here and in relation to the longer-term structural changes which were outlined earlier.

The adoption of this particular order of exposition should not be held to imply that the direction of causation runs entirely from changes in prices and margins to changes in the pattern of distribution. As we have intimated earlier, there is likely to be a considerable degree of interaction between the various elements. We discuss events in this order principally because both the ending of r.p.m. and the imposition of S.E.T. affect the pattern of distribution through their impact on prices and margins. This is not to say the process stops there or that these factors necessarily represent the main influence on the distributive process in the period since 1965. Thus the 'second round' effects − of changes in the pattern of distribution on prices and margins − may be equally as significant as the 'first round' effects (if not more so), while the growth of large retail organisations, although possibly facilitated by the abolition of r.p.m., has almost certainly had the most important bearing on the discount policy of manufacturers over this period.

1. Price Competition at the Retail Level since the Abolition of R.p.m.
As would be expected from our discussion in the previous chapter, there has been a good deal of variation in the extent of price competition between product groups following the ban on r.p.m. To begin with an overall view, however, where the practice of maintaining resale prices has been prohibited, manufacturers have in general replaced it by one of recommending retail (and, in some cases, wholesale) prices. These have been widely used by the traders offering price reductions as a selling aid to emphasize the cut being made. Thus competition at the retail level has, in many instances, been in terms of percentage or cash reductions off the recommended price. Such competition has, however, for many product groups, been concentrated among the larger retail organisations and upon the leading

brands of a particular line, 'whose quality and value in the consumer's eye (are) assured'.[1] In other words, there is some tendency on the part of consumers to associate relative prices with quality differences, so that the brand loyalty created by manufacturers has played an important role in breaking this link.

To turn to the experience of our commodity groups, it is clear that price competition at the retail level has been most prevalent in the case of domestic electrical appliances. This is immediately apparent from casual observation and is supported by a survey carried out in March, 1968, a year after the abolition of r.p.m., by a market research team. Their findings were that much less than half of retail sales took place at the recommended price (47 per cent of refrigerators, 36 per cent of washing machines and vacuum cleaners). Moreover, in some cases, price reductions were substantial: for instance, 14 per cent of washing machines were sold at over 20 per cent off the list price.[2] It is almost certain that the proportion of sales taking place at the recommended price has since declined in each case, while the size of cut has increased, and that for many appliances the vast majority of purchases by consumers are made at 'cut-prices'. This is even truer if we include in this category the sales of products carrying the retailer's own brand, which are essentially identical to the manufacturer's branded product apart from bearing a different name-plate and a lower price. Cookers represent an exception to this general situation, as these almost always are sold at the manufacturer's recommended price,[3] Electricity Boards having little incentive to compete among themselves.[4]

In contrast to the domestic electrical appliance group, most consumer purchases of tobacco, confectionery and hardware are made at the price recommended by the manufacturer concerned. With regard to the former two groups, price cuts were only really at all prevalent for a short time immediately after the ban on r.p.m. Since then, price reductions on tobacco have largely been confined to periodic promotions on selected brands run by the supermarket outlets of the larger multiple grocers and coops, to variety stores and to certain off-licences, a limited number of which sell cut-price cigarettes on a regular basis. With regard to confectionery, price cuts have become mainly concentrated on 'multi-packs', which combine a number of units of a popular count-line in a single pack. These for the most part are sold only by the larger grocery and variety store outlets.

A survey conducted by the National Hardware Alliance in 1967–8, among retail ironmongers, found that it was the policy of 91 per cent of the respondents to charge recommended prices. The products which were sometimes sold at below this price tended to be those for which the competition of neighbouring discount stores,

---

1 N.B.P.I. Report No. 165, *Prices, Profits and Costs in Food Distribution*, p. 5.

2 See N.B.P.I., Report No. 97, *Distributors' Costs and Margins on Furniture, Domestic Electrical Appliances and Footwear*, Appendix 10.

3 *ibid.*

4 This is not to say that periodic promotions are not important in this area, but these have usually taken the form of a free gift – a small appliance for instance – with the purchase of a cooker.

194

department stores or supermarkets was relatively intensive. Moreover these products largely consisted of non-hardware lines, such as paint and small electrical appliances.[1] In general, price cuts on hardware have usually been confined to the leading brands of certain household goods or appliances — discount stores and supermarkets tending to limit the range of goods stocked to this type of product.

The factors underlying this variation between commodities were outlined in the previous chapter, and their influence can be illustrated by comparing the domestic electrical appliance group with the other products covered.

Thus electrical appliances tend to carry a high unit price and to be purchased at relatively infrequent intervals by individual consumers. Moreover a high degree of standardisation has been attained and a substantial proportion of retail sales takes place in shops owned by a few large retail organisations. These factors combine to increase the incentive to potential purchasers to 'shop around' and compare the price offered by different retailers, insofar as possible savings in the price paid are important in relation to the cost of travel and time spent, and insofar as the difference between brands is comparatively small.

However it is difficult to ascribe the extensive retail price competition in recent years to the *legislation* against r.p.m. alone. While it is certainly true that this facilitated the development of the situation, the latter must be considered against the market conditions prevailing at the time. Thus, as we have described above, there was a significant decline in domestic sales in 1965 and these remained at a relatively low level during the subsequent two years, only increasing to their 1963 level in the 'honeymoon period' immediately preceding the budget of 1968.[2] What is important, however, is that this period of stagnation followed a long period when the trend in sales was strongly upward (albeit with a few stops along the way) which saw a substantial expansion of both manufacturing and distributive capacity. For example, the number of manufacturing enterprises increased by 37 per cent between 1958 and 1963 and that of specialist retail outlets by 23 per cent between 1957 and 1961.[3] At the same time imports showed a marked upward trend after 1963 (their share of the domestic market more than doubled between 1963 and 1968) while exports declined. It is therefore fair to describe the period after 1963 as one of excess capacity, which was extremely conducive to an increase in the degree of competition among producers and among distributors. Consequently, it is feasible to argue that the practice of r.p.m. would have been under great strain even without the 1964 Resale Prices Act. Indeed, one leading manufacturer (Hoover) voluntarily abandoned r.p.m. in June 1965, and although the remainder of the industry continued the policy until its formal removal in January 1967, the degree of enforcement was in general less stringent than it had been before 1964.

In this regard, it is instructive to look at events in the years preceding the Act. Thus in 1960 and most of 1961 the market for appliances was relatively depressed,

1 See the Monopolies Commission, *Recommended Resale Prices*, p. 35.

2 After the devaluation of November, 1967 it was announced that stringent measures were to be taken in the March budget.

3 See Tables XV.1 and XV.3 above.

the volume of sales falling by about five per cent. During this period cut-price appliances were widely on sale, in some cases at substantially below the maintained price,[1] and it was not until sales began to show a significant increase in 1962, that manufacturers exercised their legal right to prevent price-cutting.[2] Moreover even when the explicit price reductions were made difficult, retailers were always able to circumvent r.p.m. by offering attractive trade-in allowances on used goods or low rates of interest on hire purchase agreements. While practices tantamount to a breach of r.p.m. were actionable, it was more or less impossible for manufacturers to prove such a breach, and in fact no attempt was made to control the two types of practice mentioned.[3]

Domestic electrical appliances therefore provide an example of a commodity group for which the underlying conditions were virtually all favourable to the development of extensive retail price competition at the time when r.p.m. was removed.

If we consider the other groups, however, it is clear that for most products the price variable has a much less important bearing on the consumer's choice of retail outlet, and that this, in many instances, is primarily determined by the 'convenience' factor, which broadly means the location of the shop. This tends to increase the total number of outlets for any given volume of sales and to reduce the degree of competition between them, as each enjoys some advantage over other retailers, in respect of the customers living in their immediate vicinity.

Thus in the case of tobacco, consumers show a strong tendency to buy the same brand of cigarette, from the same outlet, at regular intervals. This reduces the attraction of a marginal reduction in price, and clearly the size of the retail margin makes anything but a small reduction difficult (although, of course, an attempt can be made to persuade consumers to buy cigarettes in larger units). Consequently, after an initial period immediately following the ban on r.p.m. when price reductions on tobacco attracted a good deal of publicity and additional custom, supermarkets and other traders have generally tended to treat tobacco in a similar way to most of the other goods they sell. In other words, they have for the most part aimed at making a 'reasonable' return rather than used this product as a 'loss-leader'.[4] Moreover the periodic promotions have in a number of cases been supported by the two smaller tobacco manufacturers. However, as we mentioned, there are a limited number of outlets, especially certain off-licence chains, which regularly sell the leading brands of cigarette at cut-prices.

In the case of confectionery, as we have said, a large proportion of sales can be

1 Examples of reductions of 30 per cent off the maintained price were quoted by *Which?* at the time.

2 On this, see J.F. Pickering, *Resale Price Maintenance in Practice*, Allen and Unwin, 1966, p. 76.

3 *ibid*. pp. 111–112.

4 The magnitude of the price cuts made at the time of the abandonment of r.p.m. could have produced *at best* an extremely low gross margin, and indeed the evidence points to the probability that some stores were selling tobacco at below cost. See *Financial Times*, October 18, 1968, where examples are quoted of retailers selling at a price significantly below the very best terms apparently available from manufacturers.

characterised as impulse rather than planned purchases, which tends to reduce the significance of the price variable in relation to other factors. This provides an explanation of why the fears expressed during the r.p.m. case, that supermarkets would use confectionery as a 'loss-leader', have not been fully realised. As the essential function of a 'loss-leader' is to attract customers into the store, it is clear that other commodities — the staples, such as tea and sugar, which are purchased with great regularity — fit the bill much more suitably than does confectionery. Thus, even more than tobacco, the offer of cut-price confectionery is only likely to have had any great publicity value immediately after the ban on r.p.m.

Nevertheless a small number of lines are fairly regularly sold at below the manufacturers' recommended price by a few retail organisations. These consist predominantly of the most popular 'count-lines' (Mars bars, for instance) marketed in the form of multi-packs, and, as we have said, are almost entirely confined to the variety store and grocery trade. Indeed the object underlying their introduction was to expand confectionery sales through this type of retailer following the Restrictive Practices Court's decision on r.p.m. Thus multi-packs served to raise the size and unit value of individual confectionery items, and therefore to facilitate handling, reduce pilferage and increase the feasibility of retailers being able to cut prices. This last point is important in respect of this particular commodity group as in 1967 it was estimated that items sold at a retail price of less than one shilling accounted for almost half of all sales, and further than individual purchases for an aggregate value of less than this amount represented over a third of all expenditure on confectionery.[1] A penny off a sixpenny bar of chocolate, which was then by far the most popular price (accounting for 32 per cent of all chocolate sold, in volume terms), would therefore have represented a reduction of almost 17 per cent in relation to a maximum distributive margin of about 22 per cent.

Perhaps of greater importance from the retailers' standpoint, however, was that the manufacturers concerned were in many instances prepared to bear part, and sometimes all, of the cost of any price reduction on multi-packs.[2] Thus it was not infrequently the case that the manufacturer reduced the listed retail selling price of the line in question, but at the same time maintained the distributive margin at its usual level and correspondingly accepted a lower margin for himself on such sales. While certain retailers often added a further price cut of their own to that made by the manufacturer, this was by no means invariably so, and indeed the extent of this practice tended to decline over the period 1967 to 1970. Since then, however, there are signs of a resurgence and of an increase in price competition at the retail level, although there is also evidence of greater manufacturer participation in this area. We can therefore conclude that multi-packs have been as much a part of the

1 See *Reports of Restrictive Practices Cases, Volume 6*, p. 389.

2 The importance of this point should be emphasized. Thus one leading supermarket representative envisaged, during the r.p.m. case, that manufacturers would need to make 'more than a nominal contribution' if confectionery were to be offered at cut prices, and that the margin on confectionery was similar to that expected on the majority of products sold. At the time, the gross margin aimed for was usually 20 to 25 per cent, except on the 'staples' such as sugar and tea. See H. Crane, *Sweet Encounter*, p. 155.

manufacturers' promotional effort as of the retailers', and further that they are indicative of a diversion of promotional expenditure from specialist outlets to more general stores.

A point which might be of some significance in this context is that the development of multi-packs may possibly have been associated with a reduction in the importance of impulse purchases of confectionery, by virtue of its introducing a greater element of 'planning' into the purchasing decision. Thus it might be expected on *a priori* grounds that the greater availability of confectionery in this form, in supermarkets especially, would lead to the housewife catering for her family's weekly confectionery consumption at the same time as its grocery needs. If this is so, it might imply that price would tend to become a more relevant factor. Alternatively it might well be that the impulse to purchase under the circumstances of grocery shopping is intensified by a reduction in price. In this regard it can be argued that while cut-prices on confectionery are unlikely to attract customers into the store to any significant extent, this does mean that they have no effect on sales. Moreover, the relative prices of different manufacturers' brands is also likely to be a crucial factor underlying consumer choice, which implies that competition between manufacturers in this area may be at least as important as between retailers.

At the same time price competition at the retail level has failed to materialise in respect of seasonal sales of confectionery, at least to the extent envisaged at the time of the abolition of r.p.m. Thus confectionery sold during the Christmas and Easter periods was expected to provide the greatest opportunity for price-cutting, in as much as it typically carries a much higher unit price than at other times of the year and tends to be far less of an impulse purchase. In addition seasonal sales represent a substantial part of annual consumption.[1] On the other hand, it is perhaps relevant to bear in mind that the relatively high priced items bought at such times of the year are largely intended for giving as gifts, which might be a factor in reducing the significance of the price variable and therefore in explaining the failure of retailers to comply with expectations. At the same time it is only fair to add that the absence of price cuts on seasonal sales was less apparent in 1972 than it had been over the period 1967 to 1970.

Gift purchases are also of some importance with regard to certain products included in the hardware group. Indeed they form a substantial part of department store sales of this type of commodity, which is clearly a factor underlying the relatively limited extent of price competition on such products. Moreover many of their sales of the lower-priced items in the kitchenware category can probably be described as impulse purchases, which has similar consequences. Nevertheless, sales at below the recommended price are much more prevalent with regard to the goods commonly sold by department stores than for those sold by specialist ironmongers. The absence of price competition on the latter trade has been explained in terms of the range of goods stocked and the typical size of such businesses. Thus, according to the evidence given to the Monopolies Commission, the average ironmonger may stock between 2,000 and 4,000 items, varying 'widely in their size, unit value and

---

1 The evidence of one of the larger specialist multiples in the r.p.m. case was that the seasonal trade accounted for about 20 per cent of its annual chocolate sales. See *Reports of Restrictive Cases, Volume 6*, p. 372.

rate of stock-turn', with the result that 'however desirable it might be in theory for the ironmonger to undertake his own pricing, in practice it was beyond his resources'.[1] Equally, a large part of the turnover of this type of outlet consists of convenience goods, on which price cuts would probably attract little extra custom.

2. Retail Price Competition on Carpets and Pharmaceuticals

Although r.p.m. did not apply to carpets, at least at the retail level, and still exists on pharmaceuticals, it is still of interest to consider, firstly, the extent of retail pricing competition with regard to the former group and, secondly, its likely extent with regard to pharmaceuticals if the Restrictive Practices Court's decision had been otherwise.

While retail selling prices were not maintained on carpets, the majority of manufacturers were, until 1959, signatories to an agreement which exercised a close control on both wholesale and ex-factory prices for certain grades of carpet. This state of affairs is a reflection of the importance to producers of 'selling in', or getting retailers to stock their products, and of the significance of factors other than price in determining sales at the retail level. Thus colour and design tend to be the major determinants of consumer choice on which carpet to purchase, within certain limits. Although the price is clearly likely to be important in imposing these limits, variations in price tend to be closely associated in the mind of the customer with differences in quality, because of the difficulty of forming an assessment of this, independently of the unit value of the carpet.[2] Moreover these factors tend to outweigh any brand-name considerations — indeed the process employed in the production of a carpet is usually more significant than the actual name of the manufacturer concerned.

We would therefore expect the extent of price competition between retailers to be rather limited. Not only do other factors tend to outweigh price considerations, but the features of the trade outlined above — a low degree of brand-promotion and of standardization — make it difficult for consumers to compare prices between shops, even if they so desired. This difficulty is further compounded by the practice of some retailers of including fitting and laying in the price, while others charge for this service separately; in addition, free underlay may or may not be provided with the purchase.

However prices do vary between shops; indeed, in some cases, there is apparently a marked difference for certain lines, as we mentioned earlier.[3] Furthermore it is likely that the extent of such variations has been increased by the development of discount stores and 'carpet supermarkets', although these tend to concentrate on the cheaper end of the market, for which price is probably a more important factor.

1 The Monopolies Commission, *Recommended Resale Prices*, p. 36.

2 However it should be said that manufacturers have recently tended to increase the amount of information made available to consumers, by adopting common labelling schemes, which attempt to convey such details as the type of use for which the carpet is suitable and its colour fastness. But such schemes are as yet far from being widespread. See *Which?* September, 1970, pp. 264–8.

3 Moreover, *Which?* op. cit. conducted a survey over 73 shops and found that for the same carpet, 'variations of over one pound a yard were fairly common.'

Turning to pharmaceuticals, the present arrangements with regard to ethical drug sales are for the N.H.S. to compensate retail chemists on prescriptions dispensed at the prices recommended by manufacturers, while the actual consumers pay, in many instances, only a nominal fee. As both the pattern and level of demand are effectively determined by doctors, rather than by consumers, it is difficult to conceive of a situation arising in which retailers compete among themselves in terms of price rather than service. On this type of product, r.p.m. is enforced at the wholesale stage, and we postpone a consideration of the implications of this until later.

R.p.m. is enforced at the retail stage in respect of proprietary medicines, but again it is difficult to envisage any extensive price competition developing if the practice was prohibited. Thus 'convenience' is clearly likely to represent the main factor behind any individual's choice on the retail outlet from which to buy, rather than the price charged. Nevertheless there has been a tendency for price reductions supported by manufacturers to increase in importance over recent years.

3. Changes in Distributive Margins, Overview

In general the method of pricing employed by the manufacturers of the six groups has remained much the same over the period since 1965, as described for that year in an earlier chapter. This applies equally to the basic retail and wholesale margins (shown in Table XIV.1 above). The main change in most trades has been an improvement in terms to the larger distributors, which has been associated with an increase in the importance of special discounts, taking the form in particular of allowances given for promotional purposes. This has led to a widespread expansion of 'below-the-line' expenditure on advertising relative to expenditure 'above-the-line', or national advertising.

These developments are basically related to the growth in the proportion of sales made by the larger distributive organisations, and to a consequent shift in bargaining power in favour of these and against manufacturers. However they appear to have been accentuated by the ban on r.p.m., and in a number of cases, manufacturers made some changes in their policy on discounts once this practice was prohibited. To generalise, one effect of the ban seems to have been to increase manufacturers' awareness of the change in the pattern of retailing, or of the potentiality for such change, by highlighting the position of the larger traders *vis à vis* their competitors, and *vis à vis* manufacturers themselves. However there are marked differences between product groups which stem as before from variations in the nature of the commodity and in the conditions of manufacture and distribution, or, in other words, from differences in the ability of producers to withstand pressure from distributors. This is illustrated by the experience of our six groups over the period since 1965. The main changes in the policy of manufacturers with regard to the margins allowed to retailers and wholesalers, and in the pricing policy of the latter, are considered below for each of the groups in turn. We begin by examining domestic electrical appliances, which appear to have been subject to the greatest changes and which again provide a 'yardstick' for the other five groups.

4. Changes in Distributive Margins on the Six Commodity Groups

(i) Domestic Electrical Appliances

We have seen earlier in the chapter that, over the period since 1965, price competition among retailers has been more intense on electrical appliances than on any of the other goods covered. The effect of this on distributive margins is by no means simple to predict. Thus individual manufacturers have an incentive to keep prices to consumers at a competitive level, and therefore to prevent margins from rising, but they also need to ensure that their products are as widely distributed as they desire and are 'actively' promoted, which implies that margins need to be 'attractive' to distributors. At the same time, competition among the latter is likely to reduce the actual margin earned, but also to lead to intensified pressure on suppliers for improved terms.

What has happened since 1965 is that the *basic* margins allowed to distributors on the basis of recommended prices have remained virtually constant, with a few exceptions, although there has been a widespread tendency to quote prices net rather than in terms of percentage discounts.[1] But this says little or nothing about actual developments. The basic margin is no way reflects the total margin earned in certain cases, and retailers have not adhered to recommended prices. These same considerations, however, make it difficult to describe actual developments. Moreover a good deal of variation is evident in the pricing policy pursued by different manufacturers, and in the changes made over recent years.

Nevertheless it is possible to make the broad generalisation that trade terms have become more closely related to order sizes, and therefore in some degree to the cost of supplying individual distributors. It further appears that the end of r.p.m. acted as a major stimulus in this direction. Thus the most widespread changes since 1967 seem to have involved an extension of discount structures to cover retailers previously supplied through wholesalers and the imposition of a minimum order requirement on the latter, where previously they had received a standard discount irrespective of the size of purchase made. In addition, a number of manufacturers have replaced pricing systems based on the annual value of purchases by ones related directly to individual order sizes.[2]

It is clear that such changes have favoured the larger distributive organisations as against independent retailers and these have also gained from an increase in the incidence of 'special' terms following the ban on r.p.m. In other words, instances where the actual buying price is individually negotiated with a particular concern have become more important. The outcome of such negotiations tends to depend crucially on relative bargaining strengths, and, in many cases, the overall market share of the distributor concerned is of almost as much significance as the size of order involved.

In this connection, the same features of the trade which help to explain the extensive price competition at the retail level are of some relevance. Thus the

1 An important point to be borne in mind throughout the subsequent discussion is that any comparison between the level of margin in the early 1960's and that after 1965 has to take account of one particular change in selling methods that occurred. Thus some companies used to employ their own force of door-to-door salesmen who were attached to local retail outlets and who had the task of drumming up custom for these. It is clearly difficult to make any estimate of the implicit deterioration in terms caused by the disappearance of this practice.

2 Other manufacturers have introduced or increased the extent of annual rebates but these have usually been additional to a price structure for individual orders based on volume off-take.

group can be characterised in terms of high unit value, highly standardised products, which are purchased relatively infrequently by any individual consumer. These factors imply that producers are likely to have some difficulty in building up brand loyalty, which in turn means that retailers are in a relatively strong bargaining position. Moreover their position may be expected to have been further strengthened in recent years with the increase in concentration both in production and in distribution. In other words, up to a certain point at least, both tendencies are likely to have increased the ability of retailers to play one manufacturer off against another. This is clearly so in the case of rising concentration in retailing, but is perhaps less obvious with regard to production, except insofar as it leads to greater standardisation. The argument is that any growth in concentration in production tends to increase the degree of inter-relation between manufacturers, in the sense that any action taken by one company – to raise trade discounts, for example – has a greater and more immediate effect on the performance of any other – in terms of its sales record, for instance. This is not to deny, however, that after a certain point has been reached, further concentration is liable to tilt the balance of bargaining power in the reverse direction, because of such factors as the increase in opportunity cost to the distributor of not stocking a given manufacturer's products or the greater scope for collusion among manufacturers.

The pressure on manufacturers has therefore been not only for general increases in trade discounts but also for selective improvements, in order that a favourable position might be gained *vis à vis* competitors. This has been associated, for example, with an average expansion of promotional allowances to large retail organisations, at the expense of those to independents and relative to expenditure on national advertising.

To illustrate this tendency with the most prominent example, we need only note the often substantial improvements in terms that Electricity Boards have succeeded in negotiating in recent years, especially on those types of appliance for which they dominate the market. For instance, in the case of electric cookers, the domestic sales of which are produced by just four independent concerns and retailed almost exclusively through Electricity Board showrooms, the Board improved their buying terms, over the period 1965 to 1970, from about $23\frac{1}{2}$ per cent off the recommended price to at least 30 per cent plus flat rate promotional and service allowances.[1] In addition with regard to storage radiators, the discount was raised from 45 per cent to 50 per cent over the same five-year period.[2] Moreover a similar tendency is evident even on lines for which other outlets are equally

---

1 The promotional allowance in 1970 was £1·50 per cooker and the service fee £1. It should be added that the actual terms negotiated in each case depend on the quantity ordered, which is determined, in advance, on an annual contract basis. An under-estimate of annual purchases on the part of the Boards produces a rebate from manufacturers on the difference; no compensation is forthcoming for an over-estimate, though the Boards do endeavour to 'push' the particular brand concerned.

2 In this case, the Boards have established a national consortium which negotiates centrally on behalf of the 14 area Boards *via* a system of tenders from interested suppliers. It should also be noted that the Boards have promoted these appliances very intensively, which is reflected in the annual rate of sales growth of 16 per cent between 1968 and 1970.

if not more important. Thus to take as an example an appliance produced by one company interviewed, the (implicit) maximum discount off the trade price in 1970 was 17½ per cent on a drop of 12 to Electricity Boards, as compared with 15 per cent on a drop of 36 to wholesalers, even though the market shares of the two types of distributor were similar. In 1965, terms would almost certainly have been the same for both.

It is difficult, however, to attach much importance to the end of r.p.m. in this context. Rather, for some reason, Electricity Boards seem to have become far more aware of their dominant position in certain areas of the market and to have taken advantage of it — which, of course, is an entirely rational policy to pursue. What needs to be explained, therefore, is why such a policy was not adopted earlier.

On the other hand, it is true in general terms that the distributive margin allowed by manufacturers has increased significantly since the abolition of r.p.m. For example, one manufacturer interviewed estimated that the differences between the net price and the recommended price increased in his case by about five percentage points between 1967 and 1970. While this has been associated with a substantial rise in the average size of order placed and hence with a reduction in delivery costs, this has not been sufficient compensation for the higher margin given. Correspondingly, recommended prices have been raised to enable manufacturers to grant bigger discounts, which in turn enable retailers to offer price cuts to consumers. As an illustration of this tendency the recommended price of Hoover washing machines increased by about one per cent between 1963 and 1968, but the price actually paid by final consumers decreased on average by over ten per cent.[1]

The question — which in some degree was begged earlier in the chapter — therefore arises of whether the end of r.p.m. resulted in an overall reduction in the prices paid by consumers for appliances, as compared with the prices that would have prevailed had the practice continued. The reduction clearly is in no way represented by the size and extent of discounts off the recommended price offered by retailers. The main influence on prices has probably resulted from the diversion of sales towards the larger retailers, which, as we have seen, is a tendency which was already evident before r.p.m. ended, although it can be argued that the diversion was less than it might have been without the restriction on price competition. Thus although multiple retailers usually impose a slightly higher mark-up than independents,[2] this has to be set against the higher wholesaling costs borne by the former. In other words, the total distributive mark-up (that is, including the wholesale margin) over the ex-factory price tends to be less on appliances sold by multiples than on those sold through independent outlets.

As far as the wholesale margin is concerned, there has been a significant reduction since 1965 in the percentage actually realised, particularly on major appliances which are usually distributed direct to retailers. It is clear that

1 See N.B.P.I. Report No. 73, *The Prices of Hoover Domestic Appliances*, H.M.S.O., June 1968, p. 2. It should be recalled that Hoover abandoned r.p.m. in June, 1965.

2 See, for example, N.B.P.I. Report No. 97, *op. cit.*

wholesalers have been in an extremely exposed position over this period, especially between 1964 and 1968 when there was a marked downturn in total appliance sales, as we have seen. Thus, at the same time as competition both between wholesalers and between wholesalers and manufacturers has intensified, such traders have faced increased pressure from their retail customers for improved terms, to enable the latter to compete effectively with larger organisations. Moreover the imposition of S.E.T. reduced the ability of wholesalers to improve their terms and further weakened their competitive position *vis à vis* manufacturers, particularly as *overall* terms to wholesalers appear to have *worsened* in relation to those to retailers over the period since 1965, and since the ban on r.p.m. especially. Thus, in some cases, multiples as well as Electricity Boards are able to purchase from manufacturers at lower prices than wholesalers, although the differential is usually small.[1] On the other hand, to emphasize the variation within the trade, there are some manufacturers which have not improved the relative retail terms and indeed have continued to apply a standard discount on sales to wholesalers, irrespective of the size of order placed. This tends to be in cases where wholesalers represent the main method of distribution, but it is also true that a number of producers have consciously encouraged the wholesale trade as a defensive measure against too great a reliance on a few retail organisations. In other words, favourable terms to wholesalers are seen as a means of promoting sales through independent outlets.

(ii) Tobacco

Broadly speaking, tobacco manufacturers have continued to relate trade terms to the quantity purchased. Although the two smaller concerns have from time to time granted special discounts to certain distributors, these have usually been on a relatively small-scale. Wholesalers have continued to have access to the same price schedule as retailers, which implies that the distortion created by the imposition of S.E.T. has not been alleviated. Between 1965 and 1970 there was some decline in the percentage margin allowed to trade customers on cigarettes and tobacco (by less than half of a percentage point), which can be attributed to the rise in the rate of excise duty over this period. *Cash* margins however increased between these two years, but generally be less than ten per cent. At the same time, there was a tendency for manufacturers to improve the best available terms to those on smaller orders, as a reflection of the change in the cost differential of servicing various sized accounts.[2] This change has been associated with a growth over the period in the proportion of business taking place at the best available terms.[3]

The comparative failure of the larger distributive organisations to gain preferential rates (other than those based on size of purchase) in some degree explains the limited extent of price-cutting on tobacco (given the size of retail margin). The

---

1 For example, one manufacturer interviewed estimated that the mean discount off the recommended price for a particular appliance was $33\frac{1}{2}$ on sales to wholesalers and 34 per cent on those to multiples. This compares with a basic discount of $22\frac{1}{2}$ per cent.

2 Comprising mainly the costs of processing customers' orders, packaging and delivery and travellers' time.

3 To about 80 per cent by the end of 1970, in the case of one company.

failure itself is explicable in terms of the characteristics of the trade, which tend to weaken the bargaining position of distributors. Firstly, the large organisations are responsible for only a small part of total tobacco sales — in contrast with the situation in the grocery trade, for example — which directly limits the amount of pressure which they can bring to bear on manufacturers. Secondly, the extent to which they are able to play off one manufacturer against another is severely restricted. Thus there is a high degree of brand loyalty among consumers of tobacco (fostered by national advertising and coupon trading, in particular) which reduces the amount of switching between brands resulting from a marginal change in their relative prices. Moreover the total demand for tobacco products is likely to be inflexible in an upward direction, as a consequence of government policy and the general recognition of the inherent danger to health. These two factors imply that special promotions among selected outlets may have a limited effect on the total sales of a particular manufacturer's products, causing perhaps a switch in sales between retailers, rather than between brands or any increase in total sales. It also follows that retailers need to stock a particular manufacturer's brands if they are not to lose sales. This is a particularly important consideration in the case of Imperial Tobacco, which produces about two-thirds of all tobacco sold in the domestic market. Thus the opportunity costs of not stocking the Imperial brands tend to exceed the potential loss to the company which would result from such an action.

Nevertheless there has been a significant increase in the amount of promotional activity undertaken by manufacturers in supermarket and other such outlets. This has partly taken the form of the provision of kiosks or sales points within the store — usually free of charge as long as a certain minimum level of business can be assured — which has facilitated the spread of tobacco sales in such outlets, given the difficulty of selling this product on a self-service basis which we have mentioned.

The abolition of r.p.m., however, has had an important influence on the wholesale trade. As we have seen, r.p.m. was enforced at the wholesale stage, and two selling rates were specified. Since September, 1968, manufacturers have continued to suggest these rates, but wholesalers have tended to adopt a more 'logical' pricing system, relating terms more closely to the quantity delivered, on the lines of the price structure operated by manufacturers. In addition, and of particular significance, the ban on r.p.m. meant that wholesalers could take account of the method of trading in setting their prices, which has enabled cash-and-carry sales of tobacco to develop. This in turn has resulted in competition not only between tobacco wholesalers but also between those operators mainly concerned with the grocery trade and the cash-and-carry departments of traditional wholesalers, which is essentially a similar situation as that between supermarkets and specialist retailers. Thus the former are potentially in a position to offer better terms on tobacco sales than the latter, to the extent that they are able to recoup any 'losses' (in the sense of profit foregone) on tobacco, over the remainder of their turnover. Indeed grocery traders have been accused of using tobacco as a loss-leader, and selling virtually at cost on occasions.[1]

1 In fact if cash-and-carry operators sell immediately for cash and at the same time receive up to five weeks' credit from suppliers, they are able to earn some return in the form of interest, even if they sell at cost. In other words, such traders effectively receive an interest-free loan from manufacturers, while their method of operation spares them the cost of extending credit.

(iii) Confectionery

A similar method of pricing has continued to apply with regard to confectionery as for tobacco. Between 1965 and 1970, the distributive margin, calculated as a percentage of the recommended price, showed a slight tendency to increase (by about half a percentage point on average), particularly towards the end of the period, although there was some variation between lines. At the same time, the margin expressed in cash terms increased significantly owing to the rise in recommended price, which in turn was partly a result of an increase in the rate of purchase tax. Thus between these two years, the distributive margin (on the basis of recommended prices) increased by an average of almost 39 per cent per ton of sales, whereas the rise in consumer prices averaged less than 34 per cent and in ex-factory prices, only 24 per cent.[1] The rate of purchase tax on confectionery was raised, by stages, from 15 to 22 per cent, and there was a common policy among manufacturers to at least maintain percentage margins, at those times when such rises caused an increase in recommended prices. In general, the cash margin earned by distributors on chocolate rose relative to that on sugar confectionery, principally as a result of the greater increase in chocolate prices, reflecting the marked rise in the cost of cocoa relative to sugar over the period.[2]

Broadly speaking there has been little change in the discount structure since 1965, in the sense that relative terms to different sizes of trader have remained much the same. However there has been a fairly widespread tendency on the part of manufacturers to increase the minimum size of order which they were prepared to deliver direct to retailers, with the object of reducing the number of small accounts. This typically represented a rise of about 50 per cent in the quantity of goods qualifying for direct supply. Such changes were generally made – with a few exceptions – before June, 1967, and do not appear to be directly linked with the abolition of r.p.m., but rather with the increasing costs of transportation and of servicing small accounts.

This cannot be said of the tendency for special terms and overriding discounts (based on a trader's annual turnover) to increase in importance, which is a marked feature of the period since 1967. This applies particularly with regard to the dealings with the large multiple grocery organisations and the 'symbol' wholesale groups (such as Spar and Mace), as witnessed by the development of 'multi-packs', which are largely confined to these traders, and generally carry special terms. Overall it appears that more attention has been paid by manufacturers to merchandising policy and to persuading distributors to display their products in a prominent position. This is reflected in the expansion of marketing expenditure directed 'below-the-line' (to finance the promotional activities of retailers), while at the same time national advertising has tended to contract, and in the growth in the provision of 'sales aids'.

These tendencies are associated with the improvement in the bargaining position of distributors *vis à vis* manufacturers, which seems to have resulted from the

1 See The Cocoa, Chocolate and Confectionery Alliance, *Annual Report 1971–72*, p. 29.

2 There was also some relative increase in the percentage margin on chocolate, with the result that the traditional five per cent gap between chocolate and sugar confectionery margins was closed a little.

abolition of r.p.m. and the transfer of 'the final marketing initiative' from the latter to the former. More fundamentally, they are related to the features of the confectionery trade which tend to limit the bargaining power of manufacturers, as compared with that held by the tobacco companies, for example. Thus the importance of impulse purchases reduces the degree of brand loyalty and increases the significance of the positioning of products within the store and display arrangements in general. These factors imply that the opportunity costs to a particular retail organisation of not stocking a manufacturer's brands are less in the case of confectionery than in that of tobacco, and the potential loss in sales to the manufacturer of losing these outlets, or having his products displayed in a poor position, tends to be greater. The retailer is therefore more able to play off one manufacturer against another, to achieve an improvement in buying terms. A further consideration is that as brand loyalty is likely to be a function of national advertising, any reduction in expenditure on this may tend to accentuate the situation, by weakening the position of manufacturers. However, it must be borne in mind that, as in the case of tobacco, large retail organisations accounted for a relatively small proportion of total confectionery sales in 1965, which serves to limit the bargaining power of such concerns.

As far as the wholesale trade is concerned, the ban on r.p.m. did not directly change pricing policy, as manufacturers had not controlled wholesale prices. However the lifting of the wholesale price agreement in 1965 is likely to have had some influence on policy over the period since that year. The changes that were made in discount structures in general tended to discriminate against relatively small deliveries, and in a number of instances cash-and-carry facilities were introduced with the object of replacing the traditional service to small retailers and thereby reducing operating costs.

Unlike tobacco, there was a tendency among confectionery manufacturers to increase the margin allowed to distributors when S.E.T. was introduced. The rise represented an addition of approximately half a percentage point to the distributive margin and was intended to cover increases in costs generally rather than S.E.T. alone, although the latter was used as the major element in the distributors' case for more (but as 'the last straw', rather than the only straw). Subsequent rises in the rate of tax have not elicited further support from producers. However terms to wholesalers were not improved in relation to those to retailers, and hence manufacturers did not directly correct the distortion created by the imposition of S.E.T. on wholesalers, although the increase in the minimum size of order qualifying for direct supply can be interpreted as a move in this direction.[1]

(iv) Hardware
The pricing policy of hardware manufacturers has in general shown considerable stability over a great many years, and there have been relatively few changes in the period since 1965. However while the traditional standard discount of $33\frac{1}{3}$ per cent

1 One manufacturer interviewed stated that he was 'worried' about the long-term consequences of S.E.T. on the wholesale trade, but considered that any remedial action his company could take would have a negligible effect without other producers following suit.

still applies to retailers, the wholesale discount on domestic hardware has been raised in a number of cases from 20 per cent (off the trade price) typically to 21½ or 22½ per cent. These changes were made soon after the introduction of S.E.T. and were intended to cover rises in a number of cost elements, particularly on the transport side, rather than S.E.T. alone or even principally (the same considerations applying as mentioned in connection with electrical appliances and confectionery). But there is little evidence of any significant changes in the structure of discounts. Thus there has been no marked tendency to relate wholesale buying terms more specifically to the quantity purchased, the same discount generally applying irrespective of the value of order placed (although some producers give an additional five per cent on orders above a certain value). A number of manufacturers operate annual rebate schemes, as we have mentioned, but both the incidence and structure of these appears to have remained much the same since 1965. Similar stability applies to the discounts given to most retailers.

On the other hand, it is probable that there has been some overall improvement in the terms negotiated with large distributive organisations, principally department store chains, mail-order companies and gift catelogue operators, but the nature of these dealings makes it difficult to assess general variations over time. Moreover terms to the latter two types of trader tend, in the current situation, to include an allowance for future possible price rises between the time of negotiations and the times of actual delivery, as is also true with regard to electrical appliances. We can therefore only rely on the impressions received from manufacturers that such terms have improved over recent years, in response to increased pressure from the organisations concerned, specifically to cover higher 'overhead' costs (S.E.T. being considered an important factor). However at the same time account should be taken of the fact that many manufacturers do not negotiate buying prices individually with each organisation, but relate these directly to wholesale terms.

The general failure to move to a net pricing system (or one in which terms are based directly on the quantity purchased by any trade customer at any one time) on sales other than those to the organisations mentioned above, is explicable in terms of a number of characteristics of the trade. In particular, the wide range of goods stocked by any wholesaler or retail outlet and the structural features of the specialist retailer trade, tend to imply that the value of the majority of individual purchases from any one manufacturer is relatively low. Furthermore if a manufacturing concern has interests in a number of sections of the trade, it often happens that different lines are produced at different factories (unlike tobacco and confectionery) which in turn means that an order is likely to comprise goods from different points of supply. Therefore any economies in distribution to be gained are not directly related to the overall order size, but to the amount from individual shipping points. To relate terms to the latter might clearly create problems of goodwill.

Such factors as these also serve to increase the importance of the service performed by wholesalers. As far as the latter are concerned, although manufacturers have never generally specified wholesale selling prices explicitly, the prevalence of retail price lists and of standard trade discounts has effectively imposed an upper limit to the price which can be charged. On the very small items, such as screws, nuts and bolts, wholesale prices have always tended to vary with the size of order, but even here common price lists, often published independently, are in widespread use and hence the 'going' price is usually known by the retailer. However competition between wholesalers has apparently intensified since 1965, and this has resulted in some increase in the discounts given. Although the small scale of order usually supplied limits the extent to which these apply, it is nevertheless true that this tendency has largely offset the average rise in the margin allowed by manufacturers. Moreover the development of voluntary group trading has increased the incidence of such discounts.[1] This has also been associated with a rise in the extent of special terms granted by manufacturers, to support the periodic promotions mounted by this type of wholesale group.

Indeed a significant proportion of the sales which are made at below the recommended price is a consequence of direct support from the manufacturer concerned. Thus promotional activity in this trade has always been largely directed at the consumer rather than the retailer, as one might expect in view of the relatively low degree of concentration at the retail level (which therefore reduces the importance of 'selling-in' deals).[2]

(v) Carpets

The features of the carpet trade discussed in the previous chapter imply that retailers are inherently in a strong bargaining position *vis à vis* manufacturers, insofar as it is comparatively easy for them to 'push' one brand against another, and that the price to the distributor represents an important area of competition. As we have pointed out, this area was severely limited before 1959. Since then retailers have been able to press manufacturers for improved terms, in the form of discounts off the trade price, but their success in so doing was delayed to some extent by the traditional nature of the trade − carpet manufacturers tending to be old-established family concerns with 'traditional' views on discounts − and by the buoyant state of the market after 1961. However over the period since 1965 or so, there has been a marked change in the situation, as a result of the entry of new firms, some decline in the rate of growth of sales, especially relative to the growth of productive capacity,[3] and an increase in operating costs among distributors, partly, of course, because of the imposition of S.E.T.

The average discount given (and the pressure from distributors) has therefore increased over this period, although it is difficult to assess the magnitude of the rise, owing to the variation between manufacturers in the pricing procedure adopted (terms are either based on annual purchases or individual orders). In addition, special deals with large organisations, for bulk supplies of a particular type of carpeting, have tended to increase in importance. Moreover terms appear

---

1 For example, one scheme adopted by a wholesaler operating on this principle is to relate discounts to the total monthly account of each individual retail participant, so that quantity terms apply to the whole of a retailer's purchases. See Distributive Trades E.D.C., *Voluntary Group Trading, op. cit.*, pp. 6−7.

2 In the case of one major company interviewed, it was estimated that as much as 25 per cent of current domestic sales was the by-product of promotions.

3 Woven carpet sales have fallen in absolute terms, and there has been a tendency for woven carpet firms to enter tufted production.

not to be solely related to the quantity purchased, but vary in some degree between distributive organisations, according to no precise criterion, except perhaps that of acceptability.[1] As far as the individual manufacturer is concerned, much depends on the terms which the retailer in question is currently able to obtain from his competitors.[2] In other words, the basic objective is to give an organisation the minimum possible discount or rebate consistent with its outlets both stocking and 'actively pushing' the particular manufacturer's products.

The clear implication of the above is that large retailers have gained as against smaller traders. It is also clear that terms to wholesalers have deteriorated relative to those to retailers. Thus the wholesale discount has remained at much the same level as that specified in the Carpet Manufacturers' Agreement (at between 11 and $12\frac{1}{2}$ per cent off the trade price), although it was increased by a number of manufacturers after (and again not solely because of) the introduction of S.E.T. (from 11 to $12\frac{1}{2}$ per cent, for example). The increase however was not confined to wholesalers, as it also benefited those retailers receiving wholesale terms. In general, the wholesale buying price shows little variation between traders, with the exception of the few large wholesale groups, which have increasingly adopted a centralised buying policy and have consequently been able to negotiate preferential terms.

A further consideration is that manufacturers have tended to increase the number of pattern books in circulation over the period since 1965,[3] and while these are supplied free of charge to retailers, wholesalers are usually required to pay a nominal fee. This is intended to promote an efficient allocation of such books, as individual retailers may be supplied by four or five different wholesalers; competition from manufacturers generally prevents the fee from being passed on. Moreover the relative deterioration in wholesale buying prices has not been accompanied in this trade by any alleviatory measures on direct supply such as the imposition, or raising of minimum order sizes or surcharges on small deliveries. As we have said, the nature of the product facilitates transportation and makes the size of the drop less relevant than in the case of most other commodities.

Although competition on discounts has certainly increased over the past decade, and since 1965 in particular, there is little sign that this has been associated with any rise in price competition among retailers. The evidence which we have on retail gross margins suggests that there has been some tendency to raise the percentage mark-up on carpets, although the increase is perhaps less than we might have expected and there are a few organisations which have experienced a decline in the margin earned. At the same time, however, there may have been some switch in sales towards lines carrying lower margins. Thus the information collected from twenty department store organisations during the course of the enquiry into the effects of

---

1 For example, one manufacturer interviewed was dealing with one of the largest retail groups at half the wholesale discount, whereas other similar concerns received the full discount.

2 The supply of information to manufacturers on the amount of the discounts given by other manufacturers has apparently represented a major growth area in recent years.

3 This represents the main form of promotional expenditure on the part of carpet producers.

S.E.T., reveals that, for this sample, there was an average increase in the gross margin earned on carpets of about one percentage point between 1965 and 1968, which represents a rise of almost two percentage points in the average mark-up applied.

(vi) Pharmaceutical Preparations

R.p.m., of course, has remained a permissible practice with regard to pharmaceuticals, and this has promoted a certain amount of stability in the trade. Both pricing methods and the level of distributive margins have remained much the same as described for 1965, except for some restructuring of discounts at the lower end of the scale to discourage small orders. The stability, however, applies much more to ethical drugs than to proprietary medicines. In the case of the latter, manufacturers have increasingly tended to concentrate their marketing operations on the larger retail organisations, as is illustrated by the relative expansion of 'below-the-line' expenditure on advertising and the incidence of special promotions directed principally at the customers of a comparatively few selected outlets. This tendency is closely associated with the growth in importance of such organisations, particularly those in the grocery trade. Terms to these have therefore improved relative to those to smaller retailers.

By contrast, in the case of ethical drugs, the bargaining position of retail organisations is inherently weak — and would be even if r.p.m. were to be abolished — as it is the prescriber rather than the consumer, or patient, who determines the pattern of sales. A retailer is therefore not in a position to push a particular brand against another. Consequently, manufacturers' promotional expenditure is devoted to persuading doctors to prescribe a certain line rather than retailers to dispense it.

5. Summary

The general reaction of manufacturers to the breakdown of r.p.m. has been to continue to suggest retail selling prices. With regard to most of the products included in our sample, the vast majority of distributors adher to these, and it is only among the larger retail organisations and for the leading brands of particular lines that price competition has become at all important. Domestic electrical appliances represent an exception to this general tendency insofar as the majority of sales takes place at below the recommended price. This we argued to be a consequence of the characteristics of this group and, in some degree, of the situation which has prevailed over much of the market since 1963. By contrast, for the other groups studied the price variable tends to have a much less important bearing on the consumer's choice of retail outlet, this being determined primarily by relative location in many instances. Thus with regard to tobacco, confectionery and hardware, cut-price sales have largely been restricted to supermarkets and department and variety stores which place a good deal of emphasis on their price competitiveness, but even here comparatively few lines have been affected. In the case of carpets, on which r.p.m. had never been prevalent, we argued that competition among retailers in terms of price tended to be secondary to other elements, such as the colour and design selection stocked, and moreover was limited by the widespread acceptance, on the part of purchasers, of relative price as an indicator of relative quality. In the case of pharmaceuticals, on which r.p.m. still exists, retail price competition is of no relevance with regard to ethical drug sales, and for proprietary medicines, price is inherently less important than the convenience factor.

A general point highlighted by the discussion is the importance of considering the nature of the product and the conditions of its distribution and manufacture when attempting to discern the likely consequence for retail prices of the abolition of r.p.m. This has not always been done by commentators, some of whom have tended to assume that the aftermath, in terms of price reductions, would be fairly uniform across the economy.

The method of pricing to trade customers has remained much the same as described in Chapter XIV, although in respect of domestic electrical appliances many manufacturers have adopted a system of quoting terms directly in the form of net prices instead of indirectly in the form of percentage discounts. There have been comparatively few changes in the basic retail and wholesale percentage margins, and, with the exception of certain products included in the hardware group, manufacturers have not tended to alleviate the distortion created by the imposition of S.E.T. on wholesalers. The main general change since 1965 has taken the form of a relative improvement in the total margin which the largest distributive organisations have been able to negotiate. This is a direct consequence of the growth in their importance which seems to have been accentuated by the breakdown of r.p.m.

The biggest changes in this area again occurred in respect of domestic electrical appliances, where the improvement in terms to multiples and Electricity Boards was especially marked, particularly if compared to the average margin allowed to wholesalers. The latter were in an extremely exposed position over the period studied, facing increased competition from other suppliers and pressure from customers for better terms. The bigger discounts granted by manufacturers were offset by rises in recommended prices, which had the effect of allowing retailers to offer more attractive price cuts. In the case of tobacco, there was a small decline in percentage margins between 1965 and 1970, but cash margins increased by about ten per cent. There was a relative improvement in terms on large orders, but the main change was stimulated by the end of r.p.m. on wholesale prices. Percentage margins in confectionery increased by about half a percentage point on average over this period, while the rise in the cash margin averaged 39 per cent per ton of sales. In addition, there was an increase in the minimum size of direct account and a marked tendency for special terms to gain in importance, particularly with regard to the multiple grocery trade. In the case of hardware, wholesalers experienced a rise in the margin allowed by some manufacturers, although this to a great extent seems to have been passed on to retail customers. The only other change of any note is the apparent improvement in the terms negotiated with large buyers, which can partly be ascribed to an increase in the average size of orders placed. This tendency is also evident in the carpet trade, the main stimulus in this case being the termination of the Carpet Manufacturers' Agreement, which eventually led to the extension of quantity discounts to retail purchasers. Between 1965 and 1968, the mark-up on carpets imposed by a sample of department stores increased by an average of two per cent. Finally with regard to pharmaceuticals, on which r.p.m. still applies, margins remained substantially unaltered, except for some attempt to discourage small accounts and an expansion of promotional allowances on proprietary medicines in respect of multiple retailers.

XVII
Changes in the Pattern of
Distribution since 1965

We come now to the evidence which we have on the changes that have occurred since 1965 in the method by which the six categories of consumer good are distributed from factory to final consumer. Our intention is firstly to outline the changes in the proportion of the sales of each group distributed through wholesalers over this period. Secondly, we consider these developments in relation to the structural changes that have taken place and in relation to the discussion of the previous two chapters.

1. Changes in the Wholesale Share of Trade

Table XVII.1 presents a summary view of the changes between 1965 and 1969 in the importance of wholesale traders in the distribution of the six commodity groups. Specifically it shows an index for each group which is derived from the average percentage of the home market sales of our sample of manufacturers distributed through wholesalers in each of the five years. As such, the figures need to be treated with a good deal of caution. We do not claim that they give a precise indication of the movements in the wholesale share of trade over this period, but we feel that they tend to reflect the direction and timing of the changes that occurred. This at least is the impression generally gained from our discussions with the manufacturers included in the sample.

Table XVII.1   *Index Numbers of the Percentage of Home Markets Sales Distributed through Wholesalers, 1965 to 1969*

Commodity Group	1965	1966	1967	1968	1969
			1965 = 100		
Tobacco	100	100	99	99	91
Confectionery	100	100	99	97	97
Domestic Electrical Appliances	100	96	92	86	84
Hardware	100	103	103	98	93
Carpets	100	92	85	83	n.a.[a]
Pharmaceuticals	100	102	100	101	101

Source: Our sample of Manufacturers
a Insufficient information available to make an estimate.

The table shows a decline over the period in the proportion of domestic sales distributed through wholesalers in the case of each group, with the exception of pharmaceutical preparations, for which the proportion increased slightly. The magnitude of the decline varied from probably over 17 per cent with regard to carpet to three per cent for confectionery, insofar as the experience of our sample is represen tative in this respect. Moreover there was apparently little similarity between the groups in the timing of the changes. Thus in the case of electrical appliances, the wholesale share shows a fairly steady downward trend from 1965, while the fall in that of hardware sales only occurred after 1967 and in that of tobacco only after 1968.

Although it is necessary to examine each group individually in order to get a clear view of the underlying factors at work, it is instructive to consider these changes in relation to the abolition of r.p.m. This was removed from tobacco in the latter part of 1968, from confectionery in mid-1967, from electrical appliances at the beginning of 1967 (although one leading company abandoned the practice in June, 1965) and from the hardware products covered during 1966 and 1967 (although again at least one important manufacturer stopped enforcing resale prices before then)[1]. Super- ficially at least, it therefore seems that the ban on r.p.m. may have had some influence on the proportion of goods distributed through wholesalers, as in three of the cases a decrease is discernible after the ban was imposed. This is particularly apparent for tobacco, the wholesale share of the sales of which showed a marked decline between 1968 and 1969. In the case of domestic electrical appliances, the table indicates some acceleration in the rate of decrease during 1968, but given the nature of the figures we would clearly not be justified in attaching much significance to this.

However we have seen that, with regard to confectionery and tobacco especially, the ban on r.p.m. had a fairly short-lived effect on price competition among retailers, and hence may have had a once-and-for-all influence on the pattern of retailing and consequently on the wholesale share. Certainly the table shows little change in the latter between 1968 and 1969 in respect of confectionery. Nevertheless the impact of the abolition of r.p.m. was not confined to retail prices but appears to have extended to the discount policy of manufacturers, which is likely to have longer-term repercussions on the method of distribution.

At the same time, S.E.T. was introduced in September 1966, and as we have seen, manufacturers, with the exception of those in the hardware trade, generally did not alter their relative terms to wholesalers to alleviate the distortionary effects of the tax. We would therefore expect the decline in the wholesale share shown in the table to be at least partly a result of this factor. Moreover there are the longer-term structural changes to consider, and the pertinent question might not be, for instance, what caused the decline after 1967, but what caused the 1966 percentage to be above trend. From our discussion of structural change, this seems particularly relevant with regard to the hardware group.

The factors underlying the changes shown in Table XVII.1 are considered in greater depth below, taking each group in turn.

2. The Six Commodity Groups

(i) Tobacco
The proportion of domestic tobacco sales distributed through wholesalers remained

---

1 James A. Jobling, manufacturer of 'Pyrex'

214

more or less constant between 1965 and 1968 and this probably continues a trend going back to 1960 or so. This contrasts with a substantial decrease between 1954 and 1959, when the wholesale share of trade fell by about 15 percentage points, as a result of the relaxation of war-time controls, which were responsible for keeping the wholesale share artificially high.

The stability of the method of distribution after 1960 is a reflection of the stability of the underlying structural factors. As we have seen the pattern of retailing showed little change between 1957 and 1966. Although there was a slight tendency for the importance of multiple C.T.N.'s to increase at the expense of independents, the latter were probably also direct account customers to a large extent. Moreover any decline in the wholesale share from this source, may have been offset by an expansion of tobacco sales in outlets other than retail shops, and by an increase at the beginning of the period in the minimum size of order qualifying for direct supply, which raised the proportion of new trade customers supplied through wholesalers. At the production level, the degree of concentration had little scope for increase, and even the distribution of sales between the three major manufacturers remained virtually constant over the 1960's.

Between 1968 and 1969, the proportion of domestic sales distributed through wholesalers declined significantly. This largely reflects the change in the pattern of retailing which occurred after the ban on r.p.m. in September 1968. Thus the initial consequence was for the tobacco sales of grocery stores, particularly the large multiples and coops, to increase in response to the price cuts offered by these, while sales through other outlets declined. However extensive price reductions on tobacco lasted for only a short period of time, and there is little evidence that the proportion of tobacco sales made by multiple grocers and coops increased significantly during 1969 or 1970. Moreover specialist tobacconists and C.T.N.'s appear to have regained, over these two years, much of the trade lost in the initial period following the abolition of r.p.m. The main long-term consequence therefore seems to be a reduction (of around five percentage points) in the tobacco sales of outlets other than grocers and C.T.N.'s, such as other retail shops and public houses, for example. These of course tend to be relatively small retailers and purchasers of tobacco products and to be largely the customers of wholesalers, which accounts for the decline in the share of the latter since 1968.

In other words, what appears to have happened is that the abolition of r.p.m. resulted in a once-and-for-all gain in the tobacco sales of the large supermarket chains, including coops, which has proved to be at the expense of retailers other than specialists, and which indirectly has reduced wholesale sales. The failure of the former type of organisation to maintain the 'initial' rate of sales growth can be ascribed to the features of the trade noted in the previous two chapters, and more directly to the limited extent of manufacturers' support for price reductions in such outlets.

Within the wholesale trade, cash-and-carry operators have increased their tobacco business significantly since 1968. By the end of 1970, they accounted for about ten per cent of the total tobacco sales through wholesalers, as compared with a negligible proportion prior to the ban on r.p.m. There is little question that the freedom of wholesalers to set their own selling prices represents the major factor — and, to some extent, the *sine qua non* — underlying this development. Thus the cash-and-carry method of trading demands that wholesalers be able to offer price reductions to customers, in return for their bearing the costs of delivery and much of the warehousing costs. As both these elements increase sharply with a fall in the size of order delivered, the substantial saving achieved means that wholesalers are able to apply a relatively low mark-up to the cost of goods purchased and yet realise a higher net margin than is customary on traditional methods of operation.[1] At the same time, the rise in the operating costs of retailers is usually very small, as they typically collect their supplies at off-peak times or out of working hours. Both parties are therefore in position to gain, and the overall costs of distribution are likely to be reduced.

As the main business of cash-and-carry operators consists of supplying the grocery trade, their growth has resulted in some loss of sales to tobacco wholesalers, although it has also been associated with the development of cash-and-carry departments among such traders. Moreover we would expect the apparent economies of scale attached to this method of operation to have led to a diversion of sales from smaller to larger distributors, to an increase in merger activity and to a decline in the number of both individual enterprises and warehouses. Clearly other factors, such as the decline in the volume of sales itself and the imposition of S.E.T., also point in this direction. What evidence we have on recent developments in the wholesale trade tends to support these expectations.

(ii) Confectionery

In many ways the changes that have taken place in the distribution of confectionery are very similar to those that have occurred in that of tobacco, which is not at all unexpected in view of the characteristics that the two types of product have in common, and in view of their being sold, in many cases, by the same retailers and wholesalers. As with tobacco, the proportion of home market confectionery sales distributed through wholesalers declined between 1965 and 1969, although the fall was much less marked and occurred in 1967 and 1968. However it is probable that wholesale share had shown a slight downward tendency over a longer period of time. Thus while the proportion of sales made by multiple retailers increased by only a relatively small amount between 1957 and 1966, it should be recalled that the degree of concentration in production rose significantly between 1958 and 1967. It is likely that the decline in the wholesale share between 1965 and 1969 would have been greater, had there not been a tendency over the period for those manufacturers with relatively extensive distribution networks to reduce the number of small accounts, as we have seen. This had the effect of increasing the wholesale share of the smaller retailer trade, especially after 1966, and therefore of offsetting in some degree the relative decline in this trade.

There is little question that this decline was accelerated by the ban on r.p.m. in June, 1967, since which time grocery stores, especially the supermarket outlets, have taken a larger proportion of confectionery sales, mainly at the expense of specialist

1 This is illustrated in the next chapter.

retailers. This type of diversion was indeed predicted by the defendants during the r.p.m. case, but while the direction of change has been realised, the magnitude seems to have been much less than was envisaged. Thus the predictions[1] were for a three-fold growth in the proportion of confectionery sold by supermarkets and a doubling in that of other self-service grocers (a combined rise from nine to 22 per cent), over a five-year period after the end of r.p.m. Overall the share of grocery and food shops was expected to increase by about 14 percentage points (from 28 to 42 per cent), while that of specialist retailers was predicted to fall by the same amount (from 48 to 34 per cent), with the largest shops experiencing the greatest loss (being in a less 'protected' position). At the same time, a small rise was predicted for variety stores and a small decline for other retailers.[2]

The evidence relating to the events since June, 1967 is by no means clear-cut as far as the magnitude of the change is concerned, but there is no doubt that it has not been nearly so great as that predicted above. Indeed the pattern seems to be remarkably similar to that described for tobacco, insofar as there was an initial gain in the confectionery sales of grocery stores immediately after the ban on r.p.m., again in response to the price reductions made, but there has apparently been little change since. Thus grocers — principally the large multiple organisations — are estimated to have increased their share of the market by about three percentage points in the latter part of 1967, while C.T.N.'s experienced a fall of similar magnitude. At the same time, there was a small rise in the share of variety stores and a small decline in that of other outlets, much as predicted. The situation appears not to have altered significantly between the beginning of 1968 and the end of 1970. On the other hand, within the C.T.N. category, the rise in sales through grocery stores seems to have been largely at the expense of independent retailers, and the evidence seems to show some acceleration in the rate of decline in the number of outlets since 1967.[3]

The marked disparity between the actual changes since the end of r.p.m. and the expected outcome can be attributed to the fact that the prevalence of cut-price confectionery in supermarkets has been much less than was anticipated — with the exception of the few weeks following the Restrictive Practices Court's decision. This in turn is explicable in terms of the nature of the product itself as we have seen, which does not appear to have been fully taken into account when the predictions were formed.

However the common view among manufacturers seems to be that the predictions were not so much wrong with regard to the size of the long-term diversion of confectionery sales from C.T.N.'s to grocery stores, as to the time-scale involved. Moreover it is argued that unforeseeable circumstances arose in the period after 1967, and these at least contributed to the failure of the expected diversion to occur. In particular, sugar confectionery sales increased between 1967 and 1970 (by about five per cent), while sales of chocolate declined (by about 13 per cent), which

1 Expounded by Mr. R.N. Wadsworth of Cadbury's before the Restrictive Practices Court.

2 See H. Crane, *Sweet Encounter*, Table 2, p.90. We have taken the mean figures of Part B and Part C of this table, as the actual outcome was expected to lie somewhere between the two.

3 The provisional results of the 1971 Census of Distribution indicate that the number of C.T.N. shops decreased by 14·7 per cent between 1966 and 1971, which compares with a decline of 9·7 per cent between 1961 and 1966; see *Trade and Industry*, 21 September, 1972.

represents a distinct contrast to the trends of preceding years.[1] It also represents the reverse of what was anticipated at the time of the ending of r.p.m., as it was presumed that supermarkets would concentrate on the most popular lines (which tend to be chocolate), and that the diversion of consumers from specialist confectioners would result in a fall in the sales of secondary lines (which tend to be sugar confectionery). The reasoning underlying this presumption is firstly that supermarkets would attempt to maximise turnover per square foot of shelf (or floor) space, and secondly that consumers are attracted into confectionery shops by the leading lines and, while there, may purchase secondary lines 'on impulse'. The implications are that chocolate sales would increase at the expense of sugar confectionery, and consequently that small manufacturers would suffer a loss of business and would decrease in number, so producing a decline in the variety of confectionery on sale.

The growth of sugar confectionery consumption relative to chocolate that has in fact taken place since 1967 is largely a result of the significant change in the relative prices of the two types of product, which in turn is a reflection of the marked rise in the price of cocoa over this period. This has clearly been a major factor in lessening the diversion of trade to supermarket and variety store outlets, and therefore in ameliorating the anticipated decline in the sales of C.T.N.'s. Moreover it is generally considered that the latter have themselves been partially responsible for maintaining their position by exploiting their inherent advantages over supermarkets and pursuing such policy measures as opening late hours and encouraging impulse trade.

However the above predictions were not entirely ill-founded. Thus there does seem to have been some growth in the sales of leading lines *vis à vis* secondary lines, but it appears that supermarkets have added to the consumption of the former rather than caused a diversion of such sales from C.T.N.'s. It is also true that supermarkets have concentrated on the products manufactured by the three major groups, although they have extended the range of confectionery sold over recent years. This has been aided by a tendency among the larger sugar confectionery manufacturers to increase the extent of pre-packaging, which simultaneously reduces the importance of the 'service' that specialist retailers are able to offer (in terms of 'weighing-out' facilities). However, the evidence is that such a policy is part of a long-term trend, and was not initiated or accelerated by the relative growth of self-service sales. Thus the proportion of sugar confectionery sales that were pre-packed represented 52 per cent of the total volume in 1963 and 59 per cent in 1966, but it had only increased to 62 per cent by 1969.

At the same time much of the extension of supermarket sales has consisted of 'own label' lines. But these have largely been confined to sugar confectionery products, and the common policy of the major manufacturers is not to participate in such trade. This is principally because of the belief that any growth of 'private label' sales would be more likely to be at the expense of their own branded products than of those of other manufacturers. In addition, such a policy would further weaken their bargaining position *vis à vis* distributors, as a result of the increased dependence on one type of outlet. On the other hand, the rise in competition in the confectionery

---

1 Between 1960 and 1966, chocolate sales rose by 15 per cent whereas sugar confectionery sales fell by 17 per cent. See The Cocoa, Chocolate and Confectionery Alliance Annual Reports.

market is likely to provide an incentive for the medium-sized producers to undertake this type of business, and to manufacture lines which closely resemble those of the major concerns.

Within the wholesale trade, there has been a significant growth in the sales of cash-and-carry operators, as in the case of tobacco, but unlike tobacco this has been a long-term, rather than a recent tendency. Thus the ban on r.p.m. was not of direct importance in expanding such sales, as confectionery manufacturers had not enforced wholesale selling prices. There may, however, have been some indirect effect, insofar as it led to a diversion of sales away from independent C.T.N.'s and small outlets, and hence provided wholesalers with an incentive to look for ways of reducing operating costs, in order to maintain net profits on a reduced level of turnover. On the other hand, rising transport costs and the imposition of S.E.T, already represented such an incentive, and were probably the two most significant factors underlying the growth of the cash-and-carry method of operation.

Our estimate is that about a quarter of the total confectionery sales of wholesalers were distributed through cash-and-carry operators in 1970, if the cash-and-carry departments of specialist wholesalers are included with grocery traders. Among the latter, 'symbol' wholesalers (those sponsoring voluntary groups of retailers, such as Spar and Mace) have tended to increase in importance, and this is reflected in the pattern of retailing. Thus there has been a marked rise over recent years in the confectionery sales of 'symbol' retailers relative to those of other independent grocery outlets. This in turn is a reflection of the fact that 'symbol' retailers were responsible for an estimated 23 per cent of the total turnover of grocery shops in 1970 while other independents accounted for only 20 per cent; the respective shares in 1961 had been 13 per cent and 40 per cent.[1]

(iii) Domestic Electrical Appliances

The main long-term influence on the position of wholesale traders in the distribution of domestic electrical appliances has been the tendency for the larger retail organisations to increase their share of the market. As we have pointed out, multiple retailers, Electricity Boards and mail-order companies all increased their appliance sales significantly between 1957 and 1966 at the expense of unit retailers. The marked improvement in the relative buying terms of the former type of organisation which has taken place since 1966, implies that they have more than maintained their competitive position *vis à vis* the latter,[2] and suggests that the growth in their share of the market has continued, possibly at an increasing rate. Indeed, as we have also pointed out, the direction of causation runs both ways here, so establishing a cumulative process. Thus a rise in the market share of large retailers affects the terms at which they can purchase which in turn influences their potential sales growth. This is not to say that the former development necessarily initiated the process. In fact it appears that the demise of r.p.m. was associated with some restructuring of pricing procedures on the part of manufacturers, which tended to favour the larger retail concerns.

1 *Nielsen Researcher*, March–April 1971.

2 In fact the survey of the prices paid for appliances, which we referred to above, found that, in March 1968, price-cuts were much more prevalent and deeper among multiples than independents. See N.B.P.I. Report No.97, *op.cit.*, p.83.

These tendencies have produced a situation in which, by 1970, well over half of all domestic purchases of electrical appliances took place in outlets owned by six potential buying units — five multiple retail organisations plus the Electricity Boards.[1] They are also reflected in the figures for home market sales, collected from our sample of manufacturers, which show a decline of 16 per cent between 1965 and 1969 in the average proportion distributed through wholesalers.

In addition, this decline has partly been caused by the extension of direct accounts on the part of a number of manufacturers and by a widening of the range of goods stocked on the part of Electricity Boards and mail-order companies. Thus, for example, small appliances have increasingly been distributed direct to Electricity Boards in recent years, whereas previously a high proportion were supplied through wholesale intermediaries. Moreover Board showrooms have tended to raise their sales of certain appliances for which their share of the market had been comparatively small. This has partly been achieved by a policy of developing 'own-branded' lines, which enables them to charge a significantly lower price than that recommended for the comparable manufacturers' brand. This applies particularly to refrigerators, the Boards' share of the sales of which increased from an estimated 15 per cent in 1960 to about a third in 1970; half of this proportion consisted of sales of their own brand, which had only been introduced in the mid-1960's.

Two further developments are worthy of note. Firstly, cash-and-carry warehouses and discount stores (the two being essentially indistinguishable) have increased in importance over the period since 1965. These operate on the same principle as cash-and-carry wholesalers in the grocery trade, except that they sell to final consumers rather than retailers. In other words, they are able to offer price reductions to customers through eliminating part of the service associated with the traditional form of retail operation, including that of locating in town-centres, which is of questionable advantage to customers at the moment. They are therefore able to achieve savings in transport, selling and rental costs, as well as in the costs of undertaking repair and maintenance work, although there has been a general reduction in after-sales service at the retail level. In 1970, these types of trader were to a large extent supplied by wholesalers, partially because of some reluctance among manufacturers to deal direct with such outlets, but they were only responsible for a small percentage of sales. In the long-term however, they are probably direct account customers for the most part, assuming that their growth continues.

Secondly, there is some evidence of an increase in the importance of voluntary retail buying groups during the period under consideration. The formation of such groups varies, of course, in its incidence upon wholesalers according to whether they are sponsored by wholesalers or whether they are independently formed by the retailers themselves, with the object of increasing the size of order which they are able to place with manufacturers. The Census of Distribution for 1966 indicates that the latter type of group was far more important than the former in respect of electrical appliances, and household goods generally, but even taken together they accounted for a very small part of turnover. Thus in 1966, buying

1 This estimate is based on figures for the turnover of the large retail groups, contained in an article in *Financial Times*, 5th December, 1970.

groups formed by radio and electrical goods retailers were responsible for 98 per cent of the sales of voluntary groups in this kind of business (and for 95 per cent of the sales of such groups in the household goods category as a whole), but for only eight per cent of the turnover of independent retailers (six per cent in the case of the household goods category). However since 1966 it seems that wholesaler-sponsored groups have grown in relative significance, both in this trade and in retailing as a whole,[1] although the must successful example of this form of organisation, Combined Independent Holdings, is not connected with a wholesaler. In 1970, this group had over 700 members and in certain areas represented a buying unit of comparable importance to Electricity Boards.

With the exception of voluntary group trading the developments noted above have been (or are likely to be) associated with an increase in direct supply, and the policy of manufacturers has generally had the effect of favouring this method of distribution. However there are certain exceptions to the latter; a number of producers have not reduced their sales through wholesalers, particularly with regard to small appliances and particularly where such traders are responsible for the majority of home market sales. In such cases, wholesale terms have not deteriorated relative to those to retailers, and often the standard wholesale discount has continued to apply (irrespective of the size of order placed). Moreover one manufacturer interviewed had adopted the policy of trying to expand sales to independent outlets *via* wholesalers, and to encourage this had, over the past few years, undertaken deliveries to retailers on behalf of wholesalers, as long as the drop size exceeded a certain number of units.

Such policies as these represent attempts on the part of the manufacturers concerned to prevent their becoming too reliant on a limited number of retailers and to maintain their bargaining position *vis à vis* the latter. They have also been associated with a tendency for a few manufacturers to extend their influence more directly over the distributive trades through the acquisition of wholesalers. These have generally continued to operate as independent traders, insofar as the items stocked are not restricted to their parent companies' brands. On the other hand this development can be viewed as a potential reduction in the number of alternative channels open to the 'non-affiliated' manufacturer, to the extent that the wholesalers acquired may 'push' the group products or ultimately may be operated as part of the particular manufacturer's distribution system. Thus the present distributive arrangements under which these subsidiaries may effectively compete with the parent company on sales to retailers, may not necessarily represent the optimal solution.

Considering events as a whole, it is possible to argue that the aftermath of the ban on r.p.m. has not produced an entirely deleterious effect on wholesalers. Thus the increasing importance of order sizes and the growth of large retail concerns and direct sales have been significant factors in forcing wholesalers to rationalise their stocks, in the sense of narrowing the range of brands carried, and to take a more active role in selling the product. This has been associated with a movement

1 We have already referred to their expansion in the grocery trade; some evidence of their development over a wider field is contained in Distributive Trades E.D.C., *Voluntary Group Trading, 6 Case Studies.*

towards special dealerships — supplies of an individual manufacturer's products being limited to one trader per area — as well as with an increase in 'package deals' with retail customers — taking the form, for example, of the formation of voluntary groups. One implication of these developments may be that the proportion of appliance sales distributed through wholesalers has declined at a less rapid rate since 1969 than was the case over the preceding four years. In addition, the evidence is that wholesalers in this trade generally became less reliant on appliance sales between 1965 and 1969, and increased their sales of electrical contractors' supplies, on which competition tended to be less intense and realised margins higher.[1] This would seem to have placed such businesses on a firmer financial footing.

(iv) Hardware

As we have remarked at a number of points, the wide range of goods included in the hardware group makes it difficult to adopt an overall view. However from our discussion of retail price competition and of distributive margins, it would appear that large sections of the trade can be characterized by a high degree of stability over the period since 1965, as far as distribution is concerned.[2] In general, the main agent of change has been the growth in the sales of large retail organisations, the proportion of home market sales distributed through wholesalers being closely related to this — which is also true of domestic electrical appliances as we have seen. Unlike this type of product, however, the organisations concerned tend not to specialise in hardware, but consist of such traders as department and variety stores, mail-order companies and gift-catelogue operators (if these can be termed as retailers), whose hardware sales represent only a small part of their total turnover. Thus, as we have noted, multiple retailers whose main sphere of activity lies in hardware account for a particularly small proportion of sales (12 per cent of those of specialist shops in 1966), and have shown little tendency to increase their share (which remained constant between 1957 and 1966).

The importance of the types of large retail organisation named above varies across the group; it is especially high for those products included in the domestic appliance, holloware and kitchenware categories, which together are commonly termed as 'Houseware'. Indeed these outlets are, on the whole, responsible for more of such sales than specialist shops, and have shown a long-term tendency to increase their share. We might therefore expect to find a corresponding decline in the proportion of this type of product distributed through wholesalers over time.

1 This is the evidence of wholesalers obtained during the course of the enquiry into the effects of S.E.T.

2 This is supported by information received from wholesalers in the hardware trade during the course of the enquiry into the economic effects of S.E.T. From this it emerged that the area of competition between manufacturers and wholesalers tended to be more limited and more clearly defined than in the other five trades included in this study. Thus, as we have mentioned, there was a widespread tendency for manufacturers to distribute only to large retailers, and to send all medium and small orders through wholesalers. There had apparently been relatively little change in this type of policy since 1965, in the sense that comparatively few wholesalers reported any diversion of their traditional trade towards direct supply over the period covered by the questionnaire, which in general related to events up to the end of 1968.

In fact, as is indicated in Table XVII.1, our sample of manufacturers engaged in this area of production showed a decline in this proportion of about seven points between 1965 and 1969, with the entire fall coming in the last two years of the period. However there is some variation between the companies included both in the size and timing of the change, which makes it both important not to attach much significance to the precise magnitude of the decline, and difficult to assess how far the 'break' in 1968 was representative of this section of the trade.

Nevertheless there are a number of factors which point to the possibility that the rate of decrease in the wholesale share of trade may have accelerated over the period under consideration and in the later years in particular. Thus, as we have mentioned, retail price competition has probably been more prevalent on this collection of commodities since the end of r.p.m. than on the group as a whole, while terms to large retail concerns have almost certainly improved relative to those to other trade customers. Moreover the growth in department store and mail-order sales has in recent years been accompanied by the expansion of discount stores, the development of which had been rather intermittant prior to the ban on r.p.m., because of the action taken by a number of leading manufacturers to prevent their selling below the specified retail price. However, as we have said, these retailers tend to concentrate on the most popular branded lines, so that we would expect there to have been a good deal of variation in the change in the pattern of distribution, even within this section of the trade.

Over the group as a whole, specialist ironmongers have also lost sales since 1965 to outlets specialising in particular parts of the trade. Under this heading we can include such outlets as 'do-it-yourself' shops and what are often termed as 'craft' shops, concentrating on a range of 'modern' household goods, which have both increased in importance over this period. In addition, there has been a long-term diversion of non-hardware sales from ironmongers to other retailers. This is especially true of paint and other decorators' supplies which have increasingly been sold through shops specialising in this field, and more recently through super-markets (as well as 'do-it-yourself' shops). The latter have also expanded their sales of hardware products since 1965, and the end of r.p.m. in particular. As with discount houses, these tend to be the leading brands of certain 'houseware' lines.

Within the wholesale trade, there has been a marked tendency over recent years towards increasing the average size of delivery and reducing the number of small orders supplied. This policy has been associated with the establishment of cash-and-carry departments and the formation of voluntary groups among retail customers. Both have fairly recent origins on any significant scale. Thus, for example, less than one per cent of independent hardware shops belonged to wholesaler-sponsored voluntary groups in 1966, as opposed to about nine per cent which formed part of retailer-controlled buying groups.[1] The growth in both these methods of trading has been accompanied by an increase in merger activity at the wholesale level, with a corresponding rise in the scale of operation, which is important to the realisation of the full advantages offered by these two methods.[2]

1 According to the Census of Distribution for that year.

2 For two examples of voluntary group trading in hardware and the importance of large-scale, see the Distributive Trades E.D.C., *op. cit.* Both groups were formed after 1966.

(v) Carpets

The past decade has seen a significant decline in the proportion of total domestic carpet sales distributed through wholesalers, which is reflected in the figures shown in Table XVII.1. This has mainly been a consequence of two factors: the substantial growth of tufted sales and the dissolution of the Carpet Manufacturers' Agreement in 1959. The former has meant that almost the entire increase in consumer expenditure on this group has been directed towards a product in the distribution of which wholesalers are relatively unimportant, while, at the same time, the gradual aftermath of the latter has been to encourage direct-to-retailer sales on the woven carpeting part of the trade. Thus while the agreement was in force, terms to retailers were the same whether they purchased from wholesalers or direct from manufacturers (or at least those that were signatories to the agreement, and for the qualities of carpet covered). This clearly had the effect of placing too much emphasis on the service offered by the two types of supplier, and tended to conceal a number of features of the trade which facilitate direct supply and reduce the importance of the service provided by wholesalers. As we have mentioned, the use of pattern books as selling aids and the general acceptance on the part of consumers of a time-lag between ordering and receiving delivery limit the stocks which need to be held and reduce the significance of a fast delivery service; at the same time, the nature of the product lessens transportation problems. In other words, the agreement was likely to have increased the wholesale share of sales above an 'appropriate' level, and the subsequent decline can be regarded, in some degree, as an adjustment to this level.

However we might expect the 'appropriate' level to have decreased between 1965 and 1969, in view of the likely expansion of large retail organisations relative to small businesses. Thus, as we have seen, the former have increasingly been able to negotiate preferential buying terms with manufacturers. Moreover the growth of tufted sales, which usually carry a much lower unit price than woven carpeting, has been associated with the development of discount stores, carpet warehouses and other such outlets, although there is some reluctance on the part of certain manufacturers to deal with this type of retailer. This applies especially with regard to woven carpeting, and their growth in this area of the market may have been hindered to some extent. Thus a number of producers have refused in the recent past to supply certain traders who were considered to be capable of 'spoiling the pitch' for other outlets in their neighbourhood, by cutting price 'too deeply'. The underlying rationale is that the practice of such traders would lead to a diversion of sales between retailers, rather than to any overall increase in total consumer expenditure on carpets. In the extreme, the outcome might be that 'traditional' retailers would cease to stock the line in question, leaving the discount trader as the sole source of supply within the region concerned, with consequent implications for the bargaining relationship between manufacturer and distributor. This reasoning is in fact not confined to price-cutting on carpets, but applies generally. (It was also encountered with regard to hardware and domestic electrical appliances.)

On the other hand, at the same time as changes in terms have favoured the larger retail organisations, the features of the trade which we have mentioned, combined with the increasing provision of free pattern books on the part of manufacturers, have aided the entry and growth of comparatively small retailers. Thus these have been able to begin trading or to expand into carpets with relatively little capital. This may be reflected in the significant rise in the floorcoverings sales of 'Furniture and allied' retailers between 1961 and 1966 (of ten percentage points), as compared with the growth in importance of other specialists, which is evident in Table XV.4 above.

(vi) Pharmaceutical Preparations

Unlike the other trades covered by this study, there appears to have been no decrease in the wholesale share of pharmaceutical sales over recent years. Between 1965 and 1969, our sample of manufacturers showed a small rise in the average proportion of domestic sales distributed through wholesalers. However there was some difference between the two sub-divisions of the group. Thus an increase in the wholesale share of the ethical drugs trade probably offset a decline in that of proprietary medicines. The latter is associated with a long-term diversion of such sales from chemist shops to grocery stores. This is reflected both in the increasing concentration of manufacturers' marketing operations on large retail organisations, particularly supermarket chains, and in the growing dependence of pharmacies on the revenue obtained from dispensary services. Thus while N.H.S. receipts are estimated to have represented about 34 per cent of the turnover of chemist shops (excluding Boots) in 1961, by 1966 these had come to account for 41 per cent, and by 1971, for 44 per cent.[1] But at the same time this development also reflects the fact that ethical drug sales increased in comparison with those of proprietary medicines over this period.

The growth of the prescription side of the trade has, nevertheless, not prevented a decline in the number of pharmacies, which appears to have accelerated in recent years. Between 1967 and 1971, the number decreased by over ten per cent, which represents an annual rate of decline of about $2\frac{1}{2}$ per cent, as compared with a fall of seven per cent, or less than $1\frac{1}{2}$ per cent per year, over the previous five-year period.[2]

Within the wholesale trade, the diversion of proprietary sales from chemists to grocery stores has been associated with a shift of business from pharmaceutical wholesalers to grocery wholesalers. It is also true, however, that pharmacists have tended to increase their use of the cash-and-carry facilities offered by the latter,[3] although the expansion of these into pharmaceutical sales is restricted in some degree by the continued maintenance of resale prices on the part of manufacturers.

The apparent rise in the proportion of ethical drugs distributed through wholesalers since 1965 is a result of a number of factors. Firstly, increasing transport costs have led manufacturers generally to reduce the number of deliveries made, by such means as increasing the average time between deliveries and by imposing surcharges on small orders. Secondly, rising interest rates and a tight money situation have

1 See *Nielsen Researcher*, November–December, 1971.

2 *ibid.*

3 In 1968, 20 percent of independent chemists obtained at least some of their supplies from cash-and-carry operators; in 1971, the proportion had increased to 32 per cent. (*ibid.*)

produced an incentive for both suppliers and retailers to keep a low level of stocks, and for the former to cut down on credit facilities. While these points are by no means unique to this particular trade and apply equally to wholesalers, competition between pharmaceutical wholesalers takes place in an environment which differs from other trades in one important feature. Thus the continued existence of r.p.m. means that such traders are not free to vary the price charged, and this has resulted in some maintenance of the services provided. Although there may have been some tendency for wholesalers to reduce the level of stocks held (which is a view encountered among the manufacturers interviewed), the evidence is that the frequency of delivery has increased significantly over the period under consideration. Over the country as a whole, each independent chemist in 1969 received, on average, 41 deliveries per month from his principal supplier alone, which compares with 35 deliveries from the same source in 1963, and represents a rise of 17 per cent. Moreover in the South East, for example, the number was 49 in 1969 as against 38 in 1963, and for large shops in Great Britain, the average number had increased from 36 to 52, which is a rise of over 44 per cent.[1]

At the same time, retailers have had an incentive to reduce the number of suppliers, and hence to increase the average size of order received, because of the surcharge imposed on small orders. It is also true that clerical costs can be reduced if there is a decrease in the number of invoices handled, which may be a minor consideration but which has increased in importance since the imposition of S.E.T.[2]

A final point of some importance is that on ethical drugs manufacturers' terms to wholesalers have not generally worsened relative to those to retailers, which has occurred in many other trades over the period since 1965, as we have seen. While this may owe something to the continuation of r.p.m., it basically reflects the inherently weak bargaining position of chemist retail organisations, which have little influence over the composition of demand and the sales of individual manufacturers' products.

3. The R.p.m. Decision in Respect of Pharmaceuticals

The continued existence of r.p.m. on pharmaceuticals has, as we have said, contributed to the stability of discount structures and distributive margins, and has also served to protect retail chemists from market forces to some extent. These two effects formed the major benefits stemming from the practice of maintaining resale prices, as claimed by the defendants to the Restrictive Practices case. The Court, in fact, found in favour of the defendants, and hence accepted, in some degree, the validity of their arguments. However it is worth considering, as an epilogue, the influence of r.p.m. on this trade in more detail, together with the likely effects of its abolition.

As we have said, with regard to ethical drugs, there is no retail market as such

---

1 See *Nielsen Researcher*, November–December, 1969.

2 Furthermore the advantages to manufacturers of dealing direct with retailers have been lessened in recent years by the introduction of a market information service, on the part of the National Association of Pharmaceutical Distributors. This, at a small cost, gives producers details of retail 'disposals' and an indication of the pattern of distribution.

and r.p.m. needs only to be enforced at the wholesale stage. Its abolition would give rise to the possibility of wholesalers competing in terms of price rather than service and developing a more 'logical' discount structure than they are at present allowed by manufacturers. This would inevitably favour large orders, and the larger chemist as against the small purchaser. The result, according to the defendants in the Restrictive Practices case, would be the emergence of so-called 'short-run' distributors who would concentrate on the most popular lines and substitute price reductions on these for service provided, thus 'creaming' other wholesalers of their most profitable trade. The consequent danger is seen to arise of a decline in the number of specialist wholesalers, and, most importantly, of a concomitant reduction both in the range of drugs offered to retailers and in the speed of delivery. Indeed the Court's decision on ethicals was primarily based on these considerations.

This argument rests upon the fact that the existence of r.p.m. enables distributors to subsidise low returns, or even losses, on slow-moving drugs by the profit made on those lines with a high rate of stock turn. In other words, within the ethical drugs category there is little relationship between the gross margin allowed on individual lines and the costs involved in their distribution. Indeed the wholesale witnesses before the Restrictive Practices Court claimed such cross-subsidisation to be a major benefit in that it permitted wholesalers to fulfill their function of holding stock for the trade. Any price competition following the abolition of r.p.m. would inevitably centre upon the fast-moving lines and would make this practice no longer possible.

However contrary to the Court's finding – that there would be a substantial reduction in the availability of ethicals at dispensaries – the most likely result would seem to be that the margins allowed on slow-moving drugs would be increased to ensure the maintenance of their supply. In other words, we can take the necessity of maintaining an adequate distribution service as given, and therefore the question is only one of means rather than ends. If wholesalers are to continue to perform this service and to continue to hold stocks of slow-moving lines, they need to be recompensed for so doing. This would seem to involve some rise in the 'recommended' price of these products (or the price to the N.H.S.); but, at the same time, this would tend to be offset by a lower price on the drugs with a relatively high rate of stock turn, if the retail chemist is not to show a substantial increase in gross profit. Thus the N.H.S. as the final buyer would have to pay, more nearly, the costs of being supplied with any particular drug. The usual economic advantages of moving towards such a system lie in terms of the reduction in waste, as buyers are forced to assess more consciously the cost of their demand.

The Court made two observations in this connection. Firstly, its view was that the interest of the public as taxpayers financing the N.H.S. was not relevant to the r.p.m. case. The implication of this is that if the existence of r.p.m. resulted in prices of ethicals being on average higher than otherwise, this would not be regarded as a detriment. Equally, any increase in the efficiency of operating the N.H.S. which might stem from the abolition of r.p.m. could not be regarded as a benefit.

Secondly, some weight was given to the administrative difficulties which would arise in compensating chemists for prescriptions dispensed, if r.p.m. was prohibited. Under the present arrangements, the payment is based on recommended prices and allows a given gross margin to chemists. Price competition between distributors is likely to lead to a good deal of variation in the actual margin earned, especially on fast-moving lines, as discounts from suppliers become more important. The maintenance of the present arrangements implies, as we have said, that retail chemists retain the extra discount received, while if alterations are made the difficulty is one of retaining the incentive to chemists to place large orders, which is likely to be important to the efficiency of the distributive system. Certainly any change would be almost bound to increase the costs of administering payments. The view of the President of the Court in expressing judgement was that it might be impossible to devise a uniform system of payment which would operate fairly in all cases. This seems to overstate the problem and moreover neglects the point that the existence of r.p.m. has not prevented discounts off recommended prices from varying between retail chemists; thus, as we have seen, multiple organisations buying direct from manufacturers are able to obtain far better terms than is a unit pharmacist supplied by wholesalers.

As far as proprietary medicines are concerned, these have more of the characteristics of the other commodity groups that we have looked at. In particular, there is a retail market, which is likely to mean that the abolition of r.p.m. would be followed by some diversion of sales towards those retailers that are able to offer price reductions from those which are not. According to the distributors defending r.p.m. on this class of product, the former type of retailer consists principally of multiple grocers, and specifically supermarket chains. We have seen that these have increased their sales of chemist goods over a number of years, but it was claimed before the Court that this increase would have been greater had r.p.m. not existed. However, as we argued earlier, it is difficult to imagine that supermarkets would use proprietary medicines as 'loss-leaders' or that price cuts on these would attract much extra custom although it may be that the possibility of price-cutting would lead such stores to extend the range of lines stocked. Nevertheless the Court's judgement was that this type of diversion would take place if r.p.m. was prohibited, and that this would be associated with a loss of sales to chemists on other lines, as fewer people had cause to shop at such outlets. Some chemist shops would therefore be forced out of business, producing a corresponding acceleration in the rate of decline of retail dispensaries.

Whereas, generally, a major benefit of the abolition of r.p.m. lies in the emergence of a more efficient distribution system as the less efficient traders lose sales, in this case, the benefit has to be set against any social cost arising from a reduction in the number of dispensaries. The argument expressed in the r.p.m. case was that small pharmacies would be particularly vulnerable to price competition, and that these tend to be located in country districts, for example, where alternative dispensary facilities are not conveniently available. If this view is accepted, then considerable hardship might be caused to certain groups of consumers. Certainly the likelihood of a decrease in the number of outlets at which prescriptions could be made up, was accepted by the Court and was the major reason underlying its decision with regard to proprietaries.[1]

1 This line of reasoning was also expounded during the Restrictive Practices case in 1958 against the Chemist Federation's Agreement, which was designed to prevent the sale of proprietary medicines other than by qualified retail chemists. Interestingly enough, it was rejected by the Court at that time, because the view that a substantial reduction in the number of pharmacies would occur if the agreement was dissolved, was held to be based on pure speculation.

The argument here is, therefore, that the profits made on non-prescription goods help to finance the provision of a dispensary service. However if these profits are dependent on the existence of r.p.m. and on the restraint to competition from other traders which this entails, then in effect the consumers of these goods are subsidising the dispensary service, to the extent that they would, on average, pay lower prices if r.p.m. was removed. (Alternatively they might be able to buy from more convenient outlets if the removal of r.p.m. resulted in more shops selling a range of chemist goods.) An alternative would be for the community to directly subsidise those dispensaries which were thought to be socially desirable, with regard to their location for example. This would at least highlight the social service performed and provide a clearer indication of the cost involved, which would seem to be important on deciding the extent and the form of the facilities which should be made available. Although the direct costs of administering the N.H.S. would be likely to rise, this would tend to be offset by a reduction in 'indirect' costs, such as by a fall in the average prices of chemist goods. There appears to be no inherent reason why this type of change would constitute a less 'efficient' means of providing the necessary medical facilities, or why the true costs of providing such facilities should not be made explicit. Indeed the development of Health Centres, operated by local authorities, is a step in this direction.

Furthermore the existence of r.p.m., while protecting retail chemists in some degree from market forces, has at the same time tended to conceal the need for them to take effective measures to improve their business footing. Thus trade associations and societies have devoted much effort to defending and extending the present position, by pressing for sales of pharmaceuticals to be restricted to recognized chemist outlets (as is the case in a number of continental countries). Relatively little diversification into other areas of trade appears to have taken place, for example, and a common criticism is that the chemist tends to consider himself primarily as a professional pharmacist rather than as a retailer or businessman.

However there are a few signs of change. Boots, for instance, has been expanding particularly rapidly over recent years and may increasingly influence operations in the rest of the trade; a few chemist supermarkets have recently been opened in the London area; moreover, one of the largest grocery chains (Tesco) has established drug stores within a few supermarkets. The latter type of development is important, insofar as the employment of a qualified pharmacist reduces some of the health hazard attached to the sale of proprietary medicines through non-chemist outlets. It therefore at least partially meets the frequent argument against the abolition of r.p.m. on this class of product: that professional supervision and advice are necessary, to prevent, for example, a too liberal use of certain drugs. In addition, such diversification represents one solution to the problem of maintaining an adequate dispensary service.

As far as the wholesale trade is concerned, the end of r.p.m. would almost certainly entail an increased diversion of sales from pharmaceutical distributors to grocery wholesalers, as a corollary to the likely change in the pattern of retail trade. On the other hand, the greater freedom to vary prices might be expected to lead to an expansion of the cash-and-carry method of operation in this field, especially on the part of traders specialising in pharmaceuticals and chemist goods, grocery wholesalers probably being unable to stock a sufficient range of lines to meet the requirements of retail chemists. More generally, a ban on r.p.m. is likely to be associated with some substitution of price cuts for services provided, with one probable consequence being a reduction in the number of deliveries undertaken which, as we have seen, has been an area of intense competition between wholesalers in recent years. Although the nature of the trade imposes a constraint on the extent to which the frequency of delivery can be reduced, it is nevertheless true that there has been little attempt on the part of wholesalers to increase the average size of drop, and that very small deliveries have by no means been restricted to ethical drugs.[1] In other words, there is no inherent reason why the delivery service in operation at the moment is any sense 'optimal' or 'desirable', or why any contraction should be regarded as detrimental to consumers, as was the judgement of the Restrictive Practices Court. After all, a contraction does not necessarily imply that the speed with which emergency supplies are distributed would be reduced.

In summary, the Court's decision in this case seems to have been based on too superficial a view of the situation following the end of r.p.m. and of the likely changes that would be associated with such a step, while the alternative policy measures open do not appear to have been fully considered.

4. Summary

The evidence is that, over the period 1965 to 1969, the proportion of home market sales distributed through wholesalers declined in respect of each commodity group, with the exception of pharmaceuticals, for which there was a slight increase. In the case of tobacco, confectionery and hardware, most of the decline — as far as our sample of manufacturers is concerned — occurred towards the end of this period, and for the former two groups in particular it can largely be attributed to the abolition of r.p.m. which was associated with some change in the pattern of retailing. Specifically supermarkets, and multiple grocers generally, tended to gain sales at the expense of small retailers. However it appears that this may have been more a 'once-and-for-all' diversion of trade than a continuous one, which would receive some support from the fact that the extent of price variations between retailers has declined significantly since the immediate aftermath of the ban on r.p.m. With regard to the hardware products covered by our sample, we would have expected a decrease in the market share of wholesalers to have taken place over the long-term, in view of the tendency for large retail organisations, such as department stores and mail-order companies, to gain trade from specialist outlets. In the case of domestic electrical appliances, on the other hand, the main development has been the relative growth of large specialist retailers, which has, however, carried similar implications for the share of wholesalers. It is plausible to suppose that such growth was aided to some extent by the end of r.p.m., particularly as this was followed by the restructuring of terms to trade customers on the part of some manufacturers. With regard to carpets, the demise in the importance

---

1 While a number of traders have imposed minimum values on monthly orders, this, of course, does not necessarily produce an incentive to retailers to increase their average off-take per delivery.

of wholesalers owes much to the growth of tufted sales, although the granting of wholesale terms to large retail organisations following the dissolution of the Carpet Manufacturers' Agreement has also played a major role.

although the granting of wholesale terms to large retail organisations following the dissolution of the Carpet Manufacturers' Agreement has also played a major role.

At the same time, we noted that important developments have occurred within the wholesale trade in respect of a number of product groups. In particular, cash-and-carry wholesalers have increased their share of tobacco, confectionery and even chemists' goods at the expense of traditional distributors. The main factor underlying this growth has been the increasing cost of servicing small orders, as a result of rising transport costs especially, although S.E.T. also seems to have contributed; the end of r.p.m. was, however, a crucial factor in the case of tobacco as it gave wholesalers the freedom to set their own selling prices. The other major development has been the expansion of voluntary group trading, particularly in the grocery trade but also in respect of domestic electrical appliances and hardware.

At the retail level, there is some indication that the end of r.p.m. had the effect of enabling outlets offering a relatively low level of service to increase their share of electrical appliance and hardware sales, although this share is still comparatively small. A similar development is evident for carpets, for which retail prices have never generally been subject to the direct control of manufacturers. In each of these trades, a widespread reluctance to deal with such outlets was apparent among manufacturers.

Finally, with regard to pharmaceuticals, we noted that the lack of any decrease in the wholesale share of home market sales probably reflected the relative expansion of ethical drug sales; in the case of proprietary medicines there was some evidence of a diversion of trade from independent chemists to large retail organisations, despite the continued enforcement of resale prices. The Restrictive Practices Court's decision on this may have the effect of lessening such diversion, but it may also hinder the development of a more 'rational' distribution of dispensary services, conceal the need for changes to be made in the operation of retail chemists, promote cross-subsidisation in respect of ethical drugs and encourage the over-expansion of service at the wholesale level.

XVIII
General Conclusions

In the foregoing we have considered in some detail the changes that have occurred in the distribution of six classes of commodity over the period since 1965. Our intention was that these case-studies would be relevant to a much wider range of consumer goods than we have been able to cover, and that they would serve to illustrate the types of development that have taken place in the distributive process in recent years. A further object was that they would indicate the nature of the influence of such factors as the structural changes in the retail trades – which formed part of the concern of the first part of the study – and the abolition of r.p.m. It is clear that while certain developments have been common to most of the groups, in one form or another, there are important areas of difference, particularly with regard to the magnitude of change. It remains to bring together those findings which appear to us to be of most significance.

The primary agent of change seems to have been the tendency towards an increasing concentration of consumer expenditure among a smaller number of retail organisations, as a result of the growth of multiples relative to independent outlets. This has been associated with a decline in the proportion of sales distributed through traditional wholesalers and a rise in the bargaining power of distributors *vis à vis* manufacturers, and has had a major effect on the level and structure of distributive margins and the prices paid by consumers. At the same time, the progressive ending of r.p.m. has given distributors greater freedom to determine their own selling prices, and while this has not been exercised in the majority of cases, it does appear that there has been some acceleration in the trend towards multiples in a number of trades. Moreover the imposition of S.E.T. increased the incentive to traders of seeking ways of increasing revenue and of reducing operating costs.

The tendency for large retailers to control a greater proportion of the retail market has involved not only the growth of specialist multiples but also the expansion of such concerns as multiple grocers, department store chains and mail-order companies. Indeed the latter have been particularly important in those trades where the growth of specialist multiples has not been conspicuous, such as in the case of hardware. In some degree this represents the continuation of a trend already evident before 1965. Thus we have noted the significant increase in mail-order sales relative to total retail business between 1957 and 1966. Over the same period, the volume of sales through 'Grocery and provision dealers' (as defined by the Census of Distribution) increased by about 20 per cent, while that through such outlets as butcher shops and greengrocers declined. In addition, the multiple share of grocery turnover increased from 22 per cent to 36 per cent, while in respect of butcher shops and greengrocers, the rise was less than three percentage points.

This type of change in the pattern of retailing is, in some degree, associated with the development of 'one-stop' shopping, and with the expansion of supermarkets and self-service stores generally. Thus there is a marked tendency for these to increase the range of lines stocked, and for a greater proportion of consumer expenditure to take place in such outlets. This is illustrated by the fact that self-service stores increased their share of the grocery trade from 21 per cent in 1961 to 45 per cent in 1966[1] and to over 60 per cent by 1970.[2] Over this period total sales through grocery stores increased at much the same rate as total retail sales, whereas there was a relative decline in consumer expenditure on groceries. The progressive abolition of r.p.m. has clearly played an important role here, in enabling retailers to attract customers into the store by means of price cuts, and to generally substitute lower prices for other elements of service — lower prices being equally part of the service provided by the retail sector as, for example, personal attention. Although this development has proceeded furthest in the grocery trade, the expansion of such outlets as discount stores and cash-and-carry warehouses has taken place at a significant rate in the durable goods market.

However price cuts have generally not been nearly as prevalent or as deep as was anticipated by many interested parties before r.p.m. was prohibited. The nature of the commodity in question has been an important factor here, to the extent that traders have concentrated price cuts on those products offering the greatest potential return. Thus supermarkets have continued to base their promotional activity on the staple commodities, like tea and sugar, while running periodic promotions of limited duration on other goods, often supported by the manufacturer concerned. With regard to durable goods, price competition at the retail level has been most prevalent on fairly standardised, high-unit value goods, such as domestic electrical appliances, and has been mostly restricted to the leading brands of other types of product.

The obvious criteria to be met in this respect, are firstly, that consumers should be aware of the price reduction being offered and secondly, that they should consider it to be sufficiently attractive to lead them to purchase from the outlet in question. In the case of certain products, such as carpets for example, there are difficulties in meeting the first criterion, insofar as customers face problems in making valid comparisons between the prices charged by different retailers. In the case of other commodities, such as confectionery, tobacco, proprietary medicines and a number of hardware lines, there arc difficulties in satisfying the second criterion, insofar as convenience tends to be the most important factor in determining a consumer's choice of the outlet from which to purchase.

Consequently the fears of the advocates of r.p.m. — expressed during the confectionery case for instance — have generally not been realised. There appears, for example, to have been no continuing large-scale diversion of trade from specialist confectioners to supermarkets, despite the ability of the latter to use confectionery as a 'loss-leader' for the remainder of their turnover (although the predictions of manufacturers are for a gradual diversion to occur). Similar considerations would

---

1 According to the Census of Distribution for 1966.

2 See *Nielsen Researcher*, March—April 1971.

seem to apply in respect of proprietary medicines, but were given little weight by the Restrictive Practices Court.

One point to be borne in mind, is that, if it is accepted that the demand for services and 'variety' is income-elastic, then we might expect sales of specialists to increase over time, in relative terms, with the growth in income per head, insofar as such outlets are able to offer a wider selection of lines and a greater element of service than can more general stores. However to the extent that the price of providing these types of service is also likely to increase, again in relative terms, there is a substitution effect to consider, which might well outweigh the income effect. At the same time it might be argued that the switch in trade that has occurred since the end of r.p.m. may represent an initial reaction to the abolition of this practice, possibly rectifying a prior over-expansion of services resulting from the restriction on retail price competition. Certainly the pattern of events with regard to both tobacco and confectionery can be held to support this hypothesis.

Nevertheless, it is true that large retail concerns, such as supermarket chains, have been generally favoured by the changes in manufacturers' pricing policies that have occurred over recent years. This is clearly a reflection of the shift in bargaining power from manufacturers to distributors that has taken place in a number of trades, and which has in some degree been associated with the end of r.p.m. It can be argued that there has been a tendency for manufacturers to relate terms more closely to the size of a distributor's order, but it is also true that terms at the top end of the scale have come to be individually negotiated to a greater extent. This has meant that the price at which the largest organisations purchase tends to be as much a function of their overall importance in a particular market as of the amount of goods bought from the manufacturer concerned. This, in turn, has been associated with an overall increase in below-the-line expenditure on promotions, relative to the amount devoted to national advertising and, in some degree, with a switch in promotional activity from small retailers to large.

Thus manufacturers have increasingly tended to concentrate their marketing effort on the larger distributors. Moreover, in a number of cases, they have raised the minimum size of order requirement applying to direct accounts or have imposed, or increased, surcharges on small orders in recent years. This type of policy, together with the widening of discount structures, has had an important bearing on the retailer-wholesaler relationship.

Consequently, while the change in the pattern of retailing has meant a diversion of business away from the traditional customers of wholesalers, the policy of manufacturers has tended to make small retailers more reliant on the services of wholesalers. They have generally found, however, that wholesalers have also adopted measures aimed at discouraging the smaller orders, in their attempt to maintain net profits. Thus wholesalers have experienced some tendency for their purchasing terms to deteriorate relative to those to large retailers, while they have faced increasing pressure from customers for improvements in their selling terms, as a result of increasing competition at the retail level. At the same time, the imposition of S.E.T., the impact of which was, with a few exceptions, not offset by any action on the part of manufacturers, both reduced the ability of wholesalers to grant such improvements and intensified the pressure from their customers.

234

Under such circumstances, there has been a marked tendency for wholesalers to introduce new methods of working, which have included the adoption of cash-and-carry trading, the formation of voluntary groups among retailer customers and a general rationalisation of the range of lines carried. These developments have been important not only in raising the wholesale net margin, but also in mitigating the relative decline in sales through independent retailers, insofar as they have enabled these to improve their buying terms significantly.

To illustrate this in respect of cash-and-carry trading we can refer to an investigation conducted for 1969 by the N.B.P.I. which collected financial data from a sample of grocery wholesalers.[1] These showed that, in the case of cash-and-carry trading, total expenses represented, on average, 4·3 per cent of turnover, as compared with a figure of 7·6 per cent in the case of traditional methods of operation. Net margins were 1·4 per cent and 0·9 per cent respectively, which means that the average gross margin, and hence the buying price of retailers, was significantly lower on cash-and-carry business.[2] Moreover it is probable that the use of such facilities does not involve retailers with any great increase in operating costs, because of the possibility of picking up suppiies in off-peak periods. The recent growth in the cash-and-carry method of operation is indicated by the fact that the value of turnover of this type of grocery trader is estimated to have more than trebled between the beginning of 1968 and mid-1972[3] which clearly represents a substantial rise in the volume of goods handled.

At the same time, this development has been associated with a diversion of trade from specialist wholesalers to those operators mainly engaged in the grocery business. These have increasingly expanded the range of products stocked, as is illustrated by the finding that in May, 1972, 71 per cent of cash-and-carry warehouses in this field stocked some hardware products and 64 per cent stocked some electrical appliances.[4] Almost all carry a range of tobacco and confectionery. A further point of interest is that a large proportion of such warehouses belong to eight organisations (57 per cent of the number of 617 in 1972).

In addition, voluntary group trading has developed furthest in the grocery field, symbol retailers being currently responsible for a large proportion of turnover than non-affiliated independents in this area. Nevertheless both this form of operation and that of cash-and-carry have become of increasing importance in the specialist wholesale trades. Indeed both are symptomatic of a general improvement in the position of wholesalers, which seems to us to have occurred since the late 1960's. This has partly been achieved by rationalisation with regard to the number of individual businesses and depots, as well as with regard to the lines stocked. It has also been influenced by the policy of some manufacturers to maintain sales through wholesalers and through independent retail outlets, in some cases, as a countervailing

1 See N.B.P.I. Report No. 165, *Prices, Profits and Costs in Food Distribution*, pp.15–16.

2 The sample also indicates that the adoption of cash-and-carry trading, as with self-service in retailing, can achieve substantial gains in the labour productivity of wholesalers, as payroll represented only 2·4 per cent of turnover in respect of this method of operation, whereas for traditional wholesaling, the average figure was 3·9 per cent of turnover.

3 See *Nielsen Researcher*, May–June, 1970 and May–June, 1972.

4 *Nielsen Researcher*, May–June, 1972.

force against the growth of large retail organisations, in others, because of the rising costs of delivering small orders direct. This, in some trades, has been accompanied by a tendency towards vertical integration on the part of manufacturers to gain a greater degree of control over 'independent' wholesalers (which as yet has not been fully exercised in may respects).

In other words, the situation confronting wholesalers has obliged them to adopt a more conscious approach to selling and marketing than was necessary hitherto. However while the growth of multiple retail organisations has played the major role in this respect, and has been a dominant factor generally in increasing the efficiency of the distributive process, it has also provided a strong incentive towards concentration not only in the wholesale trades but also in the manufacturing sector. Again the main example of the latter is the grocery trade, where the increase in the bargaining power of distributors has seemingly been an important element in reducing the profitability of food producers and in stimulating the recent rise in merger activity. The growth in concentration in retailing therefore implies a reduction in competition across the economy as a whole and possible in the variety of products on sale to consumers. Moreover while until fairly recently the expansion of large retailers has taken place at the expense of smaller traders, a situation is likely to increasingly develop in which any growth of one organisation represents a loss to another. A possible consequence of this is collusion among such concerns, and therefore the reversal of the beneficial effect which these retailers have undoubtedly had on the prices paid by final consumers. Furthermore widening discount structures and the development of a special relationship between manufacturers and large retail concerns is likely to make entry into the retail trade much less 'easy' than has historically been the case.

Nevertheless we must end by stressing the marked differences that were seen to exist between commodity groups as to the significance of the developments mentioned above and to the relevance of the generalisations which we have made. Thus we need only contrast the importance of large distributive organisations in respect of tobacco, for which small retailers account for about 80 per cent of total sales, and have shown little long-term tendency to lose trade, with their importance in respect of domestic electrical appliances, where six concerns control over half of the market and have shown a marked tendency to increase their share.

EL   O50WS

WARD